Sarah Woods

Working and Living

DUBAI

guides

Contents

09

Working in Dubai 185

10

References 205

Index 217

About the Author

Sarah Woods is an award-winning writer who has spent time travelling and working in Dubai. As part of her work for Real Estate TV and *A Place in the Sun*, *Homes Overseas* and *Homes Worldwide* magazines, she has interviewed over a thousand British expatriates about their life abroad. Sarah has also been involved with film and documentary projects about Britons who have relocated to foreign climes. She works closely with foreign embassy staff and relocation agents across the world and has contributed articles to the *Sunday Times*.

Sarah was awarded the Kenneth Westcott Memorial Prize for her writing in 2007, and the British Guild of Travel Writers 'Guide Book of the Year' Award in 2005. In the course of her work Sarah has clocked up almost three quarters of a million kilometres since the late 1980s, visiting around 50 countries. Today she divides her time between her family in the eastern Mediterranean and a flat in the UK. She is currently working on projects in the Middle East, South America and Central America and the Caribbean.

Cadogan Guides is an imprint of
New Holland Publishers (UK) Ltd
London • Cape Town • Sydney • Auckland

New Holland Publishers (UK) Ltd
Garfield House,
86–88 Edgware Road
London W2 2EA

80 McKenzie Street
Cape Town 8001
South Africa

Unit 1, 66 Gibbes Street
Chatswood, NSW 2067
Australia

218 Lake Road
Northcote
Auckland
New Zealand

cadogan@nhpub.co.uk
www.cadoganguides.com
t 44 (0)20 7724 7773

Distributed in the United States by Globe Pequot, Connecticut

Copyright © Cadogan Guides 2009
"THE SUNDAY TIMES" is a registered trade mark of Times Newspapers Limited

Cover photographs all © Fotolia.com: © Bretin, © Philippe Perraud, © jscalev, © Bea Busse, © Sebastian Walter, © Richard Morgan, © Haider Yousuf
Photo essay photographs all © Fotolia.com: © Bretin, © Jürgen Lorenzen, © Philip Chivers, © Akhilesh Sharma, © Richard Morgan, © Isabelle Barthe, © jscalev, © Bea Busse, © Haider Yousuf © Diana Gräßer
Maps © Cadogan Guides, drawn by Maidenhead Cartographic Services Ltd
Cover design: Sarah Rianhard-Gardner
Layout and editing: Linda McQueen
Proofreading: Helen Peters
Indexing: Isobel McLean

Produced by **Navigator Guides**
www.navigatorguides.com

Printed in Finland by WS Bookwell
A catalogue record for this book is available from the British Library

ISBN: 978-1-86011-416-8

The author and publishers have made every effort to ensure the accuracy of the information in this book at the time of going to press. However, they cannot accept any responsibility for any loss, injury or inconvenience resulting from the use of information contained in this guide.

Please help us to keep this guide up to date. We have done our best to ensure that the information in this guide is correct at the time of going to press. But laws and regulations are constantly changing, and standards and prices fluctuate. We would be delighted to receive any comments.

Introduction

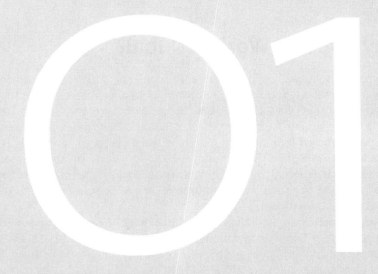

01

As the most forward-thinking of the seven sheikhdoms of the United Arab Emirates (UAE), Dubai is a hard act to follow. Although second in size to neighbouring Abu Dhabi, Dubai boasts a much larger population and is renowned for its progressive stance and dynamic buzz. First-timers in Dubai often reel at the fast-paced, consumer-driven thrust of the city-state – a land packed with iconic, dazzling architecture and world-class beach resorts. Every aspect of Dubai's ever-changing skyline appears to be lavished with gloss and glitz. Elaborate projects and much-photographed landmarks border on the ostentatious in a city where razzle-dazzle sets the tone.

It is almost impossible to believe that, just three decades ago, Dubai was little more than a ramshackle collection of fishing huts strung along a winding creek. Here, pearl trading formed the economic bedrock of an isolated, windblown settlement, sparsely populated by Bedouin. Today Dubai ranks as one of the world's most vibrant, cosmopolitan and avant-garde cities, a sophisticated tourist destination visited by global travellers, that has literally been carved from arid sand. Gleaming futuristic spires soar from former patches of desert scrubland as Dubai is continually redefined, bigger, bolder and better. The result is a hyper-globalised city-state where non-citizens make up over 80 per cent of the population and where European and Asian influences pepper a sophisticated cultural scene. A little garish and vulgar? Maybe – it's been slated as a 'Vegas-meets-Disney-in-the-desert' by its critics. Yet it is impossible not to admire the vision behind the crafting of the emirate. In economic and evolutionary terms, Dubai's transformation has been nothing short of dramatic – a rapid trajectory of change unrivalled by any other city on the planet.

Why Live and Work in Dubai?

Cosmopolitan Dubai is growing at a phenomenal rate, with a thriving expatriate community forming 82 per cent of its total population. More than 100,000 British nationals call the UAE home, with Europeans and Asians accounting for around 70 per cent of expatriate households. In 2007, some 24,333 people moved to Dubai each month, to add an extra 292,000 people in just a year – at a rate of 800 per day or 33 every hour. In 2008, the total number of new arrivals is expected to be closer to 100,000. Today, more than 1.4 million people live in the city-state compared to 1.1 million in 2005, according to the Dubai Statistics Department.

It's a young population. More than 40 per cent of the UAE is aged 25 and under, and 19 per cent of Dubai's population is aged between 30 and 34. It's also a male-dominated one: in Dubai, 75.5 per cent of the population is male and only 24.5 per cent female. Dubai's political stability, low crime rate and exceptional healthcare facilities are highly appealing to foreign workers, many of whom benefit from the strong economy, healthy social climate, first-class recruitment market and tax-free salaries. The launch of Dubai Healthcare City in 2002 at a cost of more than US$6 billion has further enhanced the city's lifestyle benefits. Pension reforms are also currently under way, and it is rumoured that they will encompass the expatriate community as well as local citizens.

Language

The prevalence of English as Dubai's *de facto* national language makes it easy for English-speakers to make the move although learning some key Arabic phrases will certainly endear you to the locals (*see* pp.23–4 and pp.151–3). An exotic mix of international races has added a host of nuances to everyday communication. However, language itself poses no barrier to living, working and integrating in Dubai – and experiencing all it has to offer. Newspapers, radio, TV are all available in English language format. Such basics as menus and road signs as well as red-tape and business dealings and everyday banter are all in English, too.

Lifestyle and Standard of Living

It's hard not to be seduced by Dubai's expatriate lifestyle: a glamorous cocktail of tax-free salary packages, high living standards and year-round golden skies. Although the cost of living in Dubai is quite high, personal taxes are non-existent, reducing the overall financial burden for expatriate residents.

Accommodation in the emirate is pricey and represents a major outlay, despite moves by the government to cap rental rates. However, many properties are on swish private estates in magnificent landscaped gardens complete with beach, or pool, terraces and barbecue areas – often with shops, restaurants and cafés on-site. Those who are head-hunted, relocated or who land a dream job in Dubai are often able to negotiate a housing package as part of their deal.

Dubai's flourishing expatriate community enjoys a highly social lifestyle. Eating out is a popular pastime (*see* pp.51–5), with hundreds of restaurants to choose from, from five-star fine dining to Tex Mex joints. Almost every expatriate family is a member of a private beach club or golf club, and nights out with friends tend to centre on Dubai's many nightclubs, bars and music hang-outs. Opulent, decadent and luxurious, Dubai offers real glitz and razzmatazz. It is also very family-orientated, offering many sporting and leisure clubs and amenities and an environment in which children can thrive.

Healthcare (*see* pp.162–6) and education services (*see* pp.180–84) are also world-class in Dubai; standards are exceptionally high. Fuel, taxis and domestic help – such as a maid or cleaning services – are all relatively inexpensive. An array of shops (*see* pp.168–73) stocks a wide range of local and international goods, from colourful markets and small boutiques to sprawling air-cooled malls and big supermarkets. Tax-free designer brands and keenly priced gold are just two of the draws of Dubai's shopping; the city was a major trading centre for over six centuries and is still a hotbed of commercial activity today.

Climate and Leisure

Dubai's 350 days of glorious sunshine allow residents lots of opportunity to enjoy outdoor life, from family cook-outs to shoreline strolls. An impressive number of tennis clubs, leisure parks, football centres and volleyball courts ensure plenty to do away from the hustle and bustle of Dubai's full-on, fast-paced commercial sector. Miles and miles of gorgeous beaches offer water-sports galore, from scuba diving and snorkelling to waterskiing, wake boarding, jet skiing and boating. Large expanses of palm-hemmed manicured grass, flower-filled gardens and lakeside green spaces provide good spots in which to enjoy lazy picnics. Camping trips out to the mountains, camel-trekking and 4x4 dune-bashing (*see* pp.56–8) provide a fascinating foray into the wilds of the desert – occasionally with the added excitement of spotting an oryx or eagle-owl.

Crime

Although Dubai is renowned as crime-free, no country in the world can claim this status. However, incidents of crime are low and Dubai is viewed as a safe place by its residents. Strict laws keep the streets largely free from danger and theft and violent crime is rare. Deportation is assured for any non-national involved in crime, however petty the incident.

In 2007 Dubai's Police Executive Symposium released its annual crime figures: serious crime accounted for between 0.5 and one per 100,000 people, compared with the international average of four to six per 100,000 people. A super-efficient police force prides itself on being one of the most modern on the planet. Ten police stations serve the city. *See* pp.178–80.

Getting to Know Dubai

Historical Overview

The Distant Past

Archaeological excavations – which unearthed artefacts now housed in the Dubai Museum – suggest that the site of present-day Dubai was settled by fishing communities as long ago as the third millennium BC. The Dubai Creek's natural harbour was a bustling stop-off point for merchant ships on the trade route connecting Mesopotamia (now part of Iraq) and the Indus Valley in India. As trade flourished between the 8th and 13th centuries AD, merchants sailed as far as China, returning with porcelain and silk for sale in Europe and the Middle East. Camel trains also carried wares across the desert; traces of a 6th century caravan station have been discovered to the south of Dubai at Jumeirah, which is today a focal point for tourism.

Pearly Rights

No one can accurately pinpoint when the first pearls were discovered in the Persian Gulf, but they have long been a part of the historical make-up of the Emirates. For centuries traders dealt pearls from the waterfront that would become known as Dubai Creek as divers harvested pearl crops from one in every 10,000 oysters. In 1580, Venetian jeweller Gasparo Balbi made the first ever written reference to the area while on an expedition to assess its pearling potential, putting the region – and its prolific pearl beds – squarely on the map.

Pearls are believed to be the result of a tiny bead of sand, parasite or contaminant that has worked its way into an oyster. In most cases, the foreign body is simply expelled by the living organism – but, in the rare instance that it isn't, the irritation is unbearable for the oyster (rather like grit in the eye of a human). In a protective move, the oyster secretes a nacreous layer to form a barrier. In time, this cordon becomes spun into a bead until a pearl is made.

Dubai's pearling industry collapsed at the end of the 1920s, dealt a double blow by the Wall Street Crash and the invention of the artificial pearl. The introduction of scientific techniques that allow artificial irritants to nurture the bead virtually destroyed Dubai's pearling community, even though only a tiny per cent of implanted oysters will produce pearls fit for jewellery.

In 2007, the Dubai Multi Commodities Centre (DMCC) announced the establishment of the Dubai Pearl Exchange (DPE), an exclusive trading platform for pearls. This initiative comes as part of DMCC's objective to revive the UAE's historic status as a leading destination for pearl-diving and -trading. The pearl industry, which is valued at US$1 billion in rough form, has witnessed a significant recovery since 2005, with prices on a continuous upward trend, despite a 23.6 per cent rise in world pearl production. Over 1,550 tonnes of pearls were harvested in 2005, with prices that range from US$50 to US$50,000 per grain.

Pearls and the British

While most trading goods originated from outside the region, this stretch of the Gulf coastline did yield one 'home-grown' commodity – the pearl. Until the pearl trade collapsed in the 1920s, the Gulf pearl – rated the finest in the world – formed the backbone of the economy for 3,000 years.

The strategic location and promise of rich pearl harvests inevitably drew the gaze of European imperial powers. In the 16th and 17th centuries, Portuguese, French and Dutch colonialists successively struggled to maintain a grip on local trade before the British finally seized control of the waterways. From the mid-19th century until the formation of the United Arab Emirates (UAE) in 1971, Britain was the leading maritime power in the Gulf.

The British quickly realised that they had to tackle piracy and tribal skirmishes – the two genuine threats to trade and stability in the region. In 1820 they arranged for the nine rulers of the sheikhdoms along the northern coast of the Arabian Peninsula to sign a General Treaty of Peace. The independent sheikhdoms were collectively named the **Trucial States**.

A Family of Leaders

Dubai became a sheikhdom in 1833, when a branch of the powerful Bani Yas tribe migrated there from Abu Dhabi, led by Sheikh Maktoum bin Buti, a member of the **Al Maktoum dynasty** that has governed the emirate ever since. The family's rule has placed Dubai at the vanguard of progress in the region. Their enlightened policy of abolishing import and export tariffs in the early 20th century, for example, made Dubai a leading trans-shipment centre for precious metals, and earned it the label 'City of Gold' (*see* p.168). The liberal and innovative thinking of subsequent leaders further fuelled commercial prosperity and attracted an increasing number of traders to settle in the town.

The Emirates Unite

From the early 1950s, the Trucial States Council strove to bring unity to the coastal sheikhdoms – a path that was far from smooth. In 1971, after the withdrawal of the British, this relationship was formalised with the creation of the **United Arab Emirates**. The states of Dubai, Abu Dhabi, Sharjah, Ajman, Umm Al Quwain, Fujairah and Ras Al Khaimah agreed to conduct foreign affairs jointly, and to adopt common immigration, defence, security and social-service policies.

Oil and the Birth of Modern Dubai

The formation of the UAE came hot on the heels of the discovery of 'black gold' in 1966. Soaring oil prices in the 1970s brought considerable windfalls to the small oil-producing Gulf States. This revenue – together with the stability provided by the formation of the UAE and shrewd re-investment by **Sheikh Rashid bin Saeed Al Maktoum** – allowed the foundations of Dubai's modern society to be laid. Landmark building projects transformed the creekside, Port (Mina) Rashid was opened to sea traffic in 1972, and the **Dubai World Trade Centre** became a proud symbol of the state's ambitions to become an international centre of commerce.

But Sheikh Rashid's vision went further. Determined to reinforce the economy by broadening its base beyond oil, he initiated a new industrial centre with a major port and a Free Trade Zone. By the mid-1980s, the world's largest artificial harbour (**Mina Jebel Ali**) and the **Jebel Ali Free Zone (JAFZ)** were up and running 35 kilometres (22 miles) to the southwest of the city. Furthermore, **Dubai International Airport** came to serve almost 100 airlines and established the emirate as the region's aviation and tourist hub. **Emirates Airline** – created in 1985 by another progressive ruler, the pioneering then-Crown Prince of Dubai, **General Sheikh Mohammed bin Rashid Al Maktoum** – rapidly grew into one of the world's biggest and most profitable fleet carriers.

From traditional port to international commercial heavyweight, Dubai's transformation, effected by the clear-sighted guidance of the Al Maktoum family, is the stuff of fairytales. And there is no indication that Sheikh Mohammed's quest for progress is abating as the emirate continues to surge forward. As he has said himself, 'A man has two choices, either to be a follower or to show initiative, and we greatly desire to be pioneers.'

See Chapter 03, **Dubai Today**, for the economic background of modern Dubai.

United Arab Emirates Timeline: A Chronology of Key Events

1820 To combat piracy along the Gulf Coast, Britain and local rulers sign a treaty. This, and later agreements, lead to the area becoming known as the Trucial Coast.

1892 Britain is awarded control over foreign affairs after a deal with the Trucial States that affords each emirate power over its own internal affairs.

1950s Vast reserves of oil ('Black Gold') are discovered, creating massive revenues.

1952 The seven emirates combine to form a Trucial Council.

1962 Oil is exported for the first time from the UAE.

1966 Sheikh Zayed bin Sultan Al Nuhayyan takes over as ruler of Abu Dhabi.

1968 As independence looms, Bahrain and Qatar join the Trucial States. However political differences cause the union to disintegrate in 1971.

1971 After independence from Britain in December 1971, Abu Dhabi, Ajman, Dubai, Fujairah, Sharjah, and Umm Al Quwain join together to form the United Arab Emirates (UAE). The federation is presided over by Sheikh Zayed bin Sultan Al Nuhayyan.

1971 UAE joins the Arab League.

1972 Ras Al Khaimah joins the federation.

The 40-member Federal National Council (FNC) is established to form a consultative body appointed by the emirate's seven rulers.

1981 The first summit of the Gulf Cooperation Council (GCC) is held in the UAE (a founding member).

1986 UAE president Sheikh Zayed bin Sultan Al Nuhayyan is re-elected for a fourth tenure.

1987 The UAE is rocked by a coup attempt in Sharjah, after which Sheikh Sultan bin Muhammad Al Qasimi abdicates to let his brother take up the rule, but is reinstated by the Supreme Council of Rulers.

1990 After the death of Sheikh Rashid bin Said Al Maktoum, his son Sheikh Maktoum bin Rashid Al Maktoum is appointed Dubai's ruler and the vice-president of the UAE.

1991 After the invasion of Kuwait, the UAE's forces join the allies against Iraq.

The Bank of Credit and Commerce International (BCCI) collapses. Abu Dhabi's ruling family owns a 77.4 per cent share.

1993 BCCI's executives are sued for damages by Abu Dhabi's leaders.

1994 Most of the BCCI executives are incriminated over fraud allegations and sent to jail.

1996 On appeal, two BCCI executives are cleared of wrongdoing.

2001 Some 6,000 prisoners receive an official pardon from President Sheikh Zayed.

2001 In a high-profile security crackdown, the UAE government freezes the bank assets of over 60 organisations suspected by America of funding terrorism.

2004 After the death of UAE president Sheikh Zayed bin Sultan Al Nuhayyan, his son, Sheikh Khalifa, succeeds him.

2005 The UAE plans for its first elections that will see 50 per cent of the members of the consultative Federal National Council (FNC) elected by eligible UAE citizens.

2006 Sheikh Maktoum bin Rashid Al Maktoum, UAE prime minister and vice-president and ruler of Dubai, dies during a visit to Australia. He is succeeded by his brother, Sheikh Mohammed bin Rashid Al Maktoum.

A political storm brews regarding state-owned Dubai Ports World when US Forces request that it relinquish control of terminals at six major American ports for 'security reasons'.

The UAE announces a number of initiatives to bring its business style in line with Western nations, including plans to nurture local workers and steps to allow unskilled labourers to form trade unions.

Much hype surrounds the UAE's first-ever national elections to appoint members to the Federal National Council (FNC), although just a small number of cherry-picked voters are allowed to pool.

2007 The UAE's visionary National Development Strategy is launched, outlining ambitious economic goals to make it a world leader.

Dubai and Qatar become the two biggest shareholders of the London Stock Exchange (LSE), the world's third largest financial market.

2008 Dubai declares a National Holiday to honour George Bush's visit.

US regulators at the Commodity Futures Trading Commission (CFTC) impose new trading conditions on some Dubai Mercantile Exchange contracts in a bid to limit excess speculation in futures markets.

Climate and Geography

Topography

Rising from the sand and water on the northeastern coast of the Arabian Peninsula, Dubai's modern topography is newly awash in shiny towers of landmark architectural splendour. Over 300 manmade islands and an ever-expanding coastline have also rapidly redefined the landscape of the city.

Located roughly at sea level (16 metres) on the Persian Gulf coast of the UAE, Dubai is bordered by Abu Dhabi to the south, Sharjah to the northeast and the Sultanate of Oman to the southeast. The waters of the Persian Gulf hem the western coast of the emirate.

Dubai spans an area of 4,114km² within the Arabian Desert, but boasts a fine white sand landscape distinctly different from the gravel-rich deserts of the south of the UAE. A string of rolling dunes runs to the east of the city; at their furthest reaches they become red-tinged by iron oxide deposits. A vast carpet of towering sand dunes that reach 250 metres sprawls into the **Empty Quarter**, a spectacular desert that covers over 25 per cent of the Arabian Peninsula. The jagged peaks of the **Hajar Mountains** are a dominant topographical feature along the Omani border, rising to about 1,300 metres.

Dubai's natural salt water inlet, **Dubai Creek**, runs through the centre of the city, splitting it neatly in two. Although Dubai has no rivers, there are multiple gorges and waterholes along the foothills of the Hajar Mountains.

Birding Around

Strangely for a desert landscape, twitchers have plenty to rave about in the UAE. Dubai attracts a host of migratory bird species and is also home to many indigenous species, thanks to the lush botanical greenery that is now very much a part of the modern character of the city. Over 80 species breed in Dubai during the spring and summer months, while hundreds more make the emirate a stop-off en route to Africa and Central Asia.

Many migratory species are unusual, rare or just plain spectacular – and aren't found in any other areas of the Middle East. Despite its relatively small size, Dubai is blessed with a range of different habitats, from offshore islands and rocky outcrops, mangrove swamps and tidal wetlands to mountains, mud flats, lagoons and desert scrub. Birders can expect to find a wide variety of species, from parakeets, seabirds, sand grouse, bee-eaters, flamingos, eagles, king-fishers, vultures, owls, plovers, gulls, terns and flycatchers to larks, wheatears and herons. Just a few minutes from Dubai's city centre, over 1,000 greater flamingos call the protected Khor Dubai Wildlife Sanctuary home. There are also reef herons, spotted eagles, lesser sand plovers, broad-billed and terek sandpipers. The iconic Emirates Golf Club is also an outstanding birding site and is home to red-wattled lapwings, Pacific golden plovers, pintail snipe, chestnut-bellied sandgrouse and Isabelline shrikes.

For details of birding hotspots and UAE bird checklists, contact the Emirates Bird Records Committee, t 050 642 4358, **www.uaeinteract.com/nature**.

Climate

Dubai certainly doesn't suffer from a shortage of **sunshine**, with daily rays and a subtropical, arid climate that ranges from comfortably warm to unbearably hot. Dubai's busier winter season, November to March, is popular with visitors as daytime **temperatures** sit at around a comfortable 24°C. The winter season may not offer the cut-price deals of the summer but is a better option for those keen to do anything vaguely energy-sapping. Summertime sees temperatures hit the mid-40s on the coast – and even higher inland. Heatstroke and sunburn can be a real risk at this time, particularly for Westerners unused to searing heat. Even night-time temperatures rarely dip below 30°C in July – heady highs when a simple stroll can seem like a marathon run. Yet it is important to remember that everywhere in Dubai is heavily air-conditioned – so indoor temperatures can border on the chilly in some restaurants, cinemas and hotel bars.

Dubai does get a little **rain**, and these downpours generally occur in February or March. It also has thick **snow** flurries on a daily basis – but only at the toboganing hills, twin-track bobsled ride and snowball-throwing gallery of the city's **Snow Park**, where 6,000 tons of real snow and temperatures of minus 2°C provide an unworldly escape from the outside world's searing desert heat.

Sandstorms

Dubai's prevailing wind is a weather phenomenon characterised by heavy sandstorms that whip up in the desert and deluge the city. Some of these windswept assaults are dangerous, prompting the Dubai government to issue emergency warnings. Many of Dubai's famous golf courses are particularly vulnerable to incoming storms as they are exposed to desert gusts. Typically, gusts blow directly into the face and render visibility impossible as your eyes become blinded by gritty blasts. Anyone driving long distances across the desert should always be sure to check local weather forecasts to ascertain the risk of sandstorms and prevailing winds.

In January 2008, the Dubai Meteorology Office issued an extreme weather warning for an approaching sandstorm with gale-force winds. Speeds of up to 30 knots hit the UAE's west coast as a result of the high-pressure system building over Saudi Arabia, while strong northwesterly winds blew it in from Kuwait, Qatar and Bahrain. People were urged not to drive unless absolutely necessary, aircraft were prevented from landing at Dubai International Airport due to poor visibility, construction workers were told to down-tools and boats were brought back to shore. The conditions were a result of the northwesterly **shamal** wind, a wave of low pressure that funnels through the Gulf between Saudi Arabia and Iran. These ferocious gusts can last three to 40 days and are considered to be the most hazardous weather condition in the region. The 2008 sandstorm arrived hot on the heels of three days of heavy rains, causing wide-spread flooding that resulted in traffic chaos across much of the Emirates.

However, not everything about the winds is an annoyance – in the past, Dubai architecture used towers to divert the squalls towards houses to make full use of the cooling breeze. The city gets 4,000 wind hours annually, and wind turbines are increasingly being used to generate 1,200,000 kilowatt-hours of energy – another plus-point given that the annual power consumption of a family is estimated to be 24,000 kilowatt-hours (therefore each turbine can supply energy for about 50 families). Architects who design tall buildings today take the impact of the wind into consideration. A prime example of wind-harnessed energy in Dubai is the Dynamic Architecture Tower. Here, 200 apartments are equipped with four turbines to satisfy all energy needs, in what has been hailed as a positive exploitation of Dubai's dreaded sandy blasts.

The UAE is the first country in the Middle East to introduce the Satellite Delivered Information System technology (SADIS), an effective global weather forecasting technology. Supplying data on temperature, humidity, volcanoes and wind directions, SADIS also enables the UAE to receive the latest forecasts for centres all over the world through direct contact with the world centre in London. It is operated by the UAE's National Meteorology Authority-qualified forecasters and is one of the most technologically advanced weather prediction systems on the planet.

Water, Water Everywhere

The UAE has one of the highest per capita rates of water consumption on the planet, largely the result of vast amounts of urban development and rapid rates of population growth. Much of the water usage is lavished on greening the UAE's dry desert landscape to allow gardens and flowers to flourish – a decadence of wealth. In 2008, Mohammad Saeed Al Kindy, the minister of environment and water, announced plans to help rationalise water consumption levels. In addition to increased demand, scarce rainfall has seen water supplies come under strain. Between them, the seven Emirates receive rainfall of less than 115 million litres per annum – and many observers feel that the installation of water meters is just around the corner. This would measure usage and monitor usage patterns and also highlight wastage and over-consumption – and allow individual leaders the opportunity to bill for it.

Month-by-month Breakdown

January

This is the coolest month: average maximum temperatures settle at around 24°C, with an average minimum of 14°C. However, records show that January temperatures have been reported as high as 32°C and as low as 8°C, so variations do occur. The weather is typically cloudy and unsettled, as mid-latitude weather disturbances penetrate into the Gulf, bringing changeable weather and cool winter shamals (northwesterly winds) in their wake. Such shamals sweep down the Gulf frequently, producing intense convective activity resulting in squally, thundery weather with showers, storms and high seas.

On average five or six rainy days can be expected during the month; however, as many as 17 rainy days have been recorded. Rainfall is often short-lived and intense, with isolated thunderstorms producing the majority of the recorded rain. Large fluctuations in rainfall occur from year to year, with occasional dry years or as much as 82mm falling during the month. On clear, fine days the weather is pleasant and warm with weak afternoon sea breezes.

Sea temperatures are around 21°C.

February

Temperatures increase a degree or so in February, with mean maximums typically around 25°C; however, the extreme maximum temperature has reached 36°C, with a minimum as low as 7°C. Unsettled wintry weather is more frequent; winter shamals persist, with their associated unsettled weather and strong winds. This makes February one of the windiest months. Ahead of an approaching shamal, strong southeasterly winds often develop, with hot, dry conditions and occasional sandstorms. The transition from the southeasterly winds ahead of the trough to the northwesterly shamal is therefore usually associated with a marked fall in temperature.

February is the wettest month of the year, with an average of 25mm of rain; it also holds the record for the most rainfall in a day, 150.2mm in 1988 at Dubai Airport. The expected number of rainy days during the month is five, but has been as high as 12. The relatively warm, moist air over the Gulf combined with winter weather patterns helps to fuel cloud and storm development. Local convergence and the effect of the mountains in the east of the country also generate or enhance rainfall.

March

The period from March through to May is Dubai's 'spring' season, when temperatures begin to climb steadily towards the summer peaks. Average maximum temperatures rise to around 28°C in March; however, winter weather patterns continue to affect the area. This means that a more abundant supply of energy is available for the development of cloud and storms. March is therefore often a very changeable month, when Dubai can experience a wide range of weather phenomena. This is why March has the highest expected number of rainy days – six on average and up to 18 in recent years – as well as the most frequent occurrence of thunderstorms. Average rainfall for the month is 21mm but has been as high as 155mm. As in February, in between the periods of unsettled weather, winds tend to veer to the southeast and bring warm, dry desert air to the coast. Temperatures have been recorded in the low 40s later in the month; however, extreme minimums of 11°C have also been recorded.

Case Study: Clare Lewis

'Since I moved here in 2005, time has flown by. It's been a real whirlwind of new friends and new experiences – and has made me realise just how short life is. Now, I can't imagine commuting into London every day on the train in the cold, wind and rain. I'm so glad that I followed my "just do it" gut instinct – I've met some wonderful people here and have enjoyed building a brand new life in the sun. My job at an events management company brings me into contact with senior executives from across the globe from companies like Cartier, Nokia, Tommy Hilfiger and General Motors. As a sun-worshipper, I love the fact that the weather is so hot and sunny. I wake up to the sun shining into my apartment and never tire of how that makes me feel.

'It's easy to feel like royalty here thanks to free-flowing champagne brunches, polo matches, gourmet dining and days spent lazing around the pool. I also have a cleaner and get my dry cleaning done each week for around 40p per item. Although much of Dubai has been like a building site – with lots of cranes, banging and dust – the city is slowly beginning to take shape. This ongoing, relentless construction has its down-side, of course. Other crazy things include some of the drivers here – they're maniacs! I'm also bemused by the Dubai government's recent initiative to combat high humidity using chemically controlled precipitation measures to make it rain – I mean, how bizarre is that?'

April

As the sun begins to climb in the sky, April brings some beautiful weather to the Emirates, with maximum temperatures typically around 33°C. Humidity is generally low and, although winter systems are still possible, they are less frequent. Rainfall drops to around 7mm across an average of around three days (although a high of around 60mm has been recorded), while coastal afternoon sea breezes increase in strength as the temperature gradient between the land and the sea develops.

The increase in temperature does, however, mean that the occasional storms that do develop can be violent, with heavy rain and squalls. One particularly violent storm in 1981 produced golfball-sized hailstones, and in 2003 a storm and squall produced mean winds of 53 knots gusting to 71 knots. As the month progresses, the high-level Jetstream starts to move northwards, cutting off southward incursions of unsettled weather and cool northwesterly winds.

The sea in coastal waters continues to warm up, with a mean temperature for the month of about 25°C.

May

May often marks the beginning of the summer heat. Average maximum temperatures are between 37°C and 38°C, but extreme highs of 47°C have been recorded. The humidity, however, is at its lowest level for the year and rain and thunderstorms are extremely rare in coastal areas. Hot, dry southeasterly winds often prevail in May, but comfort levels remain reasonable because of the low humidity. Sea temperatures increase to around 28–29°C.

June

During June, low pressure over southern Iran, which develops in the lee of the mountains, combines with a ridge of high pressure over Saudi Arabia to produce a northwesterly gradient that can persist over the Gulf for up to six weeks. The phenomenon is known locally as the 'Forty-day Shamal'. From year to year the onset and strength of this effect can vary widely. Hot and generally dry conditions prevail throughout the month, with periods of southeasterly winds replacing the northwesterly flow when the lee low weakens. When the winds are from the northwest they bring hot and sometimes dusty conditions from the deserts of Saudi Arabia, Kuwait and Iraq. Temperatures typically reach a maximum of around 39°C but can be as high as 47°C, but low humidity at this time helps to keep stress levels reasonably low.

Rainfall is infrequent during June, with most coastal stations having a completely dry month. Over the mountains in the east of the emirate, summer storms do develop and can cause intense localised heavy rainstorms and flash flooding in the wadis. Dry squalls from these storms do occasionally reach the coast dramatically reducing the visibility for a few hours.

Sea temperatures increase into the low 30s°C.

Case Study: Richard Smith

'As managing director of Charterhouse Lombard (Dubai) Ltd, part of Charterhouse Group International Limited, I'm in Dubai as part of a worldwide operation providing offshore company, trust, private foundation and business start-up services. Prior to our move I'd visited Dubai regularly for several years as my primary role is business development. I was struck by the scope of opportunity – the place has exploded in the last few years in terms of business, and property development in particular. My wife Ingrid and I made the move in 2005 when the company opened a Dubai office. Three years later, in April 2008, we had our first child here, a daughter, Millie, born in the American Hospital.

'Change is always difficult to start with, especially as Ingrid had left a good job in London to follow me out here. Apparently 80 per cent of expat postings fail because the partner doesn't settle. But Ingrid has made friends with lots of like-minded mothers and our move was made easier by the fact that she'd previously lived and worked in Hong Kong and comes from an expat family. We also already knew a few people in Dubai through business, and it's an incredibly sociable place to be.

'Know-how is important when establishing a business presence in the UAE, as the red tape is not as straightforward as going to Companies House in the UK and incorporating a company the same day. Getting the correct advice is crucial, as it is a minefield if you don't know what you're doing. We help our clients with a range of services, from identifying the correct type of legal structure for their new venture in Dubai, to finding an office and getting a local agent/sponsor to assist with visas. Basically we will project manage the entire

July

As the summer advances and the monsoon spreads northwards over India, the lee low effect over southern Iran begins to weaken and pressure gradients become weak over the area. Land and sea breezes begin to dominate the flow and, as the sea is still warming up, thermal gradients can be strong, with a moderate-to-fresh northwesterly sea breeze most afternoons. The humidity can become extremely high at times, producing severe stress. The combination of high temperatures and high humidity can make atmospheric conditions extremely unstable, and summer thunderstorms are not uncommon. As in June, these usually develop over the mountains in the east of the emirate, where the mountains act as elevated heat sources and convergence often occurs. Sea breezes on the east coast force very humid air up the mountains, where it combines late in the afternoon with Gulf Coast sea breezes from the northwest. Inland stations frequently report towering cumulus and cumulonimbus clouds, with thunderstorms, squalls and dust or sandstorms. Mid- and upper-level easterly winds then help to propel the storms towards the Gulf Coast, where they can occasionally affect Dubai, Sharjah and the northern Emirates. Mean maximum temperatures in July are typically around 41°C, process so that people can just arrive in Dubai and hit the ground running. Our clients appreciate a personal service – attention to detail counts for a lot.

'Although the UAE is quite a tolerant, liberal country, there are special considerations as it is a Muslim country and, under Sharia law, inheritance does not necessarily go to a spouse and children. If you buy property through an offshore company, there is the potential to avoid the intricacies of Sharia law, so there is an interest for cash buyers in buying property through offshore companies. It is very important to remember the maxim 'When in Rome...' as living in a Muslim country requires a certain respect for local laws and cultures. For example, the law frowns upon public displays of affection, something that hit the headlines in 2008 when two Britons got drunk in Dubai and had sex in a public place. They are now facing three years in jail. Dubai's multi-ethnic population lives in harmony, with incidents of crime rare. Cultural differences are understood and generally well respected. For example, during the holy month of Ramadan, you are expected not to be seen eating, drinking or smoking in public during the hours of daylight; on the flip side it is very much the norm at Christmas to have trees and Santa Claus in all the shopping malls. Last year there was even a Christmas Winter Wonderland for children, with an outdoor skating rink!

'For us, the worst aspect of life in Dubai is the unbearable heat for three months a year. It is hard to cope with 80 per cent humidity, so the air-conditioning is on full all the time – from home to the car to the office and back again. It's very restrictive. The rest of the year is fantastic, especially in February, when on a warm, sunny morning I remind myself of the freezing, miserable weather we used to endure in London at that time of year.'

inland stations being the hottest, with expected maximums of 44°C and all-time extremes of around 49°C.

Sea temperatures begin to become unpleasantly warm, reaching 32–33°C.

August

Conditions during August are similar to those experienced in July in terms of temperature and humidity. During the summer, as the sea surface temperature rises, the Gulf increasingly becomes a prolific source of water vapour. Afternoon sea breezes bring this warm, humid air to coastal areas and can produce some of the year's most uncomfortable conditions. The risk of summer storms persists and, although most frequent over the mountains, these can occasionally affect coastal areas too. Inland desert areas have a rather different climate. Although summer maximum temperatures in the desert are frequently higher than those on the coast, the mean humidity is up to 20 per cent lower than coastal areas. This produces rather more comfortable conditions and is the reason that, prior to the prevalence of air-conditioning, many local families would spend the summer months away from the coast.

Mean sea temperatures are around 33°C but have been recorded up to 35°C.

September

As temperatures begin to fall after the height of the summer, there is a sting in the tail for residents of coastal cities. Sea temperatures reach a peak at the end of August while warm, humid air on the coast reaches high temperatures. Humidity soars and this is one of the months with a high occurrence of fog. Night-time temperatures begin to drop into the upper 20s and fog will often form in the early morning hours. Maximum temperatures can still occasionally reach extremes of 45°C, with extreme minimums around 22°C. Sea temperatures begin to fall later in the month, with a mean for the month of around 32°C.

October

It is the latter part of the year when the weather is the most pleasant and settled in the UAE. Maximum temperatures in October are around 35°C and, although the humidity remains reasonably high, comfort indices rise from the extreme levels experienced in the summer. As night-time temperatures continue to fall, faster than the sea temperature, fog is still a problem in the early morning. The weather is usually dry and settled, but there have been exceptional years such as 1997 when several weather systems penetrated into the area, bringing unsettled wet weather and thunderstorms.

The mean sea temperature for the month is 30°C.

November

Temperatures continue to fall sharply during the month, with mean maximums between 30°C and 31°C. As the subtropical Jetstream moves southwards and upper level winds over the Gulf strengthen, there is the increased potential for low pressure systems to propagate from the north and west into the area.

Late in the month it is possible for the first shamals to affect the Gulf, but it is not usually until December that unsettled weather reaches the region. Again, November 1997 was an exceptional year, with 12 rain days including four thunderstorm days producing 31mm of rain at Dubai International Airport. In 2004 a severe line-squall and thunderstorm brought heavy rain (24mm) and a hailstorm that produced stones of up to 150mm in diameter.

December

By the end of the year, winter systems are more frequently affecting the Emirates. The mean monthly rainfall is 15mm, with rain reported on three or four days during the month. Mean maximums fall to 26°C, with minimums typically around 16°C. The humidity is frequently high in the early morning hours, with fog still causing a problem, although Dubai and the northern Emirates tend to be a little less humid than other areas of the country. Occasionally persistent periods of unsettled and wet weather can affect Dubai in December. Rainfall totals have been as high as 130mm, with a 24-hour maximum rainfall of 73mm. Sea temperatures fall to around 23°C.

Data courtesy of the Dubai Metrological Office

Language

Language is an important marker of identity for any country, and the fact that it is possible to travel around Dubai without encountering any Arabic speaks volumes about the modern character of the city. While Arabic is the official language, English is widely spoken by the multicultural population, hailing from, it is alleged, over 160 different nations from every corner of the globe. Dubai bridges the East and West, drawing workers from an area that spans the Middle East, North and South Africa, India and Southeast Europe – that's 31 countries, 53 languages and 1.8 billion people. Over 91 per cent of the working population is non-national, with most graduate professional workers coming from Europe, America and Australia. That English is used with such prevalence is understandable, given Dubai's complex ethnic make-up.

Of course, it helps to foster relationships and win respect to throw a few words of Arabic into the conversation now and then. It isn't the easiest language to master, but a number of schools specialise in tutoring foreigners in the city (*see* p.151) and offer group schooling or one-to-one.

Arabic

Arabic is one of the most spoken languages in the world, with over 200 million speakers across 24 countries. As the official language of all the countries of northern Africa, the Arabian Peninsula and much of the Middle East, including Iraq, Syria, Lebanon, Kuwait, Saudi Arabia and Bahrain, it is the second language of millions of Muslims and one of the six official languages of the United Nations. The languages of northern India, Turkey, Iran, Portugal and Spain are littered with words of Arabic origin.

Modern Arabic varies considerably from country to country. A few introductory phrases are listed below; for more, *see* **Living in Dubai**, pp.151–3.

Pronunciation
a as in 'had'
e as in 'bet'
i as in 'hit'
u as in 'put'

Useful Greetings
hello *marhaba*
response to above *marhabtayn*

peace be upon you *salaamu alaykom*
response to above *wa alaykom is salaam*

Case Study: Viren Lodhia

'Dubai is an amazing country with so much to offer but I always tell people considering a move out here not to expect things to be as organised and systematic as they look from the outside. In many respects, Dubai is a real contradiction: extremely modern, yet a city still very much finding its feet – almost learning to become a big city. Yet it's certainly made a wonderful impact on us as a family, and our life in the Jumeirah Beach Residence (JBR) is very much the beachfront idyll. We moved to Dubai from Loughborough in 2004 for the career opportunities and assumed we'd be here a couple of years – now, three and half years later, we still love being here.

'I'm married with one son, who was born in Dubai, and living on the beach with a little child is something very special. When it came to deciding whether our son should be born in the UK or here in Dubai we were swayed by the high standard of local healthcare. Our current home is a rental apartment and we're living here while our purchased property is being built. It's a three-bedroom apartment, approximately 1,800 square feet, with a balcony and a maid's room, which is quite common in Dubai. We are within walking distance of the beach and Dubai Marina and it's a good location for families and young couples, with a "café" lifestyle available within a few minutes' stroll.

'We started learning Arabic when we arrived, although we rarely use it, since the population is highly cosmopolitan. However, it was fun learning, and a great way to meet new people.'

good morning *sabah il-khayr*
response to above *sabah in-nuwr*

good evening *masa il-khayr*
response to above *masa in-nuwr*

goodbye *ma is-salaama*

my name is... *ismiy...*

Dubai Today

A multi-billion-dollar injection of funds has transformed the former desert outpost of Dubai into one of the finest holiday destinations on the planet. No other city has developed a comparable tourism industry, with such dramatic results, in such a short period of time. Today, Dubai's main tourist website receives in excess of 250,000 hits a day. Dubai occupies 83 per cent of the UAE's total land space allotted to tourism projects and accounts for over 50 per cent of the value of the UAE's tourism, with over AED 450 billion in investments. Tourism is also at the thrust of Dubai's future strategic growth, with dozens of ambitious development projects under way to secure the ongoing loyalty of the tourist dollar.

Dubai's world-class infrastructure, air links and port facilities make it the region's best-connected city. It is politically stable, has a liberal government renowned for its efficiency and commitment to a free and balanced economic policy, and has business-friendly regulations and tax incentives. It is cosmopolitan and multicultural, with foreign nationals from (allegedly) over 160 countries accounting for over 91 per cent of the total working population. Annual job creation is predicted at 8.3 per cent, according to the website **http://BritishExpats.com**, with Dubai's population predicted to grow by 108,000 people annually to 2.1 million by 2010.

However, as it continues to mushroom and morph, Dubai is also increasingly being placed under the scrutiny of the world's human rights campaigners amid reports of industrial injuries and poor pay and conditions. Balancing such labour laws and women's rights with commercial goals and global vision has been a challenge to the Dubai administration. It is also faced with demands for greater security in the region post-9/11.

Rulers and Foreign Policy

Ruled along dynastic lines as part of system of tribal consensus without an independent parliament of political parties, the UAE administration centres on a consultative council that is nominated by the ruling family. A group of five old Arab families provides the dynamo behind emirate control, with the **Maktoum dynasty** a powerful ruling force since 1833. When Sheikh Rashid, the visionary architect of Dubai's success and financial power, died in 1990, his son Sheikh Maktoum took over at the helm. The focus of Maktoum's policies was economic freedom and the no-holds-barred promotion of Dubai to a global market. His brother, **Sheikh Mohammed bin Rashid Al Maktoum** (born November 13 1982) became the public face of Dubai's progressive charm offensive. Sheikh Mohammed assumed power after Sheikh Maktoum's death in 2006, and today is UAE prime minister and vice president, and ruler of Dubai.

The UAE's foreign policy is based on the principles outlined in the Charter of the United Nations and the Charter of the Organisation of the Islamic

Conference (OIC). Unity within the Arab world has been a consistent theme of foreign policies, and the UAE has fostered strong diplomatic relations with more than 60 countries, including the USA, Japan, Russia, the People's Republic of China, Saudi Arabia, Bahrain, Qatar, Oman and most western European countries. It has played a moderate role in the Organization of Petroleum Exporting Countries (OPEC), the Organization of Arab Petroleum Exporting Countries, the United Nations, and the Gulf Cooperation Council (GCC).

Since 1971, the UAE has enjoyed friendly relations with the USA, nurturing private commercial ties and government-to-government deals, especially in petroleum. The United States was the third country to establish formal diplomatic relations with the UAE, and has had an ambassador resident in the UAE since 1974. American-UAE relations improved dramatically in 1990 as a result of the US-led coalition's campaign to end the Iraqi occupation of Kuwait. In 2002, the USA and the UAE launched a strategic partnership dialogue covering virtually every aspect of the relationship. Today the UAE hosts over 60 embassies, compared to just three in 1971. Dubai is also home to 30 non-resident embassies and over 40 consulates.

As an entity, the UAE absolutely condemns all forms of terrorism and is a key partner in America's so-called War on Terror. It has consistently spoken out about the targeting of innocent civilians, highlighting that this is a contravention not only of human rights but also of Islamic values and ideals. The ports of the UAE host more American Navy ships than any port outside the USA. However, a decision by the Bush administration to appoint Dubai Ports World to manage American seaports in 2006 provoked huge controversy in the USA. The idea of a state-owned company from the Arab world running operations caused a huge political storm that refused to die down, uniting Democrats and several senior Republicans in opposition to President Bush. Opponents of the 6.8 billion-dollar deal have framed it as a potential threat to national security. A decision by Dubai Ports World to delay its takeover of the seaport operation averted a national crisis, but is said to have cooled relations between the USA and the UAE.

Military Might and Defence

In 1971, the British-commanded Trucial Oman Scouts – a highly respected armed force of 1,600 soldiers, long the symbol of public order – were turned over to the UAE on its independence. Today, the UAE armed forces benefit from a decade-long US$15 billion programme to modernise the country's military strength. Defence capabilities have been upgraded to centre on modern technology in a rapidly developing military power that is one of the most impressive in the region. Army, navy, and airforce troops total around 59,000 personnel, who are primarily charged with the defence of the seven emirates. Although small in number, the UAE's armed forces are equipped with some of the world's most modern weaponry. The country has been a crucial partner in the campaign against global terrorism since the September 11th atrocities.

UAE Political Alliances and Agreements

- Arab League.
- Arab Gulf Co-operation Council (GCC).
- United Nations (and specialist agencies, including ICAO, UPU and WIPO).
- World Bank for Reconstruction and Development.
- International Monetary Fund (IMF).
- International Labour Organisation.
- United Nations Educational, Scientific and Cultural Organisation (UNESCO).
- International Organisation for Industrial Development.
- World Health Organisation (WHO).
- Organisation of Petroleum Exporting Countries (OPEC) .
- Organisation of Arab Petroleum Exporting Countries (OAPEC).
- General Agreement on Tariffs and Trade (GATT).
- World Trade Organisation (WTO).
- Organisation of the Islamic Conference.
- Non-aligned Movement.

Economic Background

In 1995, Sheikh Mohammed bin Rashid Al Maktoum made clear his vision of 'Dubai for the 21st Century' – an international city with wealth and global influence. Today, this visionary ambition is rapidly becoming reality. In a decade, Dubai's GDP (gross domestic product) has nearly tripled in size to AED 136 billion – with a 16 per cent growth in 2005 alone, according to a statement from the Dubai Department of Economic Development (DED). Dubai alone contributed 28.9 per cent to the UAE's GDP last year, according to a report by the Dubai Chamber of Commerce and Industry (DCCI).

Figures from Dubai's Department of Economic Development have revealed an explosion of new business start-ups in the emirate, with more than 13,000 private companies licensed to operate in 2006 alone. A report by the DED and the Swiss-based International Institute for Management ranks Dubai 5th out of 61 countries surveyed for ease of doing business. It was polled 3rd for adaptability of government policy to change the economy and ranked 6th in economic performance. The dirham has been pegged at AED 3.6725 to the US dollar for over 20 years.

Tourism is the major income-generator, but Dubai is also setting new standards in finance, education, technology and healthcare. The non-oil economy has been predicted to contribute 96 per cent of GDP by 2010, of which 25 per cent of GDP will be created by Dubai's knowledge economy. In commercial terms, Dubai has become a pre-eminent business hub at the crossroads of trade

The Dubai Strategic Plan

His Highness Sheikh Mohammed bin Rashid Al Maktoum, UAE prime minister and vice president and ruler of Dubai, first unveiled the plan under the banner 'Dubai – Where the Future Begins'. The **Dubai Strategic Plan (DSP)** aims to triple Dubai's GDP by 2015, maintaining double-digit growth to US$108 billion from US$37 billion. The goal is also to raise per capita GDP to US$44,000 – a 41 per cent growth from US$31,140. More than 880,000 new jobs will bring employment to 1.73 million.

Sheikh Mohammed confirmed that the Dubai economy had exceeded all targets in the 2000–2010 plan in half the time allocated. 'In the year 2000 the plan was to increase GNP to US$30 million by 2010. In 2005 that figure was exceeded, with GNP reaching US$37 million. The plan also included an increase in income per capita to US$23,000 by the year 2010. In 2005 the average income per capita had reached US$31,000. In other words, we realised, in five years, economic achievements beyond those which were planned for a 10-year period.'

The Dubai Strategic Plan focuses on five areas that demonstrate the highest levels of development potential.

- Land and the environment.
- Public sector excellence.
- Economic development.
- Social development.
- Infrastructure.

Underpinning the DSP is an **Economic Development Plan (EDP)** designed to sustain the level of Dubai's economic growth to continue to outpace other emerging economies, such as China and India. The EDP will focus on prime sectors of greatest importance to the GDP, such as **Foreign Direct Investment (FDI)**. It will also bolster productivity by 4 per cent per annum using six 'key service sectors' that include tourism, trade, transportation and finance.

Sheikh Mohammed said, 'The Dubai Strategic Plan does not constitute a collection of mute words and static texts – it represents a way of thinking, a tool by which to measure and evaluate. It is a map that outlines our path to the future, helping us to make the right choices and reach accurate conclusions. It is our guide and our reference while we work to consolidate Dubai as a pioneering global city, bursting with vibrancy and creativity, and attracting the best minds and the most successful business to an environment where living and working is a pleasure.'

and commerce between East and West. This favourable gateway location offers access to a market that spans the Middle East, North and South Africa, India and southeast Europe (an area encompassing 31 countries, 53 languages, 1.8 billion people, US$1.5 trillion combined GDP, and 114 million people with a GDP per capita greater than US$2,000, according to the Dubai International Finance Centre). It's a perfect place from which to attract continued global investment.

Tourism

Some 18 per cent of Dubai's direct GDP and 29 per cent of its indirect GDP is generated by the city-state's burgeoning tourism sector, according to the Dubai Department of Tourism and Commerce Marketing (DTCM). No other city has developed a comparable tourism industry, with such dramatic results, in such a short period of time.

Since Dubai's first five-star hotel opened in 1975, the city has spawned more than 420 hotel properties, from swanky beachfront resorts to stylish boutique B&Bs. The Burj Dubai, a 347.3-metre tower, is officially the tallest hotel on the planet. The number of guests staying in Dubai's hotels and apartments has increased more than threefold in the last 10 years, with tourism up 228 per cent in the last decade, from 1.9 million visitors in 1996 to 6.3 million in 2006. In 2008, Dubai's hotel sector recorded a 22 per cent growth in revenue, reaching AED 4.26 billion during the first quarter. Between 2007 and 2008 the number of hotel and hotel apartment guests rose by 7 per cent – the highest guest increase percentage in the world. More than 20,000 hotel rooms will be added to Dubai's current total of 30,000 by 2010 (capacity increased to 45,500 rooms and apartments in 2006 and is expected to more than double to 86,600 by 2016). DTCM figures also reveal a recorded 82 per cent hotel occupancy in 2006 – the third highest levels in the world after London and New York.

A-List Good Looks

Hollywood heartthrob Brad Pitt has claimed that the Dubai-based hotel and resort he is designing will be an 'incredible attraction'. Although the exact location of the innovative project has yet to be revealed, it will include an 800-room five-star hotel, which developers hope will eventually play host to the most glamorous events and awards ceremonies. Announcing the plans for the hotel, Pitt said, 'Whilst acting is my career, architecture is my passion.' Indeed, the actor will be heavily involved in the development and, according to Christina Lawson of Zabeel Properties (the company managing the development), 'He is not going to be the face of the project but will actually be a part of the design and overall feel of the building.' Although details of the new resort have not yet been revealed, one thing's for sure – it will reflect Pitt's commitment to environmental and social issues; the flagship development is set to be a world leader in environmental sustainability.

Cruise Tourism

As the region's main trans-shipment centre, Dubai boasts sophisticated ports, with Jebel Ali and Port Rashid ranking among the leading container ports in the world. July 2007 saw the start of a two-phase expansion project at Jebel Ali Port to increase capacity by 67 per cent. Plans include a 2,500m quay to help maintain a 15–20 per cent growth in shipping lines. Works are due for completion by 2009. A total of 35,380 vessels called at Dubai ports in 2007, an increase of two per cent over the previous year. Around 77,838 passengers used marine transport, with more than 170 shipping lines serving the ports of Dubai.

Long established as a maritime city with geographical advantages, Dubai started looking at developing cruise tourism late in the day compared with other destinations. However, this has in many ways given it the edge, as few new entries into the cruise tourism sector can boast such extensive facilities and well-established services from the start.

Dubai had been tapping into the potential of the dynamic cruise sector since the mid-1990s, when it established a department to spearhead the growth in cruise tourism in 1997. In 1999, Dubai set up a dedicated cruise terminal in a temporary location while its purpose-built 3,300m^2 port was under construction. Dubai's Cruise Terminal was officially inaugurated by Sheikh Mohammed bin Rashid Al Maktoum in 2001 at the state-of-the-art Port Rashid complex. It is the world's first to receive ISO-9002 certification and also the world's only cruise facility run by the government tourism body. In 1993, Dubai welcomed one cruise ship with 703 passengers. Today, cruise ships with 7,000 passengers are more the norm.

Tourism accounts for 8.5 per cent of jobs in the UAE, a figure that is due to increase to 9.1 per cent by 2016. Some 10.4 per cent of exports are travel- and tourism-related, according to Dubai-based hospitality consulting company Roya International. Tourism generates revenues in excess of US$3 billion, with a ratio of tourists to residents now approaching five to one, according to *Gulf News*. Since 2005, the government-owned airline, Emirates, has experienced phenomenal growth, adding new direct flights from the UK to Dubai in 2007. In 2005, around 200 tour operators featured Dubai in their programmes, up from less than 50 in 1997, and Dubai's Department of Tourism and Commerce Marketing website (**www.dubaitourism.ae**) gets over 250,000 hits a day.

Celebrity A-listers are also frequently spotted in Dubai's hotspots, with Brad Pitt, George Clooney and Claudia Schiffer just a few of the city-state's Hollywood visitors. Premiership footballers are also regular holidaymakers in Dubai, with Manchester United maestro and Portuguese international Cristiano Ronaldo (PFA Player of the Year 2007) a recent star about town. Another record-breaker is the Dubai Shopping Festival, an annual month-long event that attracts around three million visitors.

Case Study: Sam Ebbs

'My life in Dubai is very, very different from what it was at home in Guildford, Surrey. For a start, I live in a really stunning apartment – it's massive at 2,000 square feet and boasts a 60ft balcony all along the back overlooking the water of Dubai Marina. Secondly, I met my girlfriend here and we now live together here at the new Emmar Yacht Club. She's the best thing that ever happened to me, so moving here has really changed my life!

'I first visited Dubai in 2000 to do some sixth form work experience at the Emirates Golf Club through family friends – and loved it. So, when I graduated from university in 2004 I moved out to start a job as a sports coach. I built up contacts and settled in a little before attending interviews with independent financial advisors Holborn Assets. I'm now an associate with a portfolio of expatriate clients. I advise them on how to make the most of their offshore tax-free money. The plans I make for most people here revolve around a loose five-year plan – I'm a bit of an exception myself, as I have absolutely no intention of moving on. My life is five-star all the way – I rarely eat in, as the restaurants are so good. I have a nice car, live in a fantastic apartment and I socialise with friends who are like-minded. We work hard and play hard here and there's a real entrepreneurial spirit.

'When I first arrived here, Dubai Marina was nothing more than a huge ditch in the ground. Today it's one of the most impressive waterside developments in the Middle East – awash with 50 high-rise residential blocks, which is quite a mammoth change in just seven years! Only 7–10 per cent of the development planned in Dubai is complete, with 40,000 new residential units opening up each year until 2013. To say that Dubai is expanding rapidly would be the understatement of the century. I enjoy being part of this growth and can't think of anywhere else comparable, so why would I want to leave?'

Business and Commerce

Dubai's forward-looking entrepreneurial attitude has raised its international profile – and the prevailing view is that, if it's good for business, it's good for Dubai. Geographical proximity to the markets and talents of the Middle East, Africa and the Indian subcontinent has served Dubai well. The sophisticated logistics and infrastructure ensure it is a location of choice for businesses serious about trade in the region, offering multinationals a foothold in one of the most dynamic global economic scenes. Currency rates are stable, inflation is low, and just 2.6 per cent of the active population is unemployed, according to a 2006 report by the Statistics Centre of Dubai. As a liberal and moderate emirate, Dubai has attracted major players from all significant business sectors. Tax-free trade zones continue to attract commercial entities of every conceivable size. Easy access to a regional talent pool of around 14 million university-educated workers is another major draw.

1 Dhow
2 Madinat Jumeirah
3 Mosque
4 Dubai skyline
5 Fujairah fortress

6 Al Qasr resort, Jumeirah

9

10

Executive Expatriate Relocations

OPENING DOORS TO DUBAI ▶▶▶▶

EER is a Dubai based company specializing in executive relocations. The business is owned and managed by Shirley Morrison. Shirley Morrison has lived in the Middle East for the last 11 years and has helped approximately 450 expatriate families settle in Dubai.

At EER we provide a personalized and consistent point of contact for the duration of the relocation. This approach brings real support to the relocating family and removes the entire administrative burden from the client. Removing this burden from the expatriate family allows the executive to rapidly become effective in the work environment at the same time as helping the family to integrate into life in Dubai.

We believe that we differentiate ourselves by offering a personal, consistent and client specific service.

International and locally based companies and their transferring employees are supported with a complete program, which will enable them to settle into their new location as quickly and as effortlessly as possible.

- PRE-ARRIVAL INFORMATION
- VISA ASSISTANCE
- ORIENTATION
- HOME SEARCH
- SCHOOL SEARCH
- ADMINISTRATION SUPPORT

- PET RELOCATION
- FULL RELOCATION PACKAGE
- COUPLE RELOCATION PACKAGE
- EXIT SERVICES
- PERSONAL SHOPPING (we will assist you in purchasing furniture for your new home)

SHOULD THE ABOVE PACKAGES NOT MEET YOUR NEEDS, WE WOULD BE HAPPY TO TRY AND ACCOMMODATE YOUR REQUESTS.

For further information on tailor made packages please contact:

Shirley Morrison   +971 (0) 50 396 55 97

P.O Box 119970 Dubai, United Arab Emirates - Email: info@eerdubai.com Website: www.eerdubai.com

2007
Winner
Best Offshore Bank Group

Wanted: Western Expatriates

Must be willing to discover the benefits of Premier offshore banking

You want to make the most of your time in Dubai. And to make the best of your financial situation. The fact is many expats just haven't discovered the benefits that offshore banking can bring.

Here in Dubai you can take advantage of HSBC Bank International's services right on your doorstep. Our Premier Service, is a gateway to a world of financial opportunity. If you have £60,000 (or currency equivalent) to deposit with us, you can take advantage of all the benefits it offers.

Award-winning offshore banking for people living and working abroad

Call: +971 4 407 9789
Click: www.offshore.hsbc.com
Email: dubai.repoffice@hsbc.com

The world's local bank

DUBAI SPORTS CITY IS MAKING FANS OF EVERYONE.

'Dubai Sports City is one of the most exciting and ambitious sporting projects in the world today...'

Sir Alex Ferguson

STUDIOS, ONE BED APARTMENTS AND TWO BED APARTMENTS AVAILABLE.

- High rental returns with strong capital appreciation
- 18-hole golf course 'The Dunes' designed by Ernie Els
- Four dedicated sports stadiums

To find out call + 44 (0) 20 7493 5577
or visit **www.profile.com**

profile
THE LAND OF OPPORTUNITY

Beach & Golf Homes Specialists
Dubai and Abu Dhabi

PALM ISLAND LIVING

Sales
Rentals
Management

GOLF HOMES LIVING

Sales
Rentals
Management

ABU DHABI HOMES

Sales
Off Plan Sales
Investments

PALM JUMEIRAH
Holiday Homes

Holiday Rentals
Caretaking
Vacation Management

MOVING TO DUBAI AND NEED SOMEWHERE TO STAY AS SOON AS YOU GET THERE?

Need to feel at home while you find your feet...without paying high hotel rates and living out of suitcases?

LET SHORT STAY DUBAI
HELP YOU

Short Stay Dubai is a dedicated specialist provider of short term accommodation in Dubai. Choose from our extensive portfolio of self catering villas and apartments in all the popular areas of Dubai – Dubai Marina, The Palm Jumeirah, The Greens, Burj Residence/ Downtown area, Jumeirah Islands, Arabian Ranches and more.

Our villas and apartments are fully furnished and equipped, offering easy access to the main motorways, beaches, shopping malls, and business areas. Each property has been carefully chosen by Short Stay Dubai to ensure that the highest quality of accommodation is available to you while still offering the comforts of a home. We pride ourselves on our commitment to customer service and have a dedicated team to help you settle in.

To view our portfolio of villas and apartments please visit our website **www.shortstaydubai.com** or email us on **info@shortstaydubai.com**

 ShortStayDubai

 +971 (4) 33280

ARABIAN ESCAPES

We cover all our clients' property requirements in
Dubai and Abu Dhabi

Property Sales
Long-term Rentals
Short-term Rentals
Private Client Investment & Management
Relocations
Finance and Mortgage Assistance

CONTACT OUR MANAGING PARTNERS

Michael Burke	**Sara Ingham**
+971 4 3414129	+971 4 3414129
+971 50 7988428	+971 50 5511397
michael@arabianescapes.ae	sara@arabianescapes.ae

'We will help you buy, sell and manage your property'

www.arabianescapes.com
Arabian Escapes LLC
Nr Mall of the Emirates   PO Box 211044   Dubai   U.A.E.

ESCAPE TO ABU DHABI

Sheikh Mohammed has nurtured large-scale internal investment via fast-track business incentives, e-commerce and new technology, and Dubai leads the way in the rapid adoption of cutting-edge advances. The regulatory environment of Dubai's famous **Free Zones** is also conducive to efficient business: there are no corporate or income taxes, foreign-exchange controls, trade barriers or quotas or restrictions on capital repatriation, and investors enjoy effective protection of their rights. Competitive energy and real-estate costs and import duties make it less expensive than other financial centres such as Singapore, Hong Kong, Cairo or Bahrain. A high level of support is offered to administrative and recruitment activities via the Free Zone authorities' comprehensive and efficient 'One Stop Shop' facilities. The **Jebel Ali Free Zone** and **Dubai Airport Free Zone** were set up with the specific purpose of facilitating investment to complement and contribute to Dubai's growth and development. Free Zone legal status is quite distinct: companies operating there are treated as being offshore or outside the UAE for legal purposes.

The addition of two educational and accelerated-learning facilities – the **Dubai Knowledge Village** and **IT Education Project** – has done much to enhance local skill sets. These centres of global excellence in academic standards and innovation continue to strengthen the city's reputation as a place where advanced technology is central to its long-term goals, as did the October 2000 launch of **Dubai Internet City**. Businesses in Dubai benefit from the support of the world's finest state-of-the-art infrastructure and digital technology.

In 2002, the **Dubai Authority for Investment and Development** was established, followed by the **Dubai Chamber of Commerce and Industry (DCCI)** in 2003. Both bodies have been instrumental in introducing Dubai to a global audience and do much to promote the city to would-be investors and the tourist trade. The launch of the **Dubai Business Bay** project in 2004 once again thrust the city into the limelight. Sheikh Mohammed pledged that the key development, centred on the city's famous Dubai Creek, would 'take Dubai to new levels of growth and development'.

Significant foreign-capital investment has been courted in almost every segment of Dubai's economy, and this capital flow show little sign of abating in 2008. Dubai's non-oil sector already contributes over 90 per cent of its total GDP, predicted to rise to 96 per cent by 2010, as manufacturing, tourism and service industries continue to demonstrate steady growth. A total of US$52 billion of non-oil trade passed through Dubai's eight Free Zones in 2006 – a rise of 8.9 per cent on the previous year. The value of the gold trade also leapt last year, up 37 per cent from 2005 to US$14.75.

Dubai's state-of-the-art **International Finance Centre** opened its doors in 2004 and today more than 50 international banking organisations, including UK banks Barclays and Lloyds, the Bank of America, Bank of Canada and Banque Paribas, have more than 150 satellite offices in the city. The total number of stocks traded on the Dubai financial market in 2006 was 39.644 billion, worth

AED 347.98 billion, compared to 25.54 billion shares in 2005. Dubai International Financial Exchange registered transactions of some 3.682 million shares in 2006, worth AED 96.777 million. Of the Global 500 multinational companies, 139 are present in Dubai, including all of the top ten, according to figures from the Dubai International Finance Centre. Membership of the DCCI rose by 10.5 per cent in 2006 to reach 87,829.

Contacts

- **Dubai Chamber of Commerce and Industry, t 228 0000, www.dubaichamber.ae.**
- **Dubai Department of Economic Development, t 7000 40000, www.dubaided.gov.ae.**

World-class Conference Facilities

Dubai has fast emerged as a number one choice for the global Meetings, Incentives, Conventions and Exhibitions (MICE) industry. The **Dubai Department of Tourism and Commerce Marketing (DTCM)/Dubai Convention Bureau (DCB)** distributed 10,000 copies of its *Definitive Meeting and Event Planners Guide 2006* throughout global MICE markets to build on its success.

Presently, Dubai has convention facilities of collectively 130,000 square metres, offering space for more than 100,000 MICE guests. In 2006 Dubai hosted 88 exhibitions and conferences, attracting a total of 984,638 visitors and delegates, with a further 23 conferences attended by 52,660 people. According to a survey by Reed Travel Exhibitions and *MICE International* magazine, Dubai ranked as the 'Number One Conference Destination in the Region', scoring 84 per cent on the basis of costs, quality of accommodation, service standards, meeting facilities and venue availability. *Conference & Incentive Travel* magazine also polled Dubai 'Top Incentive Destination in the World 2006'.

Since opening in 1979, the **Dubai World Trade Centre** – an iconic symbol of Dubai's commercial ambitions – has become one of the Middle East's largest exhibition centres and was recently voted the world's best conference venue. One of the tallest buildings in the region, the World Trade Centre comprises 39 floors, with a total floor area of approximately 87,000 square metres including 33,000 square metres of exhibition space. The centre hosts more than 60 major international events annually, and has a list of some 100 tenants that reads like a *Who's Who* of international business. Schlumberger, Johnson & Johnson, General Motors, MasterCard International, Sony Broadcast and Federal Express each have a presence here, as do the US, Australian, Swiss, Turkish, Italian, Dutch, Spanish and Japanese consulates.

The world-class **Dubai International Convention Centre** is also a dynamic international venue and an ideal space for conferences and exhibitions that can

Case Study: Cammie McWilliam

'In 2007, I realised I'd become bored and fed up with the UK (I'm from Aberdeen). One day, I switched on the TV and watched a programme on Dubai. Soon after, I booked a one-week holiday to coincide with a big construction industry exhibition in the city – I arrived armed to the teeth with CVs and a diary full of interviews. By the time I left, several organisations were interested in hiring me – and a few months later I was on a plane to Dubai. Today, I work with architectural firm Woods Bagot, who deal with some of the most prestigious projects across the globe with over 700 staff across four regions.

'Settling in has actually been pretty easy. I miss certain little things from Scotland, but Dubai feels like home now. For a rent of around £750 per month, I have a nice en suite room in a two-bedroom apartment with a balcony, great views, swimming pool, gym and a sauna. If I rented alone, the cost per annum would be about £18,000 per year. The Marina, Palm Jumeirah and golf courses are all close by, while the huge Mall of the Emirates is a two-minute drive away. I really enjoy the Dubai lifestyle, the tax-free benefits and the weather – it's a little better than Aberdeen! My weekends revolve around the beach or doing something different like quad-biking or jet-skiing. I meet friends in Dubai's best hotels for drinks and go to pool parties and barbecues.

'The expat community here is huge, with lot of Brits, Kiwis, Aussies and Canadians. I have never once felt like an outsider, as there are so many people here of different backgrounds that in fact everyone is actually in the same boat (young and away from their friends and families). I am living a lot better than I ever did in the UK: earning a lot more, making great friends and affording luxuries that I couldn't have before. The hours are long here, but the social side more than makes up for all the hard graft. My drive into work takes me past some of the most amazing buildings – many appear overnight as construction periods here are so short. However, it isn't wise to take your eyes of the road for very long in Dubai – the driving here is some of the most dangerous on the planet. It really pays to have the patience of a saint to sit behind the wheel while surrounded by gridlock and tooting horns – oh, and with all the building going on, Dubai has a LOT of dust!'

accommodate up to 11,000 delegates. Brand new US$326 million world-class convention facilities planned for **Jebel Ali** look set to further cement Dubai's status as one of the finest conference venues on the planet, with two interconnected 34-storey towers, an exhibition centre and a 600-seater auditorium.

Dubai has secured such significant events as the International Road Transport Union, ESNEP-Site European Meeting, Physio Dubai, Arabian Hotel and Investment Conference in 2008, and is preparing to host the Dertour Academy, Thomas Cook World Tour, Routes, FIATA World Congress, Annual World Dental Congress, Kuoni Golf Challenge, Point S, ACI and World Association of Cooks Societies (WACS) World Congress. Dubai is also one of the eight members of the

Date on a Plate

From humble nibble to a multi-million-dirham agricultural sector, the UAE's sweet, juicy date crops survive dust, wind and harsh arid conditions to harvest 400,000 tons each year. The date palm, *Phoenix dactylifera*, originated in the Persian Gulf and is thought to have first been planted by Bedouin nomads. Evidence of this has been found on a 7,000-year-old archaeological site on Dalma, where pips (stones) have been gathered that were cultivated many thousands of years before. Palms have been grown in the desert using sophisticated techniques for tapping underground water sources.

An erect palm that sprouts to around 30–35 metres, the date is characterised by upward-pointing, overlapping, woody, feather-like leaves that can reach up to six metres in length. The small flowers can total more than 8,000 on a single plant. Once the fruit begin to grow, the stalk holding the cluster stoops and lengthens because of the added weight of dates. Fruits are long, dark-brown, reddish, or yellowish-brown when ripe, with thick, sweet flesh that carries a hard stone grooved down one side. Traditionally, the leaves and trunks of the date palm were used for basket-making, house-building and boat-building.

Since the late 1970s, the date industry has experienced massive expansion, thanks largely due to the availability of water and technology. The UAE now has around 40 million trees (compared to just five million in 1971) and cultivates around 400,000 tons of dates a year (compared to 8,000 tons) as one of the most prolific growers on the planet. According to a study by the DCCI, around 40 per cent of the UAE's trees are in Al Ain city, with date palms covering 30 per cent of all of the land allocated for fruit farming. In 2006, Dubai's foreign trade in dates amounted to 302.4 million dirhams, according to official sources.

BestCities, the world's first and only convention bureau alliance, whose other members are Boston, Copenhagen, Edinburgh, Melbourne, Vancouver, Cape Town, San Juan and Singapore. The Dubai Convention Bureau has fixed a target of attracting around 750,000 additional guest nights from the international rotating meetings market by the end of 2008.

More than 35 malls offer MICE delegates world-class shopping, with spending by visitors in Dubai forecast to reach almost US$7.6 billion per annum by 2009, according to the Department of Tourism and Commerce Marketing. Spending continued to gather pace in 2007, with duty-free sales up 28 per cent in the first quarter of 2006, according to reports from the Economist Intelligence Unit.

Contacts

- Dubai Convention Bureau (DCB), **t** 201 0220, **www.dcb.ae**.
- Dubai's International Convention and Exhibition Centre (DICEC), **www.dicec.ae**.
- Dubai World Trade Centre, **www.dwtc.com**.

Religion

Islam forms the bedrock of daily life in Dubai and plays an important and influential role in shaping the society and culture of the UAE. As the predominant religion, it pervades relationships, legislation, education, food, clothing, conversations and routines. Islam places great emphasis on behaviour, and generosity, respect and modesty are considered important Emirati qualities.

Case Study: Chris Thompson

Mrs Thompson, aged 56, is a part-time teacher of English as a second language. She is originally from Hampshire, married with two children aged 25 and 28.

'I moved to Dubai with my husband after he landed a job with the Dubai government. We only came for two years, but have been living here now for nine! I have found living in Dubai both enriching and very frustrating. When we arrived, our daughter had just begun A-level study and attended Dubai College to complete her education. Our son was in the UK at the University of Bath. Having our daughter here helped us settle in as we didn't feel quite so cut off from family. Now that our daughter has returned to the UK we do feel very isolated – a situation that is accentuated by the fact that our son and his wife have started a family, so we now have a young grandson whom we rarely see.

'Living in Dubai has enabled us to spend time with different nationalities and has provided us with a greater awareness of different cultures – both the good and the bad. It has made us look at our home country with a more dispassionate eye. It is impossible not to learn a great deal from interacting with different people from diverse backgrounds. We've made most of our friends through the golf club, but it is not always easy for newcomers to build friendships – there are so many English people living over here that the close-knit community spirit we found in Saudi Arabia in the mid-1980s doesn't exist here.

'A few things here really drive me crazy. Heavy traffic and the number of roads under construction create a major headache for road users. An embarrassing aspect of living in Dubai is that the lack of respect shown by some expats and many tourists to the local population. My husband and I are disgusted at some of the sights we see in terms of minimal dress in public places. Local laws are often totally disregarded, as the recent media coverage of the British couple on the beach bears out. On these occasions, we feel shame at being British.

'The biggest plus to living and working here is the tax-free income – we've been able to save much more money than we could ever do back in the UK. Mind you, prices have risen markedly over the past 3–4 years, so I'm not sure that new residents will find it as easy. However, with such a huge divide here between the have and have-nots I have learnt not to complain. As one of the haves, I try to treat everyone I meet with respect and also try to be a generous tipper to workers on a minimum wage.'

Case Study: Emma Hurley

'I'm a relative Dubai newbie as I've only been here six months. Before I came to the Middle East I spent two years working in Sydney, where I had an amazing time. However, I was ready for a new challenge and psychologically Dubai was "on the way home" to the UK. Working in Dubai is the pinnacle of anyone's career in the construction industry so I'm thrilled with my senior consultant role at leading international built asset consultancy EC Harris International.

'The projects in Dubai, from a construction point of view, are like no others in the world. It's immensely rewarding to know that I have had a part to play in the growth and development of one of the most exciting cities of the future. My own home, in Al Msalli on The Palm, Jumeirah, is on a landmark development for which I pay an annual rent of £29,000. I enjoy a high standard of living in a country where five-star service prevails. In the hotel bars, you'll find attentive staff willing to accommodate even the most difficult of requests, while extravagant venues and exclusive hotspots provide choice for a social outing. My favourite Friday brunch is at the Fairmont, where high-quality plentiful fine food and wine come at a reasonable price in luxurious surroundings.

'In terms of settling in, it helped to have previous experience of relocating from the UK to Sydney. In many ways it was a dry run and ensured I was better prepared and knew what to expect regarding visa issues, opening new bank accounts, shipping belongings, etc. It can be a hassle and, as everyone says who has relocated here, "nothing is easy"! Connecting to utilities, etc. can seem a lot more difficult than it needs to be, but once you're up and running everything is quite straightforward. Having the support of your company makes a big difference and I've been lucky that EC Harris has been present in the UAE for over two decades. As a result, I benefited from their considerable experience in arranging visas and assisting with the general settling-in process.

'However, I would recommend to anyone planning a move here to clue-up on some of the cultural and religious laws that affect expats in Dubai. This mainly includes the strict drug laws imposed here (some "off the shelf" medications in the UK are "Class A" drugs in Dubai) and public behaviour (a simple show of affection, such as holding hands, is offensive, and acting drunk carries a penalty). Some expats carry on regardless without punishment but, if you are in the wrong place at the wrong time, prison sentences have been known to occur. My advice is, be sensible and exercise respect as a guest in a Muslim country – with so many watering holes and bright lights around, many expatriates find it all too easy to forget they need to abide by an Islamic system.'

Non-Muslim expatriates living in Dubai will find that learning something about Islam will provide a vital insight into the traditions and practices that rule decisions, conduct and friendships. Although the practice of some other religious beliefs is permitted by the Dubai government, Judaism is not tolerated.

Visitors are expected to respect Islamic beliefs and conventions, for example:

- It is highly offensive to walk in front of somebody when they are praying.
- Alcohol should never be consumed in the street or in public places.
- Passionate displays of affection in public are considered offensive.
- Modest dress should be observed at all times, with beachwear saved for the beach.
- The religious observances of Ramadan (in the 9th month of the Islamic calendar) should be respected.

The Five Pillars of Islam

There are five 'pillars' of Islam:

- Faith (*shahada*): The first pillar is the profession of faith, which is the belief that 'There is no God but Allah and Mohammed is the Prophet of God'.
- Prayer (*salah* or *salat*): The second pillar lays out the obligatory prayers to be performed by devout Muslims five times a day, from sunrise to nightfall. Praying signifies a willingness to be purified. Non-believers should observe prayer times with respect and should take care not to watch or walk past anyone who is praying.
- Charity (*zakat*): The third pillar of the Muslim faith involves the (obligatory) donation of one-fortieth (i.e. 2.5 per cent) of the value of your assets annually.
- Fasting (*sawm*): The fourth pillar concerns the Ramadan Fast, a daylight self-purification for Holy month that is a test of inner knowledge and strength. Muslims refrain from drinking, eating, smoking and all other physical pleasures, including sex.
- Pilgrimage (*Hajj* or *Haj*): The fifth and final pillar of Islam relates to the Muslim pilgrimage to Mecca, urging those that can afford it to do so at least once in their lifetime to receive the reward of forgiveness for all sins.

Islam asks that many complex rituals be observed with the end of the Haj, and the Eid Al-Adha (Festival of Sacrifice) and Eid ul-Fitr at the end of Ramadan are both major celebrations.

The Family

Emirati social structure is founded on family and tribal connections, and both fulfil an important role in shaping societal values, protecting honour and guiding behaviour. Ensuring financial and emotional support to family members is a priority, and loyalty is a valued characteristic.

Traditional Muslim extended families can be very large, and it is not unusual for several generations to live together under one roof. Family matters are intensely private affairs in these tight-knit units. Marriages are carefully arranged within a small social group, according to Emirati tradition. The ideal marriage is considered to be one arranged between a man and his father's brother's daughter – although other forms of union have emerged in modern Dubai. Today, more attention is paid to developing a close relationship between partners. It is no longer a union for reproduction but one based upon love, harmony, happiness, care and equality.

In 2004, the UAE government set up a **Marriage Fund** in support of the role of the family. Eligible grant recipients are men of 21 years old and over, marrying a bride over 18 years old. Payments of around 70,000 dirhams are aimed to encourage young people to marry at a suitable age.

Women in Dubai

The UAE has been keen to lead the region's reforms in women's rights and has introduced laws and incentives to give women a greater role. Great strides have been made to popularise the vision of women side by side with their male compatriots in every area. However, this is always within a framework that protects Islamic identity and Arab tradition and culture. Although women in the UAE have undoubtedly been given greater access to executive posts in local government in recent years, concerns remain about the true value of this so-called equality. That women are now allowed to play the Dubai Financial Market (DFM) and can now become traders is indeed a remarkable step, but women in the traditionally patriarchal culture of many of Dubai's large employers remain in short supply.

In some circles, it is still frowned upon for a woman to touch a man she barely knows – an act forbidden in the traditional Islamic culture of the United Arab Emirates. Women are also discouraged from being away from the home after 10pm, a difficulty when the top jobs often require client entertaining. However, there have been many notable triumphs in the appointment of women fire-fighters, police officers and business leaders – plus the high-profile economics and planning minister, Sheika Lubna Qasimi. According to the Dubai Women's College, up to 60 per cent of students are planning to enter the workplace. However, many do not work because of parental pressure or because they choose to stay at home to raise children full time.

No laws dictate whether UAE women must wear the veil and full-length cloak known as the *abaya*, although most choose to do so. Western counterparts are encouraged to adopt a conservative approach to dressing, out of respect for the Islamic culture. Women face very few problems when visiting Dubai other than suffering the curious stares of male onlookers. Men who do harass women are

Case Study: Pam Wilby

'More than a decade ago, I secured a senior position at Le Royal Meridien Beach Resort and Spa, then known as the Forte Grand Jumeirah Beach Hotel. I moved to the UAE and achieved a first for women in the Emirates as the first female general manager of a five-star hotel in Dubai. In 2005, I opened a new hotel – the Grosvenor House West Marina Beach, with 422 rooms, suites and apartment suites. Today I am general manager of both hotels, with over 1,800 associates, and have seen Dubai change from a small town to a global city.

'When I first arrived there were fewer than half a million people living in Dubai – now there are around 1.5 million, and over 100,000 of them are Brits. This has led to quite a change in the society, but I don't believe that Dubai has lost its core identity as many people fear. Not only has there been a massive change in the population, but the very face of Dubai has been transformed; the skyline is completely different, with fantastic, breathtaking structures, and the coastline and sea are also unrecognisable as more and more man-made islands are built. Everyone is trying to do things bigger and better than ever before and trying to grab the next headline.

'The transformation of Dubai and its rising reputation has made my job much more exciting, and I love the challenge of coming up with the next big thing. It has become much easier for us to be innovative as the lure of Dubai attracts more opportunity for both hotels. For example, we have signed up world-renowned Michelin-starred chefs like Gary Rhodes to open a signature restaurant – Rhodes Mezzanine – in Grosvenor House – something only made possible by the fact Dubai is now a global player in the market. Dubai has also become a much better place to work as not only is product innovation important here but service enhancement is paramount.

'Personally, I don't think I will ever get bored of living here, because it is constantly changing and reinventing itself. Even after a decade I still feel like a tourist sometimes and get caught up in the excitement – it's really not like any other place in the world, and the latest record-breaking development or event is always just around the next corner.'

liable to be 'named and shamed' in Dubai's national newspapers, complete with photograph, a directive straight from Sheikh Mohammed.

Contacts

- The American Women's Association of Dubai, **www.awadubai.org**.
- Dubai Women Association (DWA), **www.woman.ae**.
- Dubai International Women's Club, **t** 344 2389.
- German Women's Club, **www.Frauenkreis-Dubai.de**.
- Dubai Ladies Bridge Club, **t** 050 684 8544.

Belly Dancing: More than just a Wiggle and a Giggle?

Belly dancing (or 'Oriental Dancing' as it is known in the Middle East) remains a much-practised ancient Arab craft but has also transcended folkloric status in Dubai to claim a place as a popular way to get fit. Belly dancing has countless benefits both mentally and physically. True beauty, femininity, and sensuality are unveiled through the exotic moves, resulting in a self-esteem boost. The dance also tones and shapes the arms, legs, and stomach, improves coordination and breathing, and increases the libido. Dancing played a vital part in helping women prepare abdominal muscles for labour. Middle Eastern women have always danced, but primarily for their own entertainment, for the most part at festivals, wedding celebrations, and the like. Today, what Dubai refers to as belly dancing is a relatively modern invention popularised for tourists.

The term 'belly dancing' was coined by Sol Bloom, an exhibitor at the 1893 Chicago World Fair, in attempt to drum up publicity for his exhibit, 'The Streets of Cairo'. His sultry depiction became the Hollywood image that is now ingrained in tourist culture: the scantily clad harem girl with a gem in her navel.

Belly dancing is a feature in many of Dubai's late-night restaurants, where the entertainment often takes place in a dimly lit cave-like interior. Diners huddle around tables adorned with candles while the dancer enjoys theatrical lighting hung from the ceiling above a tiny stage. A band of musicians play such instruments as the half-pear-shaped 'ud, the *tablah* (a small hand drum) and a tambourine-style *taar*. Traditional Arab music plays a large part in Dubai's belly dancing experience; there is something wonderfully exotic about the dissonant pitch of Arabic vocals tumbling through the octaves, as if gradually unfurling in a rolling whirl. However it is the star of the show who truly electrifies the audience by making a grand entrance complete with dramatic, glittering twirl. Clad in a heavily bejewelled skimpy costume, the dancer shimmies and sways in undulating movements that use every curve and fold. She also ensures her long, black, flowing hair and dark eyes are seductively poised before focusing on unsuspecting members of the crowd – usually male.

Individual lessons and group tutorials can easily be found, from fun-filled lunchtime sessions to learning the more serious rigours of the age-old art. Try the Nautilus Fitness Centre at the Crowne Plaza, **t** 331 4055, the Ballet Centre, **t** 344 9776; or private tutors Isabella, **t** 050 651 2273, or Milla Tenório, **t** 331 5173.

Internal Issues in Dubai

Human Rights

While Dubai is so often held up as a shining example of an Arab culture that has embraced 21st century globalisation without losing its traditional values, the emirate has also attracted considerable criticism regarding human rights.

Specific areas of concern include religious freedom, labour laws and the role of women in society – where important advances have been made, but where there is room for improvement, according to the Amnesty International 2007 Report. Campaigners are calling for an end to regulations, restrictions and discrimination shown towards people of non-Muslim faiths, and asking to move towards the goal of full religious and cultural tolerance.

Some of the prime concerns raised are as follows.

• **The lack of women elected to the newly formed Federal National Council (sixty-three women candidates stood for election but only one was voted on to the FNC).**

• **The continuation of the death penalty (in June a Fujairah court imposed a sentence of death by stoning upon a Bangladeshi national. This decision was later appealed and the accused was given a lesser penalty).**

• **Cruel judicial punishments (these include flogging by an excessive number of lashes).**

• **The risk of forcible return (deporting people to countries where their lives will probably be at risk).**

• **The subjection to harassment of some human rights defenders.**

• **The restriction of freedom of religious assembly and association of some religious groups without dedicated religious buildings to worship and conduct their business. The UAE government recognises a small number of Christian denominations and religious groups through the issuance of land-use permits for the construction and operation of churches, including those who use rented facilities. Some groups who have assembled without such a permit have received substantial fines.**

Labour Issues

On an ever-changing cityscape of partially constructed tower blocks, an estimated 250,000 men, largely from India and Pakistan, are employed as labour on Dubai's many mega-projects. For decades, this migrant workforce worked hard to send millions of dollars' worth of remittances back to their homelands. They seemed content with poor conditions and zero rights and appeared immune to labour unrest. However, things are beginning to change. Most workers earn around US$200 per month and live in cramped, purpose-built 12ft by 12ft camps. Yet with the dirham pegged to the weak US dollar, 2008 has seen the value of wages nosedive. Many labourers have been exploited by unscrupulous recruitment agencies and so have little course of redress, according to a Human Rights Watch report. They are also exempt from healthcare.

Critics have slated Dubai's colossal new skyscrapers as monuments to labour violations. Human Rights Watch's 71-page report *Building Towers, Cheating Workers* documents serious abuses of construction workers by employers in the

UAE. These abuses include unpaid or extremely low wages, the withholding of employees' passports, and hazardous working conditions that result in apparently high rates of death and injury. Other shady practices include agencies that unlawfully force workers, rather than their employers, to pay US$2,000–3,000 for travel, visas, government fees and the recruiters' own services. UAE law expressly prohibits domestic recruiting agents from charging workers for such expenses, but the law is commonly flouted.

The average pay-packet of a construction worker at around US$110–250 per month contrasts starkly with Dubai's national average wage of US$2,106 per month. Human Rights Watch has urged the governments of the United States, European Union countries and Australia, which are currently engaged in free trade negotiations with the UAE, to ensure that respect for workers' fundamental rights is a cornerstone of any forthcoming agreements.

Strike threats have come as a shock in Dubai, a city proud of its global business standing and dazzling high-rise skyline. Asian workers angered by low salaries and mistreatment recently rioted, smashing cars and offices and causing what a government official said was almost US$1 million in damage. Over 2,500 workers were involved in the labour unrest. The stoppage triggered a sympathy strike at Dubai International Airport, prompting thousands of labourers building a massive new terminal to down tools.

Gay Rights

Homosexuality is illegal in the UAE, although discreet gay and lesbian relationships between non-Arabs are tolerated in a turning-a-blind-eye-to-it kind of way. However, openly homosexual behaviour is not subject to the same levels of tolerance. In recent years, gay Arab men have been arrested for attending homosexual parties. They not only face government-ordered hormone treatments, but also five years in jail and a lashing. In 2008, a French man raped by three Arab men was himself accused of homosexuality – and had to flee the country to avoid standing trial. In 2001, Dubai's first publicly advertised gay club – the Diamond – was shut down by the authorities after staging a Fluff Night featuring a transvestite DJ from Birmingham, England, and a 'best-dressed transvestite' contest. It was the thousands of flyers that alerted the authorities to the event. The Diamond was closed for 'violating Islamic laws and indulging in immoral activities' via an order issued by Dubai's then Crown Prince, General Sheikh Mohammed bin Rashid Al Maktoum.

Today, gay clubs and bars do exist in Dubai, but are now underground haunts with a door policy that applies great caution. Frequenting same-sex bars carries risks if the place is raided. According to the International Lesbian and Gay Association, consensual sodomy in Dubai is punishable by up to 10 years in prison, although the sentence can be more severe if defendants are charged under Islamic law, rather than under the secular penal code.

Major Media

The launch of **Dubai Media City** in January 2001 established a new relationship between the world's communicators and the fastest-growing city in the Middle East. Today broadcasters, film-makers, publishers, print companies, journalists and new media businesses are taking advantage of the incentives offered by the **Media Free Zone**, which houses a diverse international media community. Members benefit from a business infrastructure that supports their commercial activities with high-performing and adaptable technology within a community of like-minded individuals rich in networking opportunities.

Rapidly emerging as a global media hub, Dubai Media City is widely recognised within the Middle East as a place where media businesses have the 'freedom to create'. More than 850 companies are based here, including global players such as the Associated Press, Bertelsmann, CNN, CNBC, the International Advertising Association, Platts, McGraw-Hill, Sony and Reuters, who rub shoulders with regionally renowned companies such as the Middle East Broadcasting Corporation, Saudi Research and Publishing and Taj TV.

The **Dubai Press Club**, established in 1999, also fosters interaction among journalists and media professionals from around the world. It launched the region's first official accolades for journalism – the Arab Journalism Award – to recognise and stimulate journalistic excellence in Arabic media. Dubai also has the highest satellite TV penetration in the region. It is home to several analogue TV stations and dozens of FM radio stations, as well as a number of English-language and Arabic newspapers. However, the UAE does not have freedom of speech and the media is carefully monitored by the State. Government criticism is rare in Dubai's self-censoring newspapers, with government-related news stories subject to a generous helping of gloss. Most UK and US daily papers can be purchased easily from Spinneys and Carrefour.

English-language Newspapers

- *7 Days*, **www.7days.ae**: This free tabloid-style title often attempts to tackle some provocative subjects – with mixed success.

- *Emirates Business 24/7*, **www.business24-7.ae**: Launched in 2007 to replace *Emirates Today*, *EB 24/7* offers a good round-up of commerce and some in-depth business news.

- *Financial Times*, **www.ft.com/world/mideast**: Now that the *FT* is printed in Dubai, it has become an adopted UAE title. Since 2008, the *FT* Middle East edition has run a page of dedicated news from the region.

- *Gulf News*, **www.gulfnews.com**: This weighty broadsheet is a firm favourite with western expats and carries a huge classified section, from property and cars to jobs.

- *International Herald Tribune*, **www.iht.com**: There has been talk of this US publication producing a Dubai edition in conjunction with the *Khaleej Times* – but, as yet, there is no sign.
- *Khaleej Times*, **www.khaleejtimes.com**: This strong news-focused broadsheet is popular with the Asian community's English-speakers and contains a good business section.
- *Daily Telegraph*, **www.telegraph.co.uk**: The rumour-mill has been rife with tales of a UAE edition – but, so far, the gossip has remained just that.
- *Dubai Enquirer*, **www.dubaienquirer.com**: This ultra-sarcastic Dubai-based news source is only available in e-format. It specialises in blog-style nonsense stories (see their disclaimer) heavy in irony and, as a result, tends to get misunderstood.
- *The National*, **www.thenational.ae**: This Abu Dhabi-based broadsheet is a top-notch title, in print and on-line.
- *The Times*: This UK broadsheet has been printed in Dubai since 2007 and has an international edition in the UAE that is popular with western expats.
- *Xpress*: This free weekly tabloid launched in 2007 and is part of the same stable as the daily *Gulf News*. It describes itself as a 'fast read, friendly to its readers, relevant to everyone living in Dubai and the UAE'.

Television

Dubai's local TV channels aren't the best in the world, although they are much improved on years past. A revamped **One TV** (formerly Channel 33) airs an excellent range of English-language films and programmes, while **MBC2** shows some good classic 1980s films and **MBC4** is great for US chat shows, sitcoms and news. Weekly **TV listings** are produced in most newspapers and are especially comprehensive in *Gulf News*.

A variety of **satellite TV packages** offer distinctly different options – so be sure to check what's in the small print. Soap operas are well-covered by **Orbit** and **Showtime**, while Premiership football is just a Showtime thing. For reality TV and Sky News you'll need a **FirstNet** subscription. In 2007, **City 7** entered the fray, but is often sold as an add-on to existing satellite deals.

Satellite TV Providers

- Showtime: **www.showtimearabia.com**.
- Orbit: **www.orbit.net**.
- FirstNet: **www.adduniverse.com**.
- Eurostar Group: **www.adduniverse.com**.
- Bond Communications: **www.bondcommunications.com**.

Radio

English-language radio stations in Dubai and the UAE offer a range of talk and music shows that span every genre.

All broadcasting is suspended during periods of state mourning, such as when a member of the ruling family dies. The exception to this rule would be the BBC World Service broadcast, which tends to continue uninterrupted.

- **BBC World Service, www.bbc.co.uk/worldservice**: 9am–6pm, 87.9 FM.

- **Business Breakfast, www.arnonline.com/dubai-eye**: Broadcast on Dubai Eye from 6am–9am on 103.8 FM, this well-respected show was awarded the International Radio Conference Breakfast Show of the Year 2006/2007.

- **Catboy on 92 FM**: This 'love it or hate it' breakfast show airs 6–10am and features husband-and-wife host and co-host Catboy and Geordie Bird.

- **Conception**: David Newsum cranks up a 'get ready for the weekend vibe' each Friday, 5–10pm, on 92.0 FM.

- **Dubai 92.0 FM**: Check out the weekly schedule for some of the best of BBC Radio 1's music shows, from Pete Tong's Essential Selection and Carl Cox to Judge Jules.

- **Simply Classical**: Broadcast on Dubai Eye on 103.8 FM on Saturdays at noon. Presenter John Deykin is a champion of Dubai's embryonic classical music scene and has a growing loyal following.

- **Sticky Fingers**: Broadcast on Dubai Eye on 103.8 FM: pontifications about world sports. Sticky Fingers is also on 92.0 FM on Friday afternoons as host of the Sugar Lounge, when he plays ambient mood music.

- **Virgin Radio Dubai**: This Richard Branson launch first aired in January 2008 and is fast-attracting a sizeable audience. Find it at 104.4 FM.

Culture and Art

Literature

According to the Arab League Educational Cultural and Scientific Organisation (ALECSO), 100 million people across the Arab world are unable to read or write. Despite having five per cent of the world's population, the Arab world accounts for only about 1.1 per cent of book production, according to the UN Arab Human Development Report. The UAE has pledged to eradicate illiteracy by 2015.

In 2009, Dubai will be the venue for the first ever literary festival in the Middle East. The inaugural **Emirates Airline International Festival of Literature** will take place between 25th February and 1st March. It will be directed by Isobel Abulhoul, director of Magrudy's, the region's leading chain of bookshops, and Bill Samuel, vice chairman of Foyle's. Over 25 renowned authors have given their full support for the gathering, which follows the vision of His Highness Sheikh Mohammed bin Rashid Al Maktoum of eradicating illiteracy in the Arab world. Paolo Coelho, adventurer Sir Ranulph Fiennes, second Children's Laureate Anne Fine and children's writers Lynne Truss, Jeremy Strong and Lauren Child have been booked to appear at the festival, supported by Dubai Cultural Council.

A handful of bookstores offer a good range of international titles. One of the best is Al Jashanmal Bookstores on the ground floor in the Mall of the Emirates.

Contacts

- Dubai Book Club, **http://dubaibookclub.onlinegroups.net**.
- Dubai Public Library, **www.dm.gov.ae**.

Film and Theatre

Dubai has a plethora of big-screen cinemas and multiplexes, including a 12-screen complex in the Mall of the Emirates and a 21-screen outlet in Ibn Battuta Mall. Cinema-going is a popular pastime in Dubai, although almost all the films shown are mainstream Hollywood blockbusters. These are subject to heavy-handed censorship and are often subtitled, with contentious topics and racy scenes cut out. A common gripe is that cinemas are air-cooled to sub-zero temperatures and are often noisy – chatter and mobile phones can be a real nuisance. A real highlight is Dubai's celebrated **International Film Festival**, **www. dubaifilmfest.com**, which takes place in December each year. The week-long glittering US$10 million event attracts over 45,000 people, to see over 140 films from more than 40 countries. Screenings range from feature films and shorts to documentaries from around the world.

Dubai Community Theatre and Arts Centre in the Mall of the Emirates, **t** 341 4777, **www.dubaitheatre.org**, also stages some popular shows and events.

Khawla Aljodar

A native citizen of Dubai, Khawla Aljodar now bases herself in Seattle in the USA, where a loyal following of art-lovers snap up her every squiggle. Rather than focus on a particular artistic style, her paintings are highly governed by mood. This ensures each is distinctly different, using a powerful sweeping style and colour mix. Aljodar also shies away from using a single medium, flitting from acrylics, oils and pencils to soft pastels and digital art. She favours large canvases but is no stranger to minute ACEOs (Art Card Editions and Originals) at 3.5 x 2.5 inches. She also paints and illustrates for children – and is 100 per cent self-taught. At the time of writing, Khawla Aljodar is planning to open a Dubai gallery devoted to her own original pieces.

For further details visit: **www.khawlaaljodar.com** or **www.dubaiartist.com**.

Art Galleries

Dubai may not have a Guggenheim, a Tate or a Louvre, but it does have a growing number of decent galleries that exhibit modern, contemporary and traditional art. Just a couple of decades ago, Dubai wasn't on the international art radar. Today it hosts an impressive art soirée at the annual **Art Dubai**, a top-notch event in March that attracts international art buyers in their droves. The city also has an Art Society, established in 1976 but reinvented in 1980 as the ultra-swish **Dubai International Art Centre**.

Classical Music

Classical music performances are thin on the ground in Dubai, although the city does have its own Philharmonic Orchestra (UAEPO), the first in the UAE. Originally called Dubai Philharmonic Orchestra (DPO), the UAEPO consists of musicians resident in the UAE and performs regularly at private events, public concerts and corporate functions. The UAE Philharmonic Orchestra is the only full orchestra in the UAE and represents a major step towards orchestral culture and musical education within the UAE. There is an increasing interest amongst international media concerning the fact that there is a resident Philharmonic Orchestra in the UAE. Equally the interest among international artist collaborations with the UAEPO is increasing.

The Dubai International Convention Centre and the Crowne Plaza Hotel often host visiting orchestras and musicians from around the world, although performances are far from regular. Other home-spun musical organisations include Dubai Chorus, a 65-member all-woman barber-shop style group. Also the Dubai Chamber Orchestra: an ensemble comprised of amateur and professional musicians resident in the UAE, established in 2002.

Contacts

- UAE Philharmonic Orchestra, **www.uaephilharmonic.com**.
- Dubai Chamber Orchestra, **www.dubaiorchestra.org**.

Pop and Rock

Dubai hosts an impressive calendar of events featuring international acts, with big-name artists including Shakira and Phil Collins having performed at the Autodrome's large amphitheatre. In April 2008, Madonna signed a US$25 million contract for two concerts in Dubai – the most lucrative gigs of her career. She is also in talks to perform at a private party for a mystery host while she is there. Her bill for that added extra – a cool US$10 million. The Stranglers, Def Leppard, Pink and Celine Dion have also played Dubai in recent years.

Contacts

- **Time Out Ticket Line, t 800 4669, www.itp.net/tickets.**

Traditional Handicrafts

Although much of Emirati cultural life has made way for modernity, some ancient rituals and crafts on a limited scale can still be found in the city. A relative hive of cultural activity is the **Creative Art Centre**, a large art gallery on Al-Jumeirah Road with eight showrooms across two buildings that forms a hub of cultural and handicraft activities for children and adults.

The **Dubai International Art Centre** just off Al Jumeirah Road offers craft displays, with works for sale. Traditional handicrafts in the UAE are predominantly made by women, who have passed on their skills in embroidery and weaving from one generation to the next. Gold, silver and brightly coloured strings are woven on a wooden block to produce the *teli*, elaborate and colourful embroidery that adorns the collars and sleeves of women's robes. These are worn on special occasions and at feasts. Another popular handicraft is the brightly coloured *sado*, cotton and wool threads woven into elaborately designed patterns used to make Bedouin tents. Basket-weaving using palm fronds, or *khous*, is also highly popular. Other traditional handicrafts include shawls, pottery, rugs and other woven fabrics.

Contacts

- **Creative Art Centre, t 344 4394.**
- **Dubai International Art Centre, t 344 4398, www.artdubai.com.**

National Dress

Traditionally, the men of the Arabian peninsula wear the gleaming ankle-length *dishdasha* complete with a small skull cap (*gafia*) covered by a white (or red-checkered) head cloth (*gutra*) held in place by a twisted black tie (*agal*). For important occasions and men of standing, the white *dishdasha* is covered by a flowing black cloak (*bisht*) edged with gold braid.

Emirati women usually wear trousers (*sirwal*) fitted tightly at the ankles. Over the *sirwal* a floor-length tunic (*jillabeeya*) is worn covered by a black cloak (*abaya*). Women may choose to cover their face with a black cloth (*nikab*) with small slits for their eyes. Most cover their hair with a *shaila* or *hejjab* as, according to Islam, hair is private.

Traditional clothing can be purchased from all of Dubai's main shopping malls and markets, with some particularly fine *abayas* sold in a range of high-quality fabrics.

No Pain, Just Stain

Henna tattooing is all the rage in Dubai, where non-permanent body art draws from Arab art and contemporary designs.

Henna paste is a firm favourite with Madonna, Sting and Demi Moore, all of whom have indulged in a spot of body decoration using the ancient art of henna tattooing. The complex patterns seen throughout Dubai are typical of Middle Eastern designs achieved using stencils which can be bought in souks (markets) city-wide. A growing number of street artists have claimed this non-invasive ancient art as their own in major Dubai resorts, applying henna decoration of varying styles for visiting tourists of both sexes.

The custom of applying a henna tattoo can be traced back to traditional Arab weddings, when women celebrate while the bride is tattooed. Traditionally applied to the hands and feet, henna designs typically use patterns of scrolls, vines and flowers in upward strokes. Dubai's modern interpretations are often applied to the upper arms, shoulder and calf. It takes half an hour to apply a small hand design using henna paste (*mendhi*) and as long as several hours for a more complex tattoo. A cone or syringe of henna is used to draw the design in intricate detail. The paste dries and forms a crusted ridge while the colour is absorbed into the skin. To deepen the colour intensity, a mixture of sugar and lemon juice is dabbed onto the crust. For the richest colours, the *mendhi* is left to achieve depth for several hours. Once fully dry, the crust comes away without encouragement to reveal a tattoo that can range in hue from tea-coloured to almost black. Although temporary, the henna design will last for a few weeks, during which time it will gradually lighten through natural exfoliation. Some of the better henna tattooing can be found at the Bedouin party on the Lama Desert tour, a popular twilight safari that culminates in a celebration at a desert encampment.

Food and Drink

Located as it is at the crossroads between east and west, Dubai is a melting pot of cuisines, from classical European through to indigenous Middle Eastern dishes and food from the Pacific Rim. Dubai's colourful fusion of cultures and nationalities has permeated the culinary character of the city, ensuring an exciting mix of dishes and recipes that reflect a melting pot of global influences. As you'd expect from a bustling multicultural metropolis, Dubai offers a host of gastronomic options, from kerbside eateries serving flatbread-wrapped spit-roasted lamb to bistros, cafés, restaurants and diners specialising in Italian, Greek, French, Mexican, Thai and Vietnamese food.

With so much to choose from, it's little wonder that dining out is a favourite Dubaiian pastime – and as a gastronomic centre the city rarely disappoints. Hundreds of restaurants range from grilled meat joints and Oriental eateries to elegant French *à la carte* options – along with plenty of budget fast-food outlets and juice bars. Many hotels contain half a dozen themed restaurants – with alcohol licences – while Dubai's food courts serve up burgers, pizza and noodles. There are also numerous dinner cruises and an underwater seafood restaurant that is accessed via a three-minute simulated submarine voyage; you exit to an underwater tunnel where tables circle a huge ceiling-high aquarium that holds 1,000 fish, overseen by a seven-person specialist marine-care team.

Case Study: Cooking up a Storm

Andrew Gault is the former sous chef at Dubai's iconic Burj Al Arab. He is now back in the UK as head chef at the Captain's Club Hotel in Christchurch, Dorset.

'I spent three years working in one of the most recognisable landmark hotels on the planet. Coming from the UK, what struck me was how few local ingredients there were. Almost everything for the kitchen travelled a long distance. Meat, fish, herbs and vegetables are flown in from all corners of the world – and we sourced any products requested, regardless of price.

'Life in the kitchen (below sea level) was business as usual: staff training, hygiene checks (of the highest order) and room service requests. Then, of course, there were the "Sheikh Attacks" – so named because they happened without warning. We'd get a call announcing the arrival of a sheikh and his huge entourage – and pandemonium would set in. We'd have 20 minutes to prepare 200-plus dishes that would need to be served within the allotted time scale. It certainly helped to have a kitchen brigade of 168 chefs – and after this I know anything is possible! My feeling is that, within the next 5–10 years, the vision, money and creative talent in the UAE will earn it the title of culinary hub of the world. People are already sitting up and taking notice of the UAE's huge gastronomic potential.

'Away from the job, taking time off to dine out in Dubai affords such choice that you never need eat in the same place twice. I only got one day off a week, so my time was limited, but there are enough restaurants to easily offer something new 365 days a year. My favourites, to name just a couple, are the Noodle House at Jumeirah Emirates Tower Hotel, and Madinat Souk. Market food is cheap and cheerful, with communal tables, a tick box menu and good fast food. Gordon Ramsay's Verre at the Hilton Creek is fantastic. I found the food exemplary, with service to match – it also cost a fraction of the price of his English restaurants, although this may not be the case now!

'Brunch on a Friday is huge among expats and locals alike. A lot of them now include free-flowing champagne to wash it all down. It suits the locals, as the tradition is to have a full table, so you would often see little mini-buffets created at tables rather than repeatedly filling the plate. Al Muntaha in the Burj Al Arab was a particularly sumptuous experience. A real "must try" is the Arab cuisine, as nothing beats a chicken *shawarma* on the beach.'

Dubai enjoys a sterling reputation for its gastronomic scene and has fast-become a haunt for celebrity chefs from across the globe. As the Middle East's culinary epicentre, Dubai is set to welcome two bastions of London's high-profile gourmet dining venues, the Ivy and Le Caprice. A growing number of international restaurants and critically acclaimed chefs are launching in Dubai, usually affiliated to one or other of the emirate's myriad of luxury hotels. Other renowned restaurants such as Alan Yau's Michelin-starred dim-sum restaurant Yauatcha, the Wolseley and Piers Adam's Polynesian-themed nightclub Mahiki, playground of the Britain's rich and famous, including Princes William and Harry, are also rumoured to be joining the host of other celebrated chefs and restaurateurs who have chosen to showcase their food in the emirate. The Burj Al Arab and Ritz Carlton are renowned for fine dining; the Michelin-starred British celebrity chef Gary Rhodes heads up Rhodes Mezzanine at Grosvenor House, and Gordon Ramsey presides over Verre at Hilton Dubai Creek. Ramsey's first foray outside the UK grabbed the headlines when it opened in 2001 after a party of businessmen from Abu Dhabi spent a whopping US$80,000 on dinner.

Since opening in autumn 2008, Kerzner's Atlantis on The Palm, Jumeirah has added 17 restaurants, bars and lounges to Dubai's gastronomic frenzy. Headlining these is Nobu Atlantis, whose Asian-fusion cuisine has seen it become world-renowned with a celebrity status that is matched by its famous clientele. There is also Ronda Locatelli, a fashionably fun Italian restaurant run by charismatic chef Giorgio Locatelli, Santi Santimaria's signature seafood restaurant Ossiano, and Rostang – the French brasserie, by acclaimed French restaurateur Michel Rostang. Other gastronomic delights can be found at the hobnobbers' favourite, Celebrities at the Palace.

Typical Cuisine

Dubai's traditional Bedouin diet mainly comprises of fresh fish, dried fish, dates, camel meat and camel milk, but in the city today Lebanese food typifies local Arabic dishes. Choose from *hommos* (pureed chick peas with sesame oil, lemon juice and a touch of garlic), *moutabel* (baked aubergines with sesame oil, lemon juice and a touch of garlic), *tabbouleh* (parsley, tomatoes, onions, mint, crushed wheat, lemon juice and olive oil), *warak'inab* (vine leaves stuffed with rice, herbs and spices) and *laban bi-khyar* (yoghurt with cucumber) followed by *fatayer sebanikh* (pastry filled with spinach, onions, pine kernels and lemon juice), *kibbeh maqlia* (ground meat with crushed wheat, stuffed with meat, onions and pine kernels), *laham mashwi* (tender lamb cubes grilled with onions and tomatoes) and *farrouj mashwi* (baby chicken, grilled or served with chef's hot sauce or garlic). To finish, try some *baklawa* (layered pastry filled with honey, pistachio and pine nuts) with some black Arab coffee served with dates.

Smoking the traditional post-meal *shisha* (water pipe also known as *nargile* or *hookah*) is quite unlike that of cigarettes or cigars as it uses aromatic flavours,

Fatayer bi Sebanikh (Spinach Parcels)

These delicious spinach-filled turnovers are served simply with a wedge of lemon and a dollop of fresh yoghurt. Serve hot, or cold.

Ingredients
1 kg chopped spinach
2 large onions
8 tablespoons olive oil
1 tablespoon salt
1 pinch pepper
½ glass lemon juice
500g frozen shortcrust pastry

Gently rub the spinach with salt and squeeze each leaf carefully to drain out excess water. Toss the leaves in a bowl with the oil, lemon juice, finely chopped onions and pepper.

Roll out the pastry to about 5mm thick and cut round shapes out. In the centre of each circle, place a good tablespoonful of spinach mix before pinching the dough shut in a parcel shape at the top. Bake in a hot oven for about 20 minutes, until brown.

such as grape and apple. The smoke is dampened down by the water to create a softer, smoother and more relaxing effect.

Culturally speaking, enjoying food in the Middle East is a shared experience – in a group of friends or with extended family. Traditionally, food is served in a seemingly never-ending succession of communal dishes that everyone around the table dips into – a real feast. Only the **right hand** is used to touch food in Arabic circles. Using the left hand, considered unclean as it is used for ablutions, will cause considerable offence. **Pork** is taboo, and is not eaten, prepared or served by Muslims. All other meat products for Muslim consumption must be slaughtered according to **halal** rules.

Alcohol and Wine

Although Islam prohibits alcohol, Dubai allows it to be sold by licensed outlets in hotel premises and leisure clubs. Dubai is the most liberal emirate in the UAE and it is easy to forget all about the local attitudes to alcohol on a big night out in a city where the nightlife can be raucous and wild. Permanent residents who are non-Muslim will find it easy to purchase alcohol for home consumption.

It is illegal to drink in the street, in a public space or in non-licensed premises. The legal drinking age in Dubai is 21.

According to *Wine Enthusiast* magazine, Dubai is fast-becoming a major wine destination of some distinction. Certainly, the city's Annual International Wine and Beverage Fair in February is now the Middle East's premier wine forum.

Although it started with just 10 exhibitors in 2003; it attracted 120 producers from 19 countries in 2006, including South Africa, France, Spain, Italy and Australia. During the Fair a host of wine producers showcase their products at tastings, wine dinners and events. France alone sent 30 producers, including Latour and Baron Philippe Rothschild. Dubai has a decent number of wine and champagne bars. However, Dubai's heavy tax on alcohol has hiked the cost of a bottle of wine to around 100 per cent more than in the UK.

A Food Blogger's Guide to Dubai

'As you'll gather from my blog, **http://thefatexpat.blogspot.com**, everything in Dubai revolves around food. You go out to eat, you have friends around to eat, you meet to eat – dinner is a really big deal in a city whose multiculturalism means pretty much every cuisine in the world is well represented at every level. Street food is fantastic if you're adventurous, ranging from the ubiquitous *shawarma* kebab stands ($1 for a little slice of Lebanese heaven), through Iranian kebab joints and piping hot finger food from the *pakora* stalls by the dhow port on the creek. Anywhere on the Deira side of the Creek is good for a strong cup of creamy Indian *chai panjasari* tea and a sneaky bite of something hot. Try a trip to Ravis in Satwa if you want to eat at Dubai's most famous 'street' Indian restaurant, Lemongrass (by the Lamcy Plaza Mall car park) for Thai, Pars (Satwa) for Iranian, or Al Mallah and Beirut (Diyafa Street, Satwa) or Halab (Garhoud) for Lebanese.

'Alcohol can only be served legally in hotels, so it's here you'll find the most dazzling array of dining on offer, from French *steak frites*-style bistros through to fine dining. Although Dubai's eateries haven't scored any Michelin stars yet, there are plenty of names opening up, including Gordon Ramsey, Gary Rhodes, Marco Pierre White and the latest addition, Pierre Gagnaire.

'Top picks include the great-value *wagyu* burger at Blades (the Four Seasons Golf Course), old-fashioned steakhouse dining at JWs (the JW Marriott Hotel) and funkier grill-style steakhouse at the Grand Hyatt's pricey but excellent Manhattan Grill. The Grand also features über-funky Indian at Iz, which not only offers venison curry and salmon tikka, but gets away with the fusion in style. The Park Hyatt's Thai restaurant, the Thai Kitchen, is outstanding. Possibly the best Italian is to be had at the unfashionably three-star Rydge's Plaza Hotel in Satwa. Atmosphere aplenty is on offer at the Rotana Towers' funky Teatro, but it's more of a place to have fun than focus on the food. But for me, Gagnaire's Reflets is probably the best dining treat that Dubai has to offer right now. Anywhere that can please all of the following – a grumpy diner who's had a million more bad service experiences than he wanted; a very loud, straight-talking and highly entertaining redhead; an exceedingly strong-minded and crusty wine buff; a "this is how I like it and I'm not putting up with anything you choose to foist on me in the name of theatre" Diner with Attitude; two perfectly normal people and a slightly pretentious foodie – has my vote.'

Sports and Leisure

Dubai is fast shaping up as a world-class sporting destination, and is pitching hard to host a year-round calendar of prestigious events. In 2007, it won the right to host the **Rugby World Cup Sevens** in 2009. The tournament will be the first to incorporate a women's competition, according to the International Rugby Board (IRB). The **Aviation Club** is home to the annual **Dubai Tennis Championships**, while the **Dubai International Tennis Academy** remains the only full-time tennis coaching institution in the Middle East.

Dubai also continues to mature as a world-class **golf** destination, with the addition of an 18-hole Robert Trent Jones II course at the Four Seasons Golf Club. In 2007, Spain's Sergio Garcia announced his collaboration with Greg Norman to design a course at the Jumeirah Golf Estates. Tiger Woods has also chosen Dubai to debut his self-styled championship fairways. The much-awaited Tiger Woods-Dubai course will be built on 40-million square feet in Dubailand. It is scheduled for completion in 2009 at a cost of over US$65 million.

In 2005, 2006 and 2007 Dubai also staged, among other events, the **UAE Desert Challenge**, the **Class 1 World Offshore Powerboat Championship**, the **Dubai Marathon**, and the **Dubai Desert Classic Golf Tournament**. It is also home

Falconry

As Dubai's sport of kings, falconry is revered as royal by the ruling élite: a traditional pastime in the emirate for over 2,000 years. Used by early settlers to hunt desert mammals for meat to supplement a date and bread diet, falconry became a part of the social life of tribal leaders over time. Participants gathered around a campfire before pursuing their quarry on horseback or camel. Today, Dubai's falconry set prefer powerful four-wheel drive jeeps: in modern Dubai, falconry is held onto as a rich cultural legacy by the upper echelons of society, but is affected by the intrusion of dust and concrete from the emirate's rapid urbanisation. This loss of natural habitat is a real concern to conservationists, who cite falling numbers of falcons as a genuine cause for positive action.

The UAE's two main species of falcon are the saker and the peregrine. All aspects of falconry, from the trapping and taming to the training, require high levels of patience, skill and courage. Under the Emirates Bird Ringing Scheme, a microchip is inserted under each bird's skin and a ring with a unique identification number is fitted on its leg.

Dubai is home to a purpose-built AED 16 million Falconry Centre, a specialised trade and tourism facility that showcases all activities related to the sport. The centre has a Falcon Souk for falcon traders and breeders, a tent-covered courtyard, and an exhibition centre, a museum featuring the history of Dubai's falcons. The centre, spread over an area of 27,500 square metres in Al Markadh area, is located on Muscat Road near the Camel Race track and Camel Souk.

Bumps and Humps

Camels have been trusted bedrocks of Bedouin tribal life for centuries, carrying vast, weighty loads across the sands, providing milk, meat, leather, and droppings for fuel. Today they are raced, ridden and petted in Dubai in the dunes on the city's outer fringes.

Riding a camel in the UAE is like cycling in Amsterdam – a real 'must try'. Numerous tour operators run camel-riding trips as part of a desert safari across the sand dunes. Be warned, though: camels aren't renowned for their comfy seats; they have knobbly, bony ridges that provide little cushioning and plenty of bump and bash. Rides vary in length, from a short hand-led jaunt to a longer windblown trek.

Camels are able to withstand changes in body temperature that would kill most other animals, from 34°C at night to 41°C during the day. They are also able to retain body fluids, reducing the amount of water lost through respiration and sweating. A camel's thick coat reflects sunlight while their long limbs keep them high off the hot sand. Sealable nostrils, long eyelashes and ear hairs protect against wind-swept sand.

As a nomadic tribe, the Bedouin bred camels for strength and speed, and camel racing has been part of the region's sporting culture for centuries. In the Al Aweer section of the desert near Dubai, a famous racing camel named Akwara is contentedly living out the rest of his days as a stud bull in the company of a mixed herd of 500. In April 2008, Sheikh Hamdan bin Mohammed bin Rashid Al Maktoum, Crown Prince of Dubai, purchased a female camel for a record US$2.72 million, according to the official Emirates news agency Wam. The female camel was bought at an Abu Dhabi camel beauty pageant and was the most expensive of more than 10,000 camels. Females are the fastest for racing, competing across the region for prize money worth around US$9.5 million. The UAE has been at the forefront of making changes to modernise the camel-racing industry: Abu Dhabi produced the world's first test-tube purebred camel and has also begun using remote-controlled robot riders in its camel races, rather than the child jockeys of old.

to the richest horse race in the world, the **Dubai World Cup**, which attracts a well-heeled international racing crowd with a winning purse of US$6 million.

The 7,000-seater **Dubai Autodrome** – which opened in October 2004 – has already staged the **A1 Grand Prix of Nations**. A 5km circuit has an adjoining racing school and a separate kart track, and big-name artists including Shakira and Phil Collins have performed in its large amphitheatre.

Dubai Sports City opened in 2008 as the world's first purpose-built sports city, featuring four magnificent stadiums: a 60,000 seat multi-purpose outdoor stadium, a 25,000 capacity cricket stadium, a 10,000 seat multi-purpose indoor arena, and a field hockey venue for 5,000 spectators. This international arena

Off-roading in the Wild

Wadi-bashing and dune-bashing offer a chance for petrol heads to do battle with the challenges of the desert on shifting sands, unmarked trails and vast, rounded mounds. Huge expanses of untroubled desert wilderness within an hour of Dubai city centre beg to be explored.

Car and driver take a pummelling during a serious dune-bashing (or desert driving) session, as the sand is subject to constant movement. Wadi-bashing is a more predictable path, but still takes its toll. You'll need to steer a heavy-duty 4x4 to do battle with carved gullies and windblown ravines – often in poor visibility. Balance, weight distribution, power and precision are key in either discipline, as one false move could tip the vehicle over. Scorching sun, searing heat and the disorientating effect of the desert can turn even the most simple act of navigation into an ordeal. Forget brute force and a heavy pedal; in the desert it is grit and nerve that so often wins out.

Numerous local tour operators offer desert driving challenges. Some also run desert driving courses for those keen to perfect their off-road skills.

for cricket, football, athletics and golf is home to the **ICC** (International Cricket Council), **Manchester United Football Academy** and **David Lloyd Tennis School** as well as an 18-hole **Victory Heights Championship Golf Course** designed by Ernie Els in association with Nicklaus Design.

In January 2008, the **Mohammed bin Rashid International Football Championship**, the highest-quality friendly football tournament in the world, presented by National Bonds and Dubai Sports City in association with the Dubai Sports Council, hosted a number of big-name clubs, including Inter Milan, Stuttgart and Ajax. Tennis greats Jim Courier, Michael Stich, Thomas Muster and Cedric Pioline are tipped to lead a **Legends Tour** in 2010 while FIFA has announced that Dubai will host the **Club World Cup** in 2009 and 2010 after beating off rival bids from Australia, Japan and Portugal.

Dubai's Neighbourhoods and Developments

04

Much like China, Dubai is a landscape undergoing a dramatic transformation as almost every structural landmark is redefined, resurfaced or rebuilt. Vast swaths of desert have been overtaken by high-rise apartment blocks, while sleek highways are etched into the sandy, arid scrub. Swish hotels and flyovers now stand among brick dust. Junctions have been repositioned, and every spare inch of available desert has been turned into real estate gold.

There are too many stunning architectural triumphs and record-breaking spires to count. Man-made islands and huge stretches of beach have been added to the ever-changing topography – after toiling around the clock, 14,000 labourers delivered Dubai's three 31-square-kilometre palm-shaped islands, a project billed as the largest land-reclamation project on the planet, which involved the hauling of millions of tons of Gulf sand and quarried rock over a five-year period. Ancient markets have been razed to the ground to make way for swanky new multi-malls, while new buildings sprout up everywhere, taller, bolder and bigger than ever before. Bridges are being constructed, tunnels dug and entire mini-cities created. Even Dubai's focal centrepiece – the Creek – has undergone a major facelift in a metropolis where nothing stands still amid constantly shifting sands.

This mammoth reshaping of Dubai has left the city in a constant state of limbo filled with builder's rubble, traffic cones, scaffolding and partially completed property. Not only is this disconcerting for residents, many of whom are not 100 per cent sure what the view from their window will be each morning – it is also a nightmare for cartographers (and guide book writers), who, for now, are unable to accurately map a city that's still very much 'work in progress'. At the time of writing, much of Dubai is devoid even of street names as new construction projects continually remould the modern incarnation of the city.

General Orientation

To understand the layout of Dubai, climb to the observation deck of the **World Trade Centre** for a bird's eye view: it soars for 39 floors, affording an excellent perspective of the city and is duly favoured by photographers.

Despite widespread changes, one thing remains the same: Dubai still frames its namesake **Creek**, dividing the city into two halves: **Deira** to the north and **Bur Dubai** to the south. Most of Dubai's mega-development plans are focused on the Deira side of Dubai Creek, but that doesn't mean that the Bur Dubai side is untroubled by construction. However, between the Maktoum and Garhoud bridges, the Creekside Park provides a number of gentle walks that meander through landscaped gardens. A large, shallow lagoon has been spared by the diggers and planners and is preserved as a wildlife sanctuary, attracting 30,000 migrating shore birds, including greater flamingos, although the widening project on the Creek has caused the birds some disruption.

Dubai's most famous address, **Jumeirah**, with its string of luxury hotels and resorts crowned by the iconic sail-shaped structure of Burj Al Arab, is set away from the city centre, close to the Emirates Hills complex and the Dubai Marina, a network of hotels, offices, villas and apartments among picturesque water gardens and canals.

Commonly, Dubai is referred to as having five neighbourhoods in its make-up: Deira, Bur Dubai and Jumeirah, plus **Sheikh Zayed Road** and **New Dubai**. The latter is very much an all-encompassing term for all the development under way, and the vagaries of this mean that there is often an overlap when using this definition. This division of the city into residential zones offers a range of individually styled housing, from apartment-only communities to mixed-use neighbourhoods of villas, condominiums and studios. The most popular neighbourhoods with expats include Jumeirah Beach, Umm Sequim, Emirates Lakes, Emirates Hills, Mirdiff for villas, and Bur Dubai and Sheikh Zayed Road for apartments. Each of these areas is prized for its proximity to good schools and shopping and has been built to be self-supporting with local amenities very much to hand. Almost everyone in Dubai will use these neighbourhoods as landmarks when offering directions or describing the layout of the city.

Deira

Dubai's busy downtown area of Deira is a popular neighbourhood for business and leisure, located just a five-minute drive from Dubai International Airport. Conveniently near to Dubai's main business districts and shopping areas, Deira is separated from Bur Dubai by the winding curves of the mighty Dubai Creek. As a business and commercial hub, the district is home to some excellent clothing and electrical shops and is also where most of Dubai's remaining historic architecture can still be found. A highlight is **Bastakia**, with its traditional wind-tower houses and narrow streets. At the heart of Deira, you'll find **Ban Yas Square** dominated by the **Deira Tower**. The district is also home to some of Dubai's most exotic hotels and the Creekside **fish market**.

Bur Dubai

Divided from Deira by the Creek, Bur Dubai is a district now eclipsed by a skyscraper. The **Burj Dubai** (*burj* meaning 'tower' in Arabic) is poised to put Bur Dubai squarely on the global map as the home to the tallest high-rise freestanding concrete structure on the planet. It has already overtaken Taipei 101 to become the world's tallest building, and is significantly higher than the Chicago Sears Tower (not counting the spire). The final height for both towers is being kept a closely guarded secret – as is the actual date of completion, a deadline that is rumoured to have suffered untold delays. Floor 200 has already being sold to an unnamed bidder, who is said to have purchased the entire storey for a little over US$4.5 million – a very reasonable price given all the hype.

'Bur Dubai' literally translates to 'Desert of Dubai', a reflection of the era when the district contained the entire city, between the western bank of the Creek and Jumeirah. The area has undergone extensive beautification, with the district's quay walls replaced and areas neatly paved between the British Embassy and the Ruler's Diwan office. The area is also renowned as the home of the **Dubai Museum**, housed in the **Al Fahidi Fort**, built in 1787 to defend Dubai Creek. Built from coral and shell and bonded with lime, the building is supported by wooden poles with a roof of palm fronds, mud and plaster.

Jumeirah

Dubai's first luxury coastal stretch, set away from the city centre, boasts many private residences, from high-end villages on expansive plots to modest low-level town houses. A popular area with Western expatriates and tourists, Jumeirah is synonymous with Dubai's most photographed landmark, the iconic **Burj Al Arab** hotel. Today, the sail-shaped structure, based on the traditional Arabian dhow boat, epitomises Dubai's style-led, forward-thinking drive for the ultimate in luxury. Indeed, the name Jumeirah has taken on 'brand status' in many ways, such is the upscale association of this exclusive sandy coastline where property prices have soared in recent years. Today, the area is famous as home to the **Jumeirah Beach Club**, **Jumeirah Beach Hotel** and **Jumeirah City**: a new addition of malls, hotels, and residential units that has attracted Dubai's well-to-do élite.

Prime Jumeirah neighbourhoods include the Dubai Marina, the new Palm Islands, The Lakes, The Springs and The Meadows, with views across the Persian Gulf and access to golden sands.

Sheikh Zayed Road

Sheikh Zayed Road (or the E11) is the UAE's longest road, stretching from the city of Abu Dhabi to Ras Al Khaimah parallel to the coastline of the Persian Gulf. Known by a variety of names, dependent on the emirate, including Sheikh Maktoum Road in Abu Dhabi and Sheikh Muhammed bin Salem Road in Ras Al Khaimah, the Dubai strip runs 55km from the border with Abu Dhabi to Jebel Ali. However, the most renowned stretch in the city links the Trade Centre Roundabout and Interchange 2 and is home to the lion's share of Dubai's skyscrapers, including the Emirates Towers, the Fairmont and the Millennium Tower. Half a dozen interchanges manage the traffic flow from the E11 out and around the city in what is one of Dubai's busiest stretches of central arterial road – a strategic business location and city-slicker residential zone.

'New Dubai'

As Dubai has developed farther and farther out from the Creek, it has become defined by planned neighbourhoods that are very much cities within a city. Most are anchored by a specific business sector, for example **Media City**, with residential units designed with so-called 'media types' in mind. Others are centred on a hotel-residence-mall complex like **Wafi City**, or are linked to a golf club or leisure activity. Generally speaking, units are also geared towards a target income bracket in socio-economic clusters.

Property Development in Dubai

Until 2002, acquiring property in Dubai was restricted to UAE nationals and GCC citizens, so foreigners in the emirate rented their homes, usually apartments. However, H.H. Sheikh Mohammed bin Rashid Al Maktoum changed all that when he announced the liberalisation of the real estate sector. It allowed the purchase of Dubai property on a freehold basis in designated areas – a move that sparked a new era for the city's real estate sector and prompted a fast-paced consumer spree.

At present foreign and institutional investors account for 50 per cent of Dubai's financial market's volume and turnover. Major developers, such as DAMAC, reported large numbers of non-GCC purchases in 2006, citing 65 per cent of sales to foreign buyers with at least 45 per cent being UK-based. Since 2003, Dubai's major property developers have completed thousands of sales of freehold apartments and villas to foreign buyers, ranging from studio flats at US$50,000 to multi-million-dollar villas. Of these developments, key joint projects by master developer Nakheel and IFA Hotels & Resorts represent the largest investment in The Palm, Jumeirah. Emaar and Dubai Properties are Dubai's other licensed master-plan developers. The headline-grabbing, pioneering palm-shaped offshore island, The Palm, Jumeirah, contains three key IFA projects: the Fairmont Residence, together with neighbouring Fairmont Palm Hotel and Resort; The Palm Residence; and the US$400 million, 600,000-square-metre The Palm Golden Mile. In the same year, IFA Hotels & Resorts (IFA HR) announced the appointment of luxury hotel operator Fairmont Hotels & Resorts to manage The Palm Golden Mile and their two shoreline buildings, Al Nabat and Al Haseer. IFA is also behind the US$100 million, 40-storey Laguna Tower in the Jumeirah Lakes development.

Dubai's diverse range of property options available to foreigners continues to grow, with an impressive array of showcase developments; demand continues to outpace supply. A survey published by the Emirate newspaper *Al-Bayan* suggests that the Dubai real estate market needs 750,000 new housing units to fulfil demand until 2010, given the current number of potential buyers on waiting lists. With Dubai's population predicted to grow annually by 108,000

Developers

The land bank in Dubai is shared mainly among five major corporations, including Dubai World entities **Nakheel** and **Limitless**; Dubai Holding entities **Dubai Properties Group** and **Sama Dubai**; as well as **Emaar Properties, Dubai Investments** and **Union Properties**. Dubai World, Dubai Holding and Emaar Properties offer freehold land and properties, while Dubai Investments and Union Properties own land that are offered to investors on leasehold for periods of 90–99 years. The websites for the major developers (listed developments are subject to frequent change, however) are:

- Al Fattan, **www.alfattan.com**: Marine Towers; Currency House.
- DAMAC Properties, **www.damacproperties.com**: The Crescent; Largo Vista.
- DEC (Dheeraj and East Coast LLC), **www.dheerajeastcoast.com**: DEC Towers at Dubai Marina; DEC at Culture Village; Business Bay.
- Dubai Multi Commodities Centre Authority, **www.jlt.ae**: Jumeirah Lake Towers.
- Dubai Properties, **www.dubai-properties.ae**: Jumeirah Beach Residence; The Villa; Business Bay.
- Emaar Properties, **www.emaar.ae**: Dubai Marina Towers; Al Majara Towers; Al Sahab; Marina Promenade; Marina Quays; Park Island; Emirates Hills; The Meadows; The Greens; The Springs; Emaar Golf Homes; The Views; Downtown Burj Dubai; Arabian Ranches; The Lakes; Emaar Towers.
- ETA Star, **www.etastar.com**: Liberty House; The Centrium.
- High Rise Developments, **www.highrise-re.com**: The Rotating Residences.

people to 2.1 million by 2010, the Dubai Chamber of Commerce has calculated a minimum requirement of 43,233 additional residential units per year. Almost 25 per cent of the world's supplies of cranes are now at work in Dubai, on projects worth over US$100 billion. This is twice the World Bank's estimated cost of reconstructing Iraq and double the total foreign investment in China, the world's third-largest economy, and is a sure sign that Dubai's real estate sector is far from losing steam.

- **Dubai Lands Department, t** 222 2253.
- **Real Estate Department, t** 398 6666, **www.realestate-Dubai.com**.

An A–Z of Developments

Thus far, Dubai residential real estate projects have been concentrated almost exclusively in the area referred to as **uptown**, or **New Dubai**, which stretches from Jebel Ali Free Zone to Dubai Internet City and back into the desert beyond. However, **downtown Deira** is earmarked for significant future development.

- Hircon International, **www.hircon-me.com**: 23 Marina.

- International Hotels & Resorts (IFA), **www.ifahotelsresorts.com**: Laguna Tower; Mövenpick Hotel & Residence at Laguna; Fairmont Palm Residence; The Palm Golden Mile; The Palm Residence; The Kingdom of Sheba.

- Lake Apartments, **www.up.ae**.

- Le Reve, **www.lerevedubai.com**: Le Reve.

- Limitless, **www.limitless.ae**.

- Manal, **www.manal-me.com**: Lakeside Residence.

- Nakheel, **www.nakheel.ae**: The Palm, Jumeirah; Trump International Hotel & Tower; The Palm, Jebel Ali; The Palm, Deira; The World; Jumeirah Village; Jumeirah Heights, **www.jumeirahheights.com**; Jumeirah Islands; Jumeirah Golf Estates; Jumeirah Park; International City; The Gardens; Discovery Gardens; The Lost City; Dubai Waterfront.

- Properties Investment LLC: Green Community, **www.greencommunity.ae**.

- Sama Dubai, **www.sama-dubai.com**: The Lagoons: **www.lagoons.ae**; Dubai Towers: **www.dubaitowersdubai.com**.

- Tameer, **www.tameer.net**: Palace Towers@Dubai Silicon Oasis.

- Tatweer, **www.tatweerdubai.com**: Dubailand, **www.dubailand.ae**; **www. falconcity.com**; **www.cityofarabia.ae**; **www.dubaisportscity.ae** .

- Trident Grand, **www.tridentgrandresidence.com**: Trident Grand Residence.

- Union Properties, **www.up.ae**: UPTOWN Mirdiff; Lake Apartments; MotorCity, **www.motorcity.ae**.

Work is under way on the iconic **Burj Dubai**, which stands to become the tallest building in the world. Distinctive low-rise apartments and low- to medium-rise villas are another characteristic of this up-and-coming district – tipped to be one of Dubai's fastest-selling hotspots in 2008 and beyond.

The target market for developments comprises local, regional and international homebuyers, those seeking to purchase a second home, and investors. Many developments offer lifestyle living, with a choice of properties from small studios and apartments to townhouses, water homes and villas. In many ways, the separate developments are like little neighbourhoods in themselves, offering many integral shops, services and facilities.

23 Marina

Located at the **Dubai Marina**, this elevated development offers a total of 90 floors of duplexes and apartments. Dark blue tinted glass and an exposed concrete frame makes a 380m-high style-statement, with a vaulted entrance and imposing lobby area. Two- and three-bedroom properties face Jumeirah Beach, Burj Al Arab and Sheikh Zayed Road, with covered eight-storey car parking facilities. Amenities include round-the-clock security, high-speed internet access, data and telephone systems, a 24hr concierge, housekeeping staff and a 24hr convenience store. Each duplex boasts a private plunge pool, while residents enjoy the exclusive use of three levels of spa suites, gym and aerobics facilities.

Al Majara Towers

This five-building residence comprises high-rise waterfront towers over-looking **Dubai Marina**'s largest bay. The final phase – Al Majara Towers 4 and 5 – are ten and eight storeys respectively, with each containing a range of one- and two-bedroom suites. Amenities include a 1,350 square metre resort spa and fitness club with outdoor terraces, swimming pool, gym, and health facilities. Other features include a Hollywood-style movie theatre, games room, business centre, lounge facilities, guest suites, landscaped courtyards, underground parking and 24hr concierge and security.

Al Sahab

A twin-tower 44-storey waterfront project, Al Sahab overlooks the largest bay of water at **Dubai Marina**. From the level three Marina homes upwards, all residents have unparalleled views over the Arabian Gulf, Dubai Marina, world-class golf courses and the desert. Residential suites feature in the beachfront towers, with a range of two- and three-bedroom properties offered as Marina Homes. The project is equipped with smart technology, offering high-speed digital connection for internet, television and voice communications. Amenities include a gymnasium, squash court, aerobics studio, swimming pool, mini-cinema and sheltered parking.

Arabian Ranches

Located on the outskirts of Dubai city at the junction of three highway roads leading to Abu Dhabi, Al Ain and Dubai, the Arabian Ranches development combines championship golf with luxury properties and equestrian facilities. Nine models offer a wide range of family accommodation in Iberian-influenced architectural styles. The 18-hole **Arabian Ranches Golf Course**, designed by Ian Baker-Finch in association with Nicklaus Design Layout, sits at the centre of the complex. Additional facilities for golfers include a clubhouse, bar, function room and pro shop as well as a tuition academy and guest accommodation. A full-service **Equestrian Centre** has an Andalusian theme complete with a Spanish-style polo club, tack shop, spa, and swimming pool. Shopping, dining and entertainment amenities are centred on the **Village Community Centre**, where 20 outlets include supermarkets, cafés and restaurants plus a laundry, pharmacy and travel agency. Arabian Ranches is also home to the **Jumeirah**

English Speaking School (JESS), an education centre for children that offers primary and secondary schooling. *See also* 'Emaar Golf Homes', p.73.

Business Bay

Business Bay, a commercial and business cluster along a new extension of the Dubai Creek, will cover an area of almost six million square metres when completed. It will feature office and residential towers set in landscaped gardens with a network of roads, pathways and canals. There will also be a 303-room luxury hotel, the **Business Bay Hotel**, at the heart of the development. The hotel will feature trendy coffee shops and restaurants.

The **Executive Towers** kicks off the first phase of Business Bay, comprising a cluster of towers featuring eleven residential blocks, a luxury hotel, shopping mall, clinics and health clubs. Studios and one- to four-bedroom apartments, and executive luxury apartments on the higher floors, are on offer. A plaza level or courtyard acts as the hub of community life and amenities include landscaped plazas, children's play areas, swimming pools and health clubs.

In July 2007, Dheeraj and East Coast LLC (DEC) the joint venture between India's Dheeraj Group and the UAE's East Coast Group, announced the launch of **The Bay Residences**, its first residential project within the Business Bay precinct. The development will be predominantly residential units, with 190 one-, two- and three-bedroom apartments. Amenities include five retail units, a health club, Jacuzzi, swimming pool and cafés.

Canal Residence West

Due for completion by the end of 2009, Canal Residence West is located in the heart of **Dubai Sports City** and **Dubailand** (*see* p.71). An elegant waterside residential complex modelled on an upscale Riviera lifestyle, the project blends classic European, Mediterranean, Venetian, Spanish and traditional Arab architectural styles. Canal Residence West comprises five towers on a tree-lined promenade on the banks of a waterway. Units are spacious one-, two- and three-bedroom apartments, each wired for digital technology and equipped with CCTV. Amenities include a private health club, beauty salon, spa, reading and music room, business centre and secure parking facilities. Elevated swimming pools and sundecks benefit from shaded pavilions with communal outdoor space that includes children's play areas, gardens and barbecues.

The Centrium

This quadruple tower project offers one-, two- and three-bedroom apartments in the master-planned **International Media Production Zone** on Emirates Road. Each unit features an intercom system linking apartments and is wired for smart technology. Facilities include swimming pools, water features, barbecues, gym, health club and jogging tracks.

The Crescent

This triple-tower construction in a master-planned community just off the **Emirates Road** features a collection of one- and two-bedroom apartments and studios. A range of floor plans offers views across parklands and lakes with amenities that include shops, restaurants, swimming pools, tennis courts, sports grounds and fitness clubs. The development rises to 15 storeys and is patrolled by 24hr security.

Culture Village

Located on the **Dubai Creek** extension, Culture Village is designed as the cultural hub of Dubai. Culture Village has been designed to mix Middle Eastern old-world pleasures and entertainment with a modern, sophisticated ambiance. The project features wide open spaces and cobbled walkways around waterways topped with bridges. By a creek there will also be a market place comprising souks, restaurants and cafés. An amphitheatre has been created for cultural festivals while an exhibition centre will house a museum and a dockyard where a traditional dhow will be displayed. Architecturally, Culture Village will mix Arabic and old Dubai influences with sculpture and pottery adorning the façades of buildings. The development is divided into residential, commercial and retail zones with hospitality and entertainment sub-districts.

DEC at Culture Village

DEC's three current projects in Culture Village are Cascade Ville, Cascade Manor and The Estate. Each project has run back-to-back, with the scheme set for completion by the end of 2009.

Residences at the Culture Village comprise studios, one- two- and three-bedroom apartments in traditional low and mid-rise buildings. **Cascade Ville** is a seven-storeyed residential community comprising one- to three-bedroom apartments. Amenities will include a state-of-the-art health club, gym, boutique and café with 24hr security. **Cascade Manor** is an eight-storeyed structure housing a range of one, two and three-bedroom apartments that boast wifi and a park with landscaped gardens. Residences at **The Estate** are sited within a 21-storey building that offers a range of different-sized apartments complete with CCTV and wifi. For those working at home, a custom-built loft apartment is offered that combines living space with a work area.

Currency House

Al Fattan Currency House is located in the **Dubai International Financial Centre (DIFC)**, a Free Zone on target to achieve the same financial stature as New York, London and Hong Kong. Created to service the vast Middle East and North Africa (MENA) region between Western Europe and East Asia, the DIFC is

the world's newest financial centre. Currency House is a mixed-use development comprising office and residential space with private residences that offer
a choice of one- to three-bedroom apartments and penthouses.

DEC at Culture Village

See left.

DEC Towers at Dubai Marina

DEC is a joint venture between Dheeraj Constructions India and East Coast LLC
Dubai. The company has a handful of notable developments under way in the
city, including projects at Dubai Marina and Culture Village.

Due for completion by the end of 2008, DEC Towers is situated at the heart of
Dubai Marina, overlooking the coast. Comprising two residential towers
offering a range of one-, two- and three-bedroom apartments, the buildings sit
atop a two-storey structure containing parking space, a business centre and an
array of leisure facilities. Ideally positioned near the 5th interchange on **Sheikh
Zayed Road**, the DEC Tower project is located within an exclusive neighbourhood complete with world-class golf courses and luxury beachside resorts.

Discovery Gardens

This 240-hectare horticultural development on **Sheikh Zayed Road** sits
between Interchanges 5 and 6 and comprises flower-filled, botanically themed
communities. Drawing inspiration from The Gardens (*see* p.74), gives buyers a
choice of Mediterranean, Zen, Contemporary, Cactus, Mogul and Mesoamerican
apartments, which look out on to landscaped lawns, lush foliage and desert
blooms. Residents can take advantage of swimming pools, jogging paths and
tennis courts as well as a wide range of dining options, fine retailers, cinemas
and a hypermarket located at the **Ibn Battuta Mall**, a five-minute drive away

Downtown Burj Dubai

The Downtown Burj Dubai development will redefine the city skyline, adding
a new high-profile point of reference, including the tallest building and largest
shopping mall in the world. New vertical and lateral neighbourhoods are
reshaping this historic project, using distinctive architectural designs to form a
showpiece complex that comprises Burj Dubai, Burj Dubai Boulevard, Boulevard
Crescents, South Ridge, The Old Town, The Old Town Island, The Business Hub
and the Dubai Mall.

Burj Dubai, poised to be the world's tallest tower (*see* p.61), has already set a
new global record. It has more floors than any building on the planet (currently
at 120 storeys and 422.5 metres high). It is also one of the five tallest structures
in the world. The tower encompasses residential, commercial, entertainment,

Case Study: Gemma Mitchell

'I moved to Dubai from Scotland at the age of 24, in October 2007, to take up the role of PR and communications exec at Nakheel after seeing a job advertisement circulated to my masters course. The first six months here were a bit of a rollercoaster, but I think that's the same with every big move. I had a lot to adjust to: a new apartment, new car, new job and new friends – and getting used to it all doesn't happen overnight. I threw myself into the whole expat thing initially to get better acquainted with the city. Now, I'm more selective and keep my eye on all the guides to find out what's happening every week.

'I've approached my life in Dubai as long-term, rather than a "stop gap", as I'm pretty sure it's a better way to settle in and feel at home. I rent a two-bedroom apartment in Discovery Gardens, Jebel Ali, with en suite bathrooms, an open kitchen/living area, guest toilet and a small balcony. It was unfurnished so I've had to equip the whole apartment, including kitchen appliances. It's standard practice in Dubai to have to pay six or even 12 months' rent in cash upfront – although banks will give loans for rent if you have an account and a job.

'Dubai is a fast-paced city that is full of young professionals from all different walks of life, out to move forward in their careers. Although it's famous for its eating, drinking and socialising, Dubai also has a great number of sports clubs and leisure opportunities as well. The older part of town is a favourite with me as it moves away from the five-star glitz and glam to offer colour, hustle and bustle and plenty of life. In this part of town you can walk around and you feel you are in the Middle East surrounded by people and culture – in the new part of town where you drink and eat in five-star hotels as standard, you sometimes feel as if you could be in any city in the world. Me, I'd recommend Dubai to anyone who wants to try it, although it is important to read up before you leave home so that you know what to expect. Understanding the local customs is imperative in the UAE. Check the country advice on **www.fco.gov.uk/travel** and read a guidebook – it's all great prep ahead of arriving in Dubai.'

and hotel facilities, and the **Dubai Mall**, the world's largest shopping mall (see p.170), which forms the central core of the project in Dubai's new emerging downtown district. It is scheduled for completion by the end of 2008.

The 63-storey **Burj Dubai Lake Hotel and Serviced Apartments** will offer fully equipped serviced apartments in the elegant curvilinear tower, located on the **Burj Dubai Boulevard** next to the Dubai Mall. The five-star property will be managed by a leading luxury hotel group, which will also manage the 210-room luxury hotel. Owners of the fully furnished, serviced apartments retain total flexibility to occupy them whenever they choose, with the option to release them for rental income at times when the apartments are not in use. The property overlooks the **Burj Dubai Lake** and faces the **Old Town**. A collection of one- to four-bedroom apartments is already under construction.

Development of the Old Town is being carried out in phases and comprises five districts: the **Yansoon Quarter**, **Reehan Quarter**, **Zaafaran Quarter**, **Zanzebeel Quarter** and **Miska Quarter**. Properties range from low-rise three-storey apartment buildings to a number of exclusive mid-rise towers with penthouses. Architectural styles are heavily influenced by Arab architecture, taken from the Al Bastakia neighbourhood of Bur Dubai and the residences of Sheikh Saeed Al Maktoum and Mohammed Shareef Boukash. Textures reflect the gypsum, clay or sarjool plastering used in the early 20th century, using earthy natural tones that mirror the landscape. Terraces, balconies, parapets (*waresh*), pergolas, recesses and niches are key architectural features of the one- to four-bedroom residential suites.

Neighbourhood amenities include children's play areas and landscaped gardens. Facilities include a games room, juice bar, swimming pool, aerobics rooms, squash courts, cinema, relaxation rooms, external courtyards and under-ground parking.

At **The Residences**, in Boulevard Crescents, the amenities of a metropolitan centre are combined with exclusive community living. Nine high-rise buildings house one- to three-bedroom residential suites. Key features include a swimming pool, squash courts, a golf course, badminton court, fitness centre, mini theatre, library, meeting rooms, six guest bedrooms and a daycare centre with 24hr security, four parking levels and on-call 24hr maintenance services. Each suite has high-speed internet access, with combined IT outlets in every room for TV, phone and data, CCTV and an intercom system.

Dubailand

Dubailand is arguably one of Dubai's most ambitious tourism, leisure and entertainment developments – a project conceived on a phenomenal scale across 300 million square metres of desert. The project is destined to transform the geography of Dubai, using pioneering master-planning that incorporates a variety of themed worlds and family entertainment. A two-million-square-metre residential and retail centre, the **City of Arabia**, contains offices, shops, galleries, restaurants, schools, clinics and residential apartments. The 30-storey **Wadi Tower** and **G Tower** contain one-, two- and three-bedroom apartments and penthouses, with convenient access to the **Emirates Road** and the monorail.

For homebuyers with an active lifestyle, **Dubai Sports City (DSC)** in Dubailand offers luxury living around an 18-hole championship golf course. Located on a five-million-square-metre area, DSC is home to the Manchester United Training Academy, the Butch Harmon School of Golf and the David Lloyd Tennis Centre. The 18-hole Victory Heights Championship Golf Course has been designed by Ernie Els, in association with Nicklaus Design.

Apartments available include **Rufi Twin Towers**, **Champions Tower** and **Shami Tower**. Another development in Dubailand is the **Falconcity of Wonders**, a self-contained and multi-faceted residential, tourist and recreational destination mirroring the wonders of the ancient and modern world – including Dubai Eiffel Tower, Dubai Taj Mahal, Dubai Grand Pyramid, Town of Venice, Dubai Hanging Gardens of Babylon, Dubai Tower of Pisa and Dubai Light House. The whole development is designed to resemble the falcon, the national emblem. **The Villa** – Falconcity's residential area (*see* below) – is situated in the falcon's wings. **Dubai Eiffel Tower** and **Dubai Grand Pyramid** are multi-use buildings offering residential apartments, commercial space and recreational facilities. Meanwhile, **Dubai Hanging Gardens of Babylon** in Falconcity will house eco-friendly luxury flats, with numerous open-air restaurants and coffee shops, with the garden overlooking the Falcon commercial sector.

Dubailand is intended to rival Disneyland®, with theme parks, rollercoasters and large-scale attractions, using the latest technology for thrills and safety. As the largest theme park in the world, Dubailand promises unrivalled rides, including Pharaoh's Theme Park, Giants' World, Kids' World, Global Village, Space and Science World, Space Hotel, Tourism Park, Film World, Desert World Theme Park, Snow World, Aviation World, Water Park, The Castles, Arabian Theme Park, Eco-tourism World and Sports and Outdoor World. It will also include a themed area for wellbeing and relaxation, comprising village residences, resort hotels, wellness retreats, fitness and stress-management-focused facilities and health centres.

Retail and Entertainment World will provide retail facilities offering a wide variety of global brands as well as discount stores within one of the biggest malls in the world. Downtown features various dining establishments, clubs and entertainment venues including cinemas and street performers.

Dubailand is located on Emirates Ring Road, just 10 minutes from Dubai International Airport, 10 minutes from Emirates Towers, 20 minutes from Sharjah and 60 minutes from Abu Dhabi. Nearby developments include **Dragon Mart**, the largest Chinese goods market in the Middle East, **Dubai Design Centre**, the multicultural residences of **International City**, and the production studios of the **International Media Production Zone, Global Village**, and **Arabian Ranches** developments.

The Villa at Dubailand

The Villa offers buyers the opportunity to purchase their own plot of land and build their own Spanish villa based on one of the several architectural guidelines provided by the developer. The Villa comprises three communities, with **The Ponderosa** and **The Haciendas** offering ranch-style living and **The Cento** designed around clusters of villas. Plots of land range from 1,000 to 1,300 square metres at The Ponderosa and The Haciendas and 750 to 1,100 square metres at The Centro.

The village will house a shopping centre with restaurants and supermarket and community facilities include gym, swimming pools, children's playground, horse and bike trails, tennis courts and lakes. The US$163 million project's second phase was launched in 2006 and is scheduled for completion in 2009.

MotorCity at Dubailand
See p.82.

Dubai Marina Towers

Notable as the first phase in the construction of the landmark **Dubai Marina**, the Dubai Marina Towers project comprises six high-rise residential towers, three of which are named after precious stones. **Murjan** consists of 37 storeys, **Al Mass** 28, and **Fairooz** 20. The remaining towers are named after Arab fragrances: **Mesk** at 37 storeys, **Yass** at 24 storeys and **Anbar** at 16.

The Marina Towers are located near Interchange 5 on **Sheikh Zayed Road**, close to Dubai's well-known landmarks of **Dubai Internet City**, the **American University in Dubai** and the **Emirates Golf Club**. Amenities include a community centre, daycare facilities, fitness club, spa, business centre and barbecue areas. There is also a 24hr concierge and marina berthing.

Dubai Towers
See 'The Lagoons', p.80.

Dubai Waterfront

This impressive array of canals and islands will truly redefine the shape of modern Dubai, adding a string of luxury hotels and exclusive homes – and extending the coastline by 800 kilometres. A neighbourhood larger than Manhattan, it will offer more than 250 master-planned communities in a project that has made history as the biggest man-made development on earth.

A 70km canal forms the heart of the scheme, with a harbour providing access to the open waters. **Al Burj**, one of the world's tallest skyscrapers, will dominate the skyline, and the area will also be home to a luxury underwater hotel, **Hydropolis**. The Waterfront project will involve the construction of multiple roads, waterways and five square kilometres of coral reef. The planned communities on the waterfront are expected to house up to 400,000 people along with numerous shopping centres, entertainment complexes and nightlife.

Emaar Golf Homes

Mirador La Colección, at the **Arabian Ranches** golf course, is a collection of villas set on spacious plots, featuring the best elements of Spanish architecture and design. Also at Arabian Ranches, **Saheel Golf Homes** are contemporary villas overlooking the golf course. **Hattan III**, distinctive homes inspired by Arabia's heritage and Islamic architecture, are situated close to the Emirates Golf Club in the idyllic setting of the **Emirates Hills** community.

Emaar Towers

Located on the banks of Dubai's beautiful **Creek**, in the **Rigga Al Buteen** area, Emaar Towers is close to **Deira** city centre, Dubai International Airport and the traditional gold souk, and just seconds away from **Maktoum Bridge**, the link to Bur Dubai and Sheikh Zayed Road.

The apartments at the 16-storey Emaar Towers opened in 2003 and feature spacious accommodation with large feature windows, sweeping balconies and state-of-the-art kitchens complete with the latest in appliances. Accommodation comprises one- to four-bedroom apartments, penthouse, sub-penthouse and sky bridge suites, across two buildings linked by a central foyer. Amenities on site include a swimming pool, steam room, gymnasium and outdoor terrace.

Emirates Hills

Homes at Emaar's benchmark master-plan community look out over the lush green fairways of the Montgomerie 18-hole championship golf course, created by master architect Desmond Muirhead and seven-time European Order of Merit winner, Colin Montgomerie. Opened in April 2006 and marketed as the Beverly Hills of Dubai, this golfing haven comprises a good balance of villas in handsome, low-density private neighbourhoods with plenty of lush landscaping. At the top end of the market are the five- and six-bedroom **Dyaar Al Hambra** villas, with more affordable three-bedroom maisonettes facing the fairways. Amenities include 24hr security, satellite and cable television, broadband internet, golf clubhouse and spa. Emirates Hills is also the site of **Dubai International Academy**, which offers schooling from nursery to Grade 12.

Fairmont Palm Residence

See 'The Palm, Jumeirah', pp.83–4.

The Gardens

Located next to **Jebel Ali Village**, The Gardens spreads over 220 hectares with the first phase having been completed in 2003. The development consists of 129 low-rise buildings of 3,828 one-, two- and three- bedroom apartments set amid lush grounds. Amenities include a football field, tennis courts, swimming pools, basketball and volleyball courts, clinic, and a school. **Ibn Battuta Mall**, the largest themed shopping mall in the world, is also close by.

Green Community

Developed by Properties Investment LLC in an equal joint venture between Union Properties PJSC and Dubai Investments, the Green Community is located within the **Dubai Investment Park**, just off the **Emirates Road** at the intersection for Jebel Ali Free Zone and Jebel Ali Village. A multi-phased project costing AED 1.5 billion and spanning a total land area of 3,200 hectares, the Dubai Investment Park comprises mixed-use industrial, business, residential and recreational units. Pre-serviced sites and world class infrastructure offer investors state-of-the-art facilities and quality services.

The unique residential concept of Dubai's ecologically focused Green Community is located on 67 hectares within Phase 1 of the Park. Every aspect of the project has been designed with environmental consideration, from the infrastructure, architecture and cooling systems to the satellite TV systems, landscaping and recycling services.

A wide choice of residences including villas, townhouses and apartments are each designed to ensure that no two homes are the same. Mediterranean-style commercial and retail units will centre on a lake and canal. Other on-site facilities include a Marriott Courtyard hotel with boulevard restaurants and serviced apartments. Every common recreation area contains a swimming pool, children's pool, gymnasium and community room alongside picnic and barbecue areas, water features, children's playground, amphitheatre and tennis courts.

Green Community West, a neighbouring sister community spread across an adjoining 100-hectare plot, is currently under construction. It has been designed to mirror the ethos of the original Green Community, with the first of three build phases due for completion by the end of 2008.

Lake Apartments

These studio, one-bedroom and two-bedroom apartments offer panoramic views of the Green Community. Located next to the main communal park area, which leads down towards the amphitheatre and lake, the apartments are a short walk from the shopping and dining zone. Forming the final building of the highly successful Green Community, the Lake Apartments comprises a total of 52 units each set over three levels, with ground-level under-building parking. Tennis courts, basketball and volleyball are all close by with a swimming pool, Jacuzzi, children's pool and gymnasium on-site.

The Greens

This landscaped community is located adjacent to the prestigious **Emirates Golf Club** and comprises mid-rise buildings with studios and one- to three-bedroom apartments. Courtyards lead to gardens and a host of amenities that include a swimming pool, gymnasium and barbecue area. Each unit is equipped with state-of-the-art technology, including high-speed digital connections for internet, TV and voice communications.

International City

This 800-hectare mixed-use development comprises businesses, residences and tourist attractions in six key zones, namely the **Central Districts**, **Dubai**

Gates, the **Dragon Mart**, the **Residential District**, **Lake District** and the **Forbidden City**. Designed to reflect the cosmopolitan make-up of Dubai, International City is a melting pot of cultural influences. The residential district is set in 300 hectares of land and comprises more than 20,000 residential units in the style of Italian, Spanish, Moroccan, Persian, Greek, Chinese, Indonesian, English, Russian, Thai and French architecture.

International City is located on **Emirates Road**, near the Dubai International Airport and Dubailand. It is 20 minutes away from Dubai International Financial Centre and 15 minutes from Dubai Festival City.

Jumeirah Beach Residence

This project features a floor area of two million square metres developed across 1.7 kilometres and comprising 36 residential towers, four hotels, retail space and entertainment facilities. It is being developed by the same team that produced Dubai Internet City and Dubai Media City.

Located in the middle of Dubai's new growth corridor, the US$1.6 billion development is just a 15-minute drive from the heart of the city and offers a range of one- to four-bed properties with amenities that include a cinema, shops, restaurants, cafés, health clubs and sports facilities, as well as offices and medical centres. Each apartment comes with one or two private covered parking spaces, and larger apartments boast maids', utility and dressing rooms. Many properties will have sea views.

In addition to the standard apartments, a selection of specialised properties have been built from the 20th floor in each tower, including penthouses, loft apartments, terrace apartments, and garden apartments – all sold at a premium. Each is equipped with features such as private swimming pools and whirlpools, private terraces or gardens, full-length French windows and double height rooms. The project also includes **The Walk**, a 1.7km-long shopping boulevard covering some 70,000 square metres, including more than 400 outlets and 45 beachfront restaurants.

Jumeirah Heights

Located just off **Sheikh Zayed Road**, Jumeirah Heights is near to Jumeirah Islands and will be served by two metro stations by the time of the project is complete in 2010. Just 15 minutes from **Dubai Internet City** and **Dubai Media City** and shopping at **Ibn Battuta Mall**, Jumeirah Heights is also well positioned for easy access to Dubai's resorts and world-class beaches.

At the private launch of Nakheel's Jumeirah Heights development, more than 370 units were sold in under 24 hours. The project, which comprises 2,300 apartments and luxurious waterfront townhouses, will be home to around 11,000 people. It is scheduled for completion by 2010. Neatly divided into three distinct neighbourhoods, Jumeirah Heights is made-up of the **Village Centre**,

The Fronds and **The Clusters**. The two Fronds will each consist of two mid-rise apartment buildings and 17 town houses. The two Clusters will each house three low-rise apartment buildings of two- and three-bedroom apartments with private gardens. In the first stage of development, the Village Centre features almost 650 apartments and a variety of retail facilities including a supermarket, cafés, bank, pharmacy and a number of other outlets. Amenities include a club house, a swimming pool, a gym and a children's play area.

Jumeirah Golf Estates

Nakheel has joined forces with golfing superstars Greg Norman and Vijay Singh to create Dubai's premier residential golfing community. The 1,119-hectare development will be one of the finest golfing destinations and residential communities in the world, boasting four superstar-designed golf courses surrounded by luxury residential opportunities ranging between 500 and 1,000 square metres. The environmentally themed courses are inspired by the elements of nature – Earth, Fire, Water and Wind – integrating seamlessly with distinct gated communities. The first phase incorporates the Greg Norman-designed Fire and Earth courses and 14 residential communities across 375 hectares. Set at the centre of the two courses is the **Norman Clubhouse**, home to a golf academy, gym, racquet courts, swimming pools, a wellness centre, children's play area and restaurants. Fire and Earth are scheduled to open by the end of 2008, with the Vijay Singh-designed Water course following suit. Some 75 per cent of properties have absolute golf course frontage, with the balance facing lakes, nature strips and parks.

Jumeirah Islands

This elegant, award-winning 300-hectare waterfront community features 46 villa 'clusters' set on inland man-made islands surrounded by waterfalls, lagoons and lushly landscaped canals. The entire complex, linked by walkways and bridges, is located just off **Sheikh Zayed Road** between Interchanges 5 and 6. Each neighbourhood comprises 16 properties, many with private swimming pools, based on four individual architectural themes. The Oasis, Islamic, European and Mediterranean designs each come with a large range of options in a community designed for families and everyday living.

Jumeirah Lake Towers

Situated adjacent to **Sheikh Zayed Road**, between Interchanges 5 and 6, Jumeirah Lake Towers is a mixed-used waterfront community comprising residential and office towers alongside hotels, leisure and retail outlets.

Featuring 79 towers clustered into groups of three, the project contains four lakes, landscaped gardens and a number of waterways. At the core of the development is **Almas Tower**, a building that houses the **Dubai Diamond Exchange** and **Dubai Multi Commodities Centre (DMCC)**. Facilities include a retail area, restaurants, cafés, daycare centre and children's play area. The DMCC Authority will be the licensing authority for businesses operating in the Jumeirah Lakes Towers. Companies will benefit from **Free Zone status**, making JLT the first mixed-use Free Zone freehold development in Dubai.

Jumeirah Park

In September 2006, more than 500 people queued to buy 2,000 villas in the newly launched Jumeirah Park development, with 1,000 units sold in just one day. Jumeirah Park is the fourth and latest addition to Nakheel's Jumeirah brand of family communities and is centrally located within 'New Dubai', between **Sheikh Zayed Road** Interchange 5 and 6. Jumeirah Park offers a secure, integrated and family-orientated residential community spreading over 350 hectares. The community comprises more than 2,000 three-, four - and five-bedroom villas in three architectural styles: rustic, heritage and regional. Villas range between 360 and 456 square metres, and are designed to meet the needs of the modern family, with an emphasis on open-plan living. All villas feature private terraces and gardens and spacious double garages. Four- and five-bedroom villas have individual temperature-controlled swimming pools, which will also be available as an extra purchase on three-bedroom villas. Jumeirah Park boasts expansive parks, eco-friendly green spaces and family-orientated amenities including a community club house, children's play area and youth centre, restaurants, department and convenience stores, and a kindergarten through to secondary school. The project is scheduled for completion in 2009.

Jumeirah Village

Although initial plans for this community in 2004 detailed more than 2,900 villas and 3,200 town houses built in classic Arabian and Mediterranean architectural designs, Nakheel has been forced to scale down the project after government plans to build highways across the site, according to *Gulf News* reports. Details of revised plans for this **Emirates Road** development have yet to be revealed but it is thought to contain an international school, a town and country club, a community centre, jogging and cycling trails, sports and leisure facilities, medical facilities, and round the clock security.

The Kingdom of Sheba

See 'The Palm, Jumeirah', p.85.

Laguna Tower

This ultra-modern 40-storey high-rise overlooks the tip of the Jumeirah Lake Towers development, offering uninterrupted views over the lake, the city and the Arabian Gulf beyond. Units comprise a mix of one- to three-bedroom apartments on each level – each with smart technology. Facilities include a large swimming pool, gym and children's playground along with a fully equipped business centre. There is also a range of shops, cafés and leisure facilities. Allocated parking and 24hr security are complemented by concierge services around the clock. Owners can benefit from room service, housekeeping, dry cleaning and laundry.

Laguna Tower is well positioned close to Dubai's **Media City** and **Internet City**; the shopping and entertainment of the **Mall of the Emirates** are also nearby. It is also near Dubai's leading attractions and landmarks, including **The Palm, Jumeirah**, **Dubai Marina**, **Ibn Battuta Mall**, **Ski Dubai**, **Emirates Golf Club** and many of Dubai's finest beaches.

Mövenpick Hotel & Residence at Laguna

IFA Hotels & Resorts' freehold hotel residences in Laguna Tower offer a guaranteed return and strong capital growth potential. The concept allows investors to buy a fully furnished five-star branded hotel residence, to be professionally managed by Swiss hotel chain, Mövenpick Hotels & Resorts. Dubai's hotel market is one of the world's strongest and most dynamic, achieving record occupancy levels and room rate levies. In terms of income potential, IFA's Hotel Ownership concept delivers owners 8 per cent guaranteed returns for the first three years, thereafter 50 per cent of the hotel's room revenue. Those wishing to resell are able to monetise at any time after completion. A total of 120 hotel rooms are offered along with an additional 296 suites and apartments.

Lake Apartments

See 'Green Community', pp.74–5.

The Lakes

These family-sized homes were constructed for rental and range from two to five bedrooms, located adjacent to **Emirates Hills**. Renowned for scenic waterways, parks and landscaped greenery, The Lakes set the tone for family living in Dubai as one of the emirate's first family schemes. Villas are situated between two world-class golf courses (the Montgomerie at Emirates Hills and Emirates Golf Course) and has been rented since completion on long-term leases. However, in February 2007 Emaar Properties announced plans to offer residents of The Lakes an option to purchase their homes.

Sales of the units in the master-planned residential project have since been undertaken in phases, with the **Zulal** and **Forat** townhouses available in the first phase. Any residual stock will be released onto the open market. There are 306 Zulal townhouses and 60 Forat townhouses, all located along picturesque lakes close to other residential projects by Emaar including The Springs (*see* p.86), The Meadows (*see* p.82) and Emirates Hills (*see* p.74).

Lakeside Residence

This residential project in Jumeirah Lakes is 35 storeys high and comprises 358 apartments, each equipped with smart technology. Accommodation comprises one- and two-bedroom units with amenities that include basement parking, shops and a deck on the 15th floor.

Other features at Lakeside Residence include an electronically monitored security system, high-speed lifts, ambient lighting and a balcony in every apartment. There is also a large recreation centre with gymnasium and pool.

The Lagoons

This 6,500,000-square-metre mixed-use scheme is the brainchild of Dubai Holding's realty arm, Sama Dubai. Half of the project on Dubai Creek was sold to third party investors, with the balance developed and marketed by Sama Dubai.

A key feature of The Lagoons is seven landscaped islands interlinked by bridges comprising residential units, shopping centres, office towers and marinas. It will also include conservation areas, parks and open spaces along with resorts and five-star hotels. Cultural attractions of the project include Dubai's first opera house, a planetarium, a museum, an art centre and a theatre. A healthcare and therapy centre will also be located on-site. At the heart of the development, **Dubai Towers** forms an impressive centrepiece.

The Lagoons project is scheduled for completion in 2010.

Dubai Towers

Dubai Towers will make a bold statement on Dubai's skyline: a cluster of towers that combine to form a signature focal-point of the Central Business District of The Lagoons' development. Destined to become one of the city's iconic structures, Dubai Towers has been designed to metaphorically represent the luminous movement of candlelight. It comprises residential, commercial, retail and hospitality units and is scheduled for completion by mid-2010.

Sama Dubai is currently developing **Dubai Towers–Doha**, **Dubai Towers–Casablanca** and **Dubai Towers–Istanbul** under the Dubai Towers brand.

Largo Vista

These sleek 15-storey residential towers in the **International Media Production Zone (IMPZ)** are designed around an attractive crescent-shaped portico. Units comprise two-bedroom apartments and studios, each offering panoramic views. Individual entrance lobbies provide access to accommodation and amenities. On-site facilities include a large temperature-controlled swimming pool, tennis courts, children's play area, health club, gym, sauna, communal barbecue area, banquet/function room, coffee shop and covered parking.

The IMPZ's residential sector is located off the **Emirates Road**, a 10-minute drive from Jumeirah Beach and the theme parks of forthcoming Dubailand.

Le Reve

This celebrated penthouse-only development is contemporary in style, with units that range in size from 550–1,200 square metres. Designed by W.S. Atkins, the company behind the world-renowned Burj Al Arab, Le Reve enjoys a premier location next to **Dubai Marina** overlooking The Palm, Jumeirah. Three styles of accommodation (**Presidential Classic**, **Presidential Contemporary** and **Royal**) offer spacious modern grandeur – the largest apartments contain five bedrooms, two reception rooms, five bathrooms and a gourmet kitchen. Amenities include a gym, swimming pool, hotel services, underground parking and 24-hour concierge. Terraces are angled to ensure privacy with a 15-metre-high podium that accommodates all on-site recreational facilities at deck level.

Liberty House

This mixed-used 42-storey building in the **Dubai International Financial Centre** comprises 29 floors of apartments and eight floors of open-plan office space. A roof terrace on the 9th floor of the northeast wing has provision for a jogging track and fitness areas. Options include 208 studios, 120 one-bedroom apartments and 44 spacious two-bedroom apartments. Modern security features, such as video entry, are also part of the spec. Facilities also include two recreation and relaxation decks with pools, spa, fitness suite and gym.

The Lost City

Launched in September 2004, the Lost City is a residential development inspired by ancient civilisations, from **The Fertile Crescent** to **The Orient**, **Mediterranean Africa** to the **Arabian Peninsula**. Comprising a range of villas, townhouses and apartments, the Lost City mixes historic influences with state-of-the-art modern facilities. Located in a 560-hectare site in **Jebel Ali**, at the intersection of the Ibn Battuta Interchange Road and Emirates Road, the Lost City is close to **Ibn Battuta** shopping mall and **Discovery Gardens**. On-site facilities include a championship 18-hole golf course designed by Greg Norman.

Marina Promenade

This high-rise condo project overlooks a scenic stretch of the bay opposite the prestigious **Dubai Marina Yacht Club**. Comprising six towers containing a collection of one- to three-bedroom villas, amenities include swimming pools, fitness centre, a gym, games room, squash courts, library, badminton court and business lounges. Each property is equipped with smart technology and benefits from CCTV access control systems and high-speed internet connections. The project is located close to yachts, boardwalks, shops and restaurants at the centre of **Dubai Marina**'s vibrant lifestyle. An elegant lobby is manned by a concierge and protected by 24hr security.

Marina Quays

Extending 20m over the water, Marina Quays offers a unique outlook across **Dubai Marina** and comprises a range of one- to three-bedroom apartments and villas. Located close to shops and dining outlets, on-site facilities include a gymnasium, swimming pool, squash court, aerobics studio, mini cinema, business centre and guest suite. There is also mooring within walking distance.

Marine Towers

This mixed-use 53-storey development combines stylish residences with retail outlets in a self-contained community along the shores of the Arabian Gulf, close to **Dubai Marina**, the city's media and IT hubs, and the arterial **Sheikh Zayed Road**. The development has extensive facilities for shopping, sports and dining, with community features that include promenades, walkways and gardens, children's facilities and high-level security. A team of renowned international architects are behind the design, which features two imposing towers that rise above the beachside.

The Meadows

Part of Emaar's series of pastoral themed developments, The Meadows boasts plenty of wide tree-lined streets and large open spaces. Villas range in size from three- to seven-bedroom, with all nine phases of construction now complete. This family-orientated complex centres on gardens and water features, with numerous children's play areas and leafy enclaves. Amenities include nurseries, schools, shopping centres, cafés, restaurants and mosques, close to beaches, golf, five-star hotels and **Dubai Media** and **Internet City** and the **American University** in Dubai.

MotorCity

Dubai chose to launch this first fully integrated automotive and motor sports facility at a fitting venue at the 11th Abu Dhabi International Motorshow. Poised to become the hub of the region's automotive and motor sports industry, MotorCity spans more than three million square metres in the heart of **Dubailand**, a city within a city. It comprises ultra-modern leisure, commercial and residential facilities that include **Dubai Autodrome** (the world's first Formula One Theme Park), **Business Park MotorCity** and two high-end residential areas, **UPTOWN MotorCity** and **Green Community MotorCity**. Work on the infrastructure for MotorCity is nearing completion, with the construction of some buildings under way from the second quarter of 2007. Projects will be delivered in various stages, starting from the last quarter of 2008 to the second quarter of 2009. Construction of Green Community MotorCity started last year, with anticipated completion and handover in 2009. It will comprise high-end residential units, including apartments, town houses and bungalows. UPTOWN MotorCity will contain well-appointed apartments and town houses, built on the lines of the UPTOWN Mirdiff scheme (*see* p.87).

Mövenpick Hotel & Residence at Laguna

See 'Laguna Tower', p.79.

Palace Towers@Dubai Silicon Oasis

This twin-tower development is split between residential and office space, rising from the centre of **Dubai Silicon Oasis** on Emirates Road. Located within easy reach of **Dubailand**, the **Arabian Ranches** and the **Autodrome**, Palace Towers comprises 22 storeys of 424 spacious residential apartments. An array of modern amenities ranges from a fully equipped gym and swimming pool to shopping and dining. The project is under construction with a scheduled completion date of early 2009.

The Palm Islands

Dubai's unique trio of Palm Islands are the largest man-made islands on the planet – a multi-billion-dollar project of which The Palm, Jumeirah was the first. The islands, shaped like palm trees, sit in waters just off the coast of Dubai – The Palm, Jumeirah alone has added 78.6km to Dubai's coastline. At the peak of its construction, 40,000 employees were working on the project each day, turning 94 million cubic metres of sand and seven million tonnes of rock into a world-class leisure and lifestyle resort.

The Palm, Jumeirah

When fully complete by 2010, The Palm, Jumeirah will contain 32 five-star hotels. More than 60,000 residents will call The Palm home with over 20,000 visitors per day. Five top-class beach resorts, four marinas and thousands of metres of retail and commercial are just some of the local amenities. Luxury residences will include 7,000 apartments, and 1,700 villas and townhouses. Marinas with the capacity to berth 150 yachts and 50 'super-yachts' are also available. In 2005, the Dubai government awarded the contract for a Japanese-designed **monorail** system for The Palm. The 5.4km long transport system will run between the Gateway Station at the trunk of The Palm, Jumeirah and the Atlantis Station on the crescent, calling at two intermediate stations on the way to Trump Tower and Village Centre. It will cost US$390 million and take around three years to complete.

Fairmont Palm Residence

IFA's ultra-luxurious Fairmont Palm Residence is poised to become the premier residential development of The Palm, Jumeirah. Located at a pivotal point of the island, close to cafés, boutiques and bars, the Fairmont Palm Residence offers 558 deluxe homes, including apartments, townhouses and penthouses. Using a hybrid of Arabian and modern architectural styles that mixes Middle Eastern influences with contemporary materials, each property is directly linked to the five-star Fairmont Palm Hotel and Resort. Beach access is available on a membership basis, with on-site amenities that include a gymnasium, restaurants, kids' club and swimming pool. For a nominal fee, apartment servicing, housekeeping and maintenance, maid and childcare services can also be arranged. A full property management service to maximise rental is also offered to investor-owners.

The Palm Golden Mile

The Palm Golden Mile, located on the western side of the trunk of The Palm, Jumeirah, is hotly tipped to become one of Dubai's most prestigious addresses. More than 800 luxury homes are planned for this exclusive neighbourhood close to the boutiques and cafés that edge the half-kilometre cornice. The US$400 million development will house 220 designer stores as well as an array of fine restaurants and bars.

Residences at The Palm Golden Mile are in ten waterfront buildings on the hub of the island. Properties range from one-bedroom apartments to penthouses and townhouses, with some 50 per cent of units sold in less than 24 hours of being released. Apartments boast waterside and garden views and come complete with a large, private patio. Buyers at The Palm Golden Mile can also benefit from an extensive range of services, including owners' reception and concierge, housekeeping, maintenance, security and maid and childcare services. A rental administration programme is managed by Fairmont.

The Palm Residence

Situated on the eastern shore of the trunk of The Palm, Jumeirah, The Palm Residence comprises two blocks of units, **Al Nabat** and **Al Haseer**. Apartments in both offer views over sea or gardens and are one-, two- and three-bedroom with square footages of 1,097, 1,500 and 2,100 respectively. Two- and three-bedroom apartments have a maid's room and benefit from a wide range of services offered by Fairmount Hotels and Resorts, including apartment owners' reception and concierge services, maid and childcare services, apartment servicing, housekeeping and maintenance, condominium management, clubhouse management and services and security. Owners of The Palm Residence will benefit from the same rental administrative programme offered to owners of The Palm Golden Mile. Fairmont Hotels & Resorts will also administer the rentals on their behalf.

Trump International Hotel & Tower

This US$600-million ultra-modern split-linked tower forms the visual centrepiece of The Palm, Jumeirah, an impressive 48-storey mixed-use hotel and residential structure. The Trump International Hotel & Tower was designed to minimise shadows and will feature lots of stainless steel, glass and stone.

The first joint venture between Nakheel and the Trump Organization, the scheme comprises a 300-room condo-hotel, 360 residential apartments, office space, rooftop restaurants, bars, swimming pools, yacht club, a private marina, gym, spa and health club. Residents at the 360 two-, three- and four-bedroom apartments can also access five-star leisure and entertainment facilities. The project is scheduled for completion in 2009.

The Kingdom of Sheba

The Kingdom of Sheba is located on the Crescent of The Palm, Jumeirah, adjacent to the renowned Atlantis development. Strongly influenced by classic Arab architecture, the project's residences, hotel, private residence club, vacation club and retail plaza will be managed by Fairmont Hotels & Resorts. This large-scale project is another landmark IFA Hotels & Resorts (IFA HR) development. Spread across 141,500 square metres, the mixed-use hotel and tourism scheme has a combined value of in excess of US$1 billion. The project is scheduled for completion by mid-2010. **Balqis Residence** consists of 300 residential units, from villas and town houses to luxury penthouses and apartments. Properties overlook the sea, with views across sandy beaches with prices that range from US$1 million to over U$S7 million. A continuous walkway will connect the residences to the hotel and shops and other projects on the Crescent. Owners will have access to all other IFA HR and Fairmont products and services on The Palm, Jumeirah including The Palm Golden Mile retail area – soon to be Dubai's most prestigious retail address with 220 designer stores.

The Palm, Jebel Ali

The second of Dubai's Palm Islands is The Palm, Jebel Ali, a landmark shoreline resort development. Four main architectural styles of property boast views across the water and benefit from 24hr security. A range of **garden homes** come in a variety of different layouts. Each has an individual swimming pool and private beaches. **Town houses** are offered in three- and four-bedroom floor plans. Each has a garage, shared swimming pool and garden. **Water homes**, built on stilts, come with four bedrooms and a mooring. **Beachfront villas** sit on a private stretch of sand and come in a variety of styles. A chain of floating homes or **atolls** is awaiting the final master-plan from Nakheel but from the air it will spell out a verse from an Arabic poem written by H.H. Sheikh Mohammed bin Rashid Al Maktoum. The project is well-served by island amenities and facilities, including a marina clubhouse with pool and a gym. There is also a village centre with shops, supermarkets, pharmacies and a laundry.

The Palm, Deira

Dubai's third and largest palm island is The Palm, Deira, a 12.5km man-made atoll with 41 fronds that forms the final part of the world-famous palm trilogy.

Located 8km from The World (*see* p.88) in sheltered waters, The Palm, Deira's latest master-plan (it has been tweaked, revised and then tweaked again) looks poised to position it as one of Dubai's key leisure, residential and tourist hubs. Comprising some 8,000 villas, hotels, marinas, restaurants and shopping malls, the island contains nine separate interconnected areas, conceptually titled **Palm Crown, Palm Fronds, Palm Crescent** and **Palm Trunk**. There are also five areas along a major corniche, namely **North Island, South Island, Central Island, Al Mamzar Island** and **Deira Island**. These will be linked by bridges to the mainland that will join-up with the current road transport network as well as the planned Dubai metro system (*see* **Living in Dubai**, pp.177–8). More than 17.5 per cent of the total reclamation is complete now, placing the development on schedule. More than 198 million cubic metres of sand is already in place, with land reclamation due to be completed by 2013.

Park Island

Generous use of green space and landscaped gardens are a key feature of Park Island, a development built in four phases: **Blakely**, **Bonaire**, **Fairfield** and **Sanibel**. Each of the towers is 24–28 storeys high and offers a wide range of floor plans. Residents benefit from a pool, squash courts and cinema within walking distance of the beach and the other entertainment facilities of **Dubai Marina**.

The Rotating Residences

Dubai's first rotating tower is also the world's first such project, a US$41-million structure that comprises four rotating penthouses and a rotating villa. Blessed with a full 360-degree panoramic view, the villa is a true one-off, boasting a split-level living space and a stunning garden and private swimming pool. The tower has 16 floors of retail spaces at ground floor and 90 residential units, five of which are luxury penthouses, each unit of approximately 540 square metres and a villa of approximately 880 square feet. Rotating at four different speeds at programmable intervals of 3 hours, 6 hours, 12 hours and 24 hours, the villa has a private car and passenger lift, with three car parking bays on the roof. A state-of-the-art gym and health club and retail areas form part of the project, located in Jumeirah Village South just a 10-minute drive from the **Dubai Media Production Zone**. Construction is under way on this landmark development, due for completion for occupancy by 2009.

The Springs

This gated community of town houses is located within the **Emirates Hills** community, in close proximity to **Dubai Media City** and **Internet City**. Semi-detached single-family (three- or four-bedroom/two-bathroom) villas are the highlight of this master-planned neighbourhood, which has retail facilities, fitness centres and a playground.

Trident Grand Residence

Each apartment in this development on **Dubai Marina** has password-protected touch-sensitive smart technology systems to manage lighting, music, cooling and security. On-site swimming pools, golf, a gym, yoga suite, business centre and cigar lounge are available for the exclusive use of property-owners, while a lounge on the 41st floor offers magnificent views. Two penthouse apartments have private swimming pools, a gymnasium, sun-deck area and an internal panoramic elevator. Each unit is networked for remote access, enabling owners to check on their homes from their office or even the car.

UPTOWN Mirdiff

Architecturally designed along the lines of an ancient spa town, the UPTOWN Mirdiff development promises an excellent variety of residential properties, play areas and recreation facilities nestled within landscaped gardens and public parks. A collection of town houses, mews-style terraces and five distinct apartment designs are planned around a centrepiece grand piazza. Numerous amenities include shopping and dining outlets on UPTOWN Mirdiff's 23 hectares along with a primary school.

Trump International Hotel & Tower, The Palm, Jumeirah

See 'The Palm, Jumeirah', pp.84–5.

The Views

This waterside development overlooks the **Emirates Golf Club** and comprises Riviera-style townhouses and apartments amid landscaped gardens next to **The Greens**. Several neighbourhoods, the Arno Riverside Residence, Travo, Turia, Una, Golf Towers, The Fairways and The Links, offer a variety of housing options.

At the **Arno Riverside Residence**, accommodation ranges from studio apartments to large three-bedroom properties, and most of the 177 units within this mid-rise development have views of the adjacent riverside. Located between The Greens and Emirates Golf Club, the neighbourhood has 24hr security and offers easy access to Dubai Marina, Internet and Media Cities, the American Embassy and Jumeirah Beach.

At the mid-rise **Travo Riverside Residence**, apartments are styled after Mediterranean architecture and look out across a waterway close to the Emirates Golf Club. Travo shares many of the features of Arno, except that the range of accommodation is greater, with 34 studios and 44 one-bedroom, 86 two-bedroom and eight three-bedroom apartments. A state-of-the-art gymnasium is fitted out with free weights and a wide range of machinery, and the development also boasts an outdoor swimming pool, deck and communal area.

Golf Towers is situated on the perimeter of the Emirates Golf Club, bordered by fairways on one side and riverside on the other. With one- to four-bedroom accommodation across twin towers, the development boasts a multi-purpose entertainment room, poolside barbecue deck areas and walking trails.

The Fairways is a contemporary development of three towers, with easy access to the Emirates and Montgomerie golf courses and Dubai Marina. The North and East Towers are to be the first to be released, and offer one- and two-bedroom suites with apartment sizes ranging from 72 to 140 square metres. A total of 344 units are available (163 within the North Tower, 181 within the East Tower) and each has views over the golf course or lake. A separate podium between the buildings contains a three-level secure car park, garden, barbecue area and pool. The site also features parks and walkways.

The Links is the latest addition to The Views development, with tower apartments (one-, two- and three-bedroom) offering views overlooking the prestigious Emirates Golf Course on one side and sparkling waterways to the other. The Links Water View Apartments offer studio and one-bedroom apartments in a low-rise building.

The Villa

See 'Dubailand', p.72.

The World

This collection of 300 man-made islands forms the shape of the world map, positioned four kilometres offshore and spanning an area nine kilometres wide and seven kilometres long. The World offers private island living within close proximity of the bustling city life of Dubai. Each island costs between US$15 and US$40 million and ranges in size from 13,500 to 49,500 square metres. They are protected by a 26km circular breakwater which is approximately 4m high.

Construction is under way on this multi-billion dollar project, and is scheduled to be completed by the end of 2008. The World, whose sales are by invitation only, is now 92 per cent reclaimed, with full reclamation for all islands and breakwater expected to conclude on schedule. Nine islands including 'Ireland' have been sold so far this year. Once complete, the project will be visible to the naked eye from space.

Buying a Property in Dubai

Many Westerners move to Dubai with their job or on an offer of work. Part of the deal is that their new employer helps them secure residency and suitable housing. In order to buy or rent an apartment or villa in Dubai, you'll need a residence permit (*see* p.138) – so applying for this is a crucial first step.

Accommodation in Dubai adheres to a zoning system which stipulates the style and type of property built – and the nationality of those who can live there. Options for both purchase and rental range from studio flats, apartments, condominiums and villas, with serviced hotel apartments (self-contained units or large suites) also doing a roaring trade. Figures from Colliers International suggest that a minimum of 125,000 residential units will be released in Dubai before the end of 2009 – yet this is still expected to fall short of demand. According to *Wealth Creator* magazine, Dubai's rate of capital appreciation is tipped to achieve 18 per cent per year until at least 2015.

To help guide newcomers through the property maze, the Dubai Lands Department has released a 168-page *Guide to Freehold Property* detailing where foreign investors can legally buy. In 2007, the government pledged to make such material available in English as well as Arabic in strong support of Dubai's large number of global investors. For more information on neighbourhood and developers, *see* Chapter 04, **Dubai Neighbourhoods.**

- Dubai Lands Department, **t** 222 2253.
- Real Estate Department, **t** 398 6666, **www.realestate-Dubai.com.**

Dubai Property Investment FAQs: Your Questions Answered

- **Why buy in Dubai?**

Dubai is fast shaping up to become one of the most significant financial and commercial hubs on the planet. Its business-friendly government is committed to attracting and retaining widespread investment, with investors provided with an unrivalled package of tax advantages, encouraging both start-ups and regional expansion into the emirate, bringing with them tens of thousands of expatriates – all of whom to need somewhere to live. Property therefore continues to promise healthy returns on both capital and rental income.

Since freehold property became available to foreigners (*see* opposite), more than 20,000 non-national buyers have taken possession of freehold villa homes in Dubai. Demand for real estate continues to outpace supply by a significant margin and shows little sign of slowdown. Dubai's real estate market is also supported by its growing attractiveness as a holiday destination – in 2006, 6.3 million tourists visited the emirate. Visitors from the UK and Ireland, for example, have increased more than tenfold since 1993.

• **Can you buy property freehold?**

Until 2002, when the then Crown Prince of Dubai and UAE Defence Minister, His Highness General Sheikh Mohammad bin Rashid Al Maktoum, announced that 100 per cent freehold ownership of certain properties in Dubai was available to all nationalities, non-Gulf Cooperation Council (GCC) nationals living in the UAE were only permitted to rent property or own real estate on an approved 99-year leasehold basis.

In 2006, however, a newly decreed freehold property law was introduced to strengthen Dubai's real estate sector. The legislation enabled property purchased by foreigners to be legally assigned to them for life and permitted its registration at the Dubai Lands Department. This ensures full rights to the property, with the right to sell, lease or rent at the owner's discretion.

However, the exact rights surrounding freehold ownership – granting complete title on the property and land – in Dubai can be a source of confusion for many foreign investors, because the term 'freehold ownership' had no official definition in the UAE until the 2006 change in law. Today 'freehold' is a Dubai buzzword and a better understood concept with non-nationals.

• **How regulated is the property market?**

A legal and regulatory framework supports Dubai's real estate market. A decree firming up the legalities relating to freehold ownership in March 2006 has served to bolster the confidence of property investors. Global backers continue to demonstrate trust in Dubai's potential, with annual investment totalling more than AED 180 million forecast for the next three years.

Only developers specifically licensed by the government have the right to sell freehold real estate, so it is important for investors to identify those that do from the outset. The land bank in Dubai is mainly shared among five major corporations, including Dubai World entities Nakheel and Limitless; Dubai Holding entities Dubai Properties Group and Sama Dubai; as well as Emaar Properties, Dubai Investments and Union Properties. Dubai World, Dubai Holding and Emaar Properties offer freehold land and properties, while Dubai Investments and Union Properties own land that is offered to investors leasehold for periods of 90–99 years. *See* Chapter 04, **Dubai Neighbourhoods**.

• **Is Dubai a safe place to invest and spend time?**

In addition to year-round sunshine and a 52-week tourist season, Dubai offers high levels of safety, and the city has been rated as the world's safest travel destination for four consecutive years by Interpol. Dubai has a benign, cosmopolitan culture and a long history of political stability. It also has a near-zero crime rate and a liberal pro-West stance. Yet the government is far from complacent amid the global threat of terrorism. Dubai authorities have assumed a leadership role in Middle Eastern anti-terrorism measures and invested significant sums to better protect its borders. A number of forward-thinking counter terrorism laws were implemented post 9/11, and continue to offer Dubai's visiting and resident population a high degree of confidence, according to a survey by the Dubai Department of Tourism and Commerce Marketing. In 2007, Dubai's ruler, Sheikh Mohammed bin Rashid Al Maktoum, stated his commitment to protection, stating, 'I want each and everyone living here to be safe and secure.' The UAE has experienced no major terrorist incidents to date.

- **How big an investment-driver is tourism?**

Dubai remains wholly focused on economic diversification away from the foundations of its prosperity – oil. Today, 95 per cent of Dubai's GDP is generated by non-oil sector revenues compared to approximately 55 per cent in 1975. Tourism alone generates revenues in excess of US$3 billion, with a ratio of tourists to residents now approaching five to one, according to *Gulf News*. Dubai has set tourism as a strategic development priority, as evidenced by mega-projects like US$64 billion Dubailand with its theme parks, resorts and sports stadia, which includes a US$2 billion Universal Studios theme on a mammoth Universal development.

See **Dubai Today**, pp.28–36, for more on Dubai's economy.

- **How does economic diversification impact my investment?**

Today, just 5 per cent of its GDP is generated by oil revenues compared to approximately 45 per cent in 1975. The government is targeting other industries. Dubiotech, a new industrial park, targets international biotech companies working in the pharmaceutical, medical, genetic research and bio-defence fields. Dubai's International Media Production Zone is another ground-breaking project created to attract the world's finest printers, publishers and production companies to the city. Both are forecast to bring a sizeable foreign skill-set to Dubai's community of 160-plus nationalities, further expanding the emirate's expatriate population.

In a decade, Dubai's GDP has nearly tripled in size to AED 136 billion – a 16 per cent growth in 2005 alone according to a statement from the Dubai Department of Economic Development. The 2006 Dubai Strategic Plan (DSP; *see* p.29) has further strengthened the focus on diversification. This economic road map bodes well for investors in a nation on target to triple its GDP via double-digit growth to US$108 billion by 2015.

Property prices in Dubai represent good value by international standards, but rents are high – an attractive proposition for investors. Tony Horrell, CEO of the international capital group at Jones Lang LaSalle, said, 'Dubai, with its dynamism in pursuing significant investments within the Emirate and in global assets, has emerged as one of the leading players in the real estate market across the world.' Some 80 per cent of the Fortune 500 companies are now located in Dubai, with its Free Trade Zones continuing to nurture a substantial amount of investment. More than 300 British companies are based in the Jebel Ali Free Zone Authority alone.

• **How stable is the dirham?**

The dirham has been pegged at AED 3.6725 to the US dollar for over 20 years. A planned new single Arab Gulf currency tipped for introduction in 2010 looks likely to be delayed due to the challenges of achieving monetary union in such a short timescale. As an interim measure, the UAE government may undertake

Case Study: Mark Emlick

'I'm originally from Edinburgh but currently based in Dubai, where I rent a three-bedroom serviced apartment in the Governor House hotel in Dubai Marina. Living in hotel accommodation is a lot more convenient from a business perspective, as I tend to travel a lot to various international professional commitments. I am the chairman and founder of Dunedin Independent plc, one of the UK's leading IFA businesses with £500 million in assets under management. I am also the chairman and co-founder of Strategic Investment Management, which is a FSA-regulated business with the main goal of identifying and developing niche property investment opportunities, predominantly in the hotel sector, including some of the top-rated hotels in Scotland, like, for example, Radisson SAS in Glasgow city centre. Up until now we have managed £350 million in compound deal flow.

'I first came to Dubai about five years ago on holiday – although I was also interested in exploring it as a new and potentially lucrative business destination. I liked what I saw: the city was rapidly growing and developing, quickly gaining its own unique presence on the international map. The business opportunities, particularly in real estate, were plentiful and I had soon purchased a number of residential units to "test the water". Since then my portfolio has grown considerably to include a large number of varying properties as well as land for development or resale. I have also gone further by establishing Strategic Property Investment Group in the city – we have already completed many attractive transactions with returns on assets averaging to 50 per cent per annum, and there are many more in the pipeline. I am happy to say that Dubai's real estate market has not suffered from the effects of the credit crunch, and the annual growth rates can still be as high as 60–70 per cent, which is unbelievable when you compare it with anywhere else in the world.

'I like living in Dubai. The expat community is very diverse, both culturally and ethnically, which makes the social life an exciting experience. Also, from a business perspective, mixing different mentalities and life experiences promotes a rich exchange of ideas and opportunities. The business mentality is a unique mix between Eastern sentimentality and Western pragmatism. Arab businessmen will be more inclined to do business based on their level of familiarity towards you, so it is worthwhile to work on your networking if you want to succeed here. I would also recommend securing some reliable recommendations, if possible. Knowing people is key in this country.'

a revaluation, but in the meantime the exchange rate remains entirely dependent on the £/US$ rate. However, Kuwait's announcement that it is abandoning its currency peg against the dollar may also have an impact on Dubai's currency plans.

- **What costs are involved when purchasing a property?**

No stamp duties or property taxes apply, although there may be a fee for facilitating a transfer on the secondary market ('flipping') of 2–7 per cent, see p.102.

If you are buying an 'off-plan' property (one that is inder construction) you will be expected to pay in stages; see p.99.

Mortgage-lenders (see below) typically charge a processing fee of 1.25 per cent of the loan.

Insurance is often mandatory when funding a property purchased via finance. Expect to take out building, contents and/or life assurance policies. Some lenders require all three.

For more on costs, see p.105.

- **Are home finance products available?**

Dubai's mortgage sector opened up considerably during 2006, and from 2007 a widening range of mortgages became available to non-Gulf Cooperation Council (GCC) nationals. Mortgages are available to foreign buyers on a fixed-rate and variable-rate basis, linked to the Dubai Interbank Offered Rate. At present, there are 14 lenders in Dubai – 10 local banks and four international. The key lenders are HSBC, Amlak, Tamweel, Al Mashreqbank, Lloyds TSB, Dubai Islamic Bank, Abu Dhabi Commercial bank (ADCB), National Bank of Dubai (NBD), Rakbank and Emirates Islamic Bank (EIB). Barclays Bank also entered the market in 2006.

Mortgage terms vary (as do the lending criteria) but loans of up to 80 per cent of the value for purchase are offered on completed properties; up to 70 per cent for re-mortgages; and up to 70 per cent for properties under construction. Variable and fixed rate loans range from 15–30 years. Specific lenders work with selected developers only. Available loans include a range of Sharia-compliant contracts. Non-Gulf Cooperation Council nationals pay a slightly higher interest rate than residents, of generally 8–11 per cent.

See pp..105–14 for more on home financing loans.

- **How does Dubai compare with other property hotspots?**

Reports by The Economist suggest that the total value of residential property in the world's developed economies rose by more than $30 trillion during the last five years, to over $70 trillion – an increase equivalent to 100 per cent of those countries' combined GDPs. According to the latest global real estate capital report from international capital group Jones Lang LaSalle, Dubai's total property market transactions totalled around US$600 billion. The company placed Dubai property on a par with that of other major financial centres such as London, Hong Kong, Sydney and New York – although considerable disparity remains between the average values in the prices of the real estate, for example, in Dubai and London.

Even allowing for skyrocketing prices, Dubai's real estate continues to represent good value when compared with other developed nations, with an absence of income tax on rentals, and capital gains tax and stamp duty on property sales, an attractive prospect for investors. At present, the supply of real estate is falling short of demand and this particular trend is set to continue until at least 2015. Additionally, the high rental yields achieved by investors (currently 7–8 per cent for long-term rentals and 12–15 per cent for short-term) seem to justify further capital appreciation in the market.

While future capital growth is difficult to predict in an immature market, this is expected to achieve around 18 per cent per annum up to mid-2010, according to *Wealth Creator* magazine. Property prices in Dubai have recorded high levels of capital growth in recent years. Average property prices in Marina Terrace, for example, have appreciated by 207 per cent since the launch of the development in 2002, while residential units in The Waves, also located in Dubai Marina, have appreciated by 162 per cent since its launch in 2002.

Dubai's property rights, transaction costs and capital gains taxes are all critical issues for real estate investors. Direct comparisons with many other countries favour Dubai in several key areas. Part of the reason for the gap between Dubai property prices and those of, say Singapore, has been the lack of finance options available. The widening of Dubai's mortgage sector has effectively eliminated this factor, so any disparity in real estate prices is forecast to be short-lived. Many other real estate markets prohibit foreigners from owning property, especially on a freehold basis. In addition, transaction costs (registration fees, stamp duty, etc.) are often high and property taxes common. Dubai's favourable approach to foreign ownership, combined with the performance of the real estate sector, makes it an attractive prospect for investors – especially given the economic objectives of the Dubai government.

Finding an Apartment or Villa

Buying a property anywhere in the world isn't something to do lightly and Dubai is no exception. Visiting Dubai twice, before committing to a purchase, is heartily recommended, preferably at different times of year. It is also important to do as much research as you can on specific developments before beginning your search for a villa or apartment. Each neighbourhood is very, very different and it is vital to make sure the one you pick is right for you. *See* **Dubai's Neighbourhoods and Developments**, pp.59–88. Remember, Dubai is a modern city where construction has only really been prolific since 2002, so if your heart is set on a charming period house with a sense of history you'll be sadly disappointed. What Dubai does have in abundance is cutting-edge architecture and bold design, with villas, townhouses and apartments the most common. Even the oldest villas and apartments are under 20 years old, with most property on the market sleek, futuristic and minimalistic in style.

House-hunting in Dubai can be done from your armchair using the internet, enabling some much-needed research to take place while on home soil. Every developer or agent selling Dubai properties has a presence on the web, be they Dubai-based or in the UK. Scanning these sites will help you to form an opinion on what is right, and wrong, for you. Several factors should be considered when searching for the ideal apartment or villa, including:

- **Size of property you require.**
- **Proximity to your place of work.**
- **Local amenities and facilities.**

Estate Agents

Any agency worth its salt will minimise the leg-work of trawling through the vast portfolio of available Dubai properties on your behalf. This includes:

- **Accurately matching properties to your individual requirements.**
- **Arranging flights and property viewings.**
- **Updating you on changes in the Dubai property market.**
- **Providing you with advice and support throughout.**

A few of the estate agencies offering property in Dubai include:

- **FPD Savills (UK), t (020) 7016 3740; www.savills.co.uk/abroad.**
- **Homes Dubai (UK), t 08700 992400; www.homesdubai.com.**
- **DAMAC (Dubai), t 390 8804; www.damacproperties.com.**
- **Oryx Real Estate (Dubai), t 348 0598; www.oryxrealestate.com.**

Property Exhibitions

Throughout the world, property exhibitions have gained popularity as a good source of information for would-be purchasers. Some are tailored specifically to buying real estate in the UAE, others are more general, but each will offer guidance on apartments and villas on the market in Dubai.

In the UK, the largest property shows are advertised in the national press – with some of the largest linked to TV property programmes. For details visit:

- **A Place in the Sun Live, www.aplaceinthesunlive.com.**
- **Home Buyer Show, www.homebuyershow.co.uk.**
- **Oman International Property Exhibition, www.oite.com/ipe.**
- **Dubai Property Investment Show, www.internationalpropertyshow.ae.**

Inspection Trips

All reputable selling agents and developers will make provision for viewing trips to allow potential buyers to inspect a shortlist of properties in Dubai. To avoid a wasted journey, be sure to do as much homework as possible about the properties that have been earmarked for inspection. Otherwise, it will be an expensive trip (even if it is subsidised by the agent) and a fruitless one at that. It is much better to take your time and be spoilt for choice by properties that are 100 per cent spot-on.

Orientation Tours

A number of relocation specialists offer orientation tours of Dubai. Costs vary but expect to pay around US$650 per day for a comprehensive 'newcomer's guide' to the city. Other drive-by tours offer would-be residents a blow-by-blow explanation of Dubai's layout, from the locations of the best supermarkets and food shops, speciality shops, hospitals, police stations, post offices, libraries, hairdressers, banks, furniture stores, electricity and phone companies, to advice on road laws, police and emergency services – and where to find the major shopping malls.

Many orientation tours include some useful background information on local culture, from Dubai's heritage houses, *abras* (water taxis) and dhows on the creek as well as the famous gold and spice souks. Some provide lots of tips and advice on Dubai from an expatriate lifestyle perspective, with a strong focus on exploring the various expatriate residential areas, beach clubs, public parks and recreational amenities as well as popular sports facilities. This type of service can prove invaluable in a city like Dubai where the landscape is subject to change – and roads can be torn up overnight to add new lanes.

Typically, the best orientation tours in Dubai include the following: a welcome pack, with the *Dubai Explorer* guide book and sample newspapers; an arrival agenda; and the use of loan mobile phone for one week. They will aim to inform you of the location of the following: residential areas; schools and other educational establishments; kids' clubs and play areas; clothes, uniform and shoe shops; dry-cleaners; municipal parks and recreation areas; golf clubs; beach clubs; furniture stores; soft furnishings stores e.g. curtain-makers, upholsterers; supermarkets, groceries, household, appliances stores; hardware and DIY stores; banks; employment agencies; points of interest; places of worship; medical facilities (hospitals and clinics); police stations and emergency services; post office, utilities and telecommunication services; transport services; pet stores and veterinary surgeries; pet relocation companies; beauty salons, hairdressers and spas; restaurants and fast food outlets; car showrooms.

Buying Off-plan

Dubai has become the self-proclaimed 'Off-plan Property Capital of the World', shifting more units at pre-construction phase than any other nation. Over the past five years, successive real estate projects have sold out in less than 24 hours, with waiting lists drawn up for entire developments before a brick has been laid. In every way, Dubai's off-plan sales have achieved record-breaking status, setting a formidable benchmark for future emerging real estate markets keen to steal its crown.

Case Study: Alan Errington

'I'm originally from South Wales but have lived in the UAE for 16 years now, working in both Dubai and Abu Dhabi. When Dubai's first freehold developments were offered to the market in 2002, my wife Naomi and I made our first off-plan purchase at Dubai Properties' Jumeirah Beach Residence (JBR) development. We had previously looked at the Palm Islands, Emaar Towers at Dubai Marina and The Greens. JBR is the largest single-phase residential development in the world, comprising 36 residential towers, four hotel blocks and four beach clubs. The development offers a wide selection of residential units ranging from studio, one-, two-, three- and four-bedroom apartments with sea view, marina view, and other views to suit different budgets and needs. JBR was also very competitively priced, so we purchased a four-bedroom terrace apartment overlooking the beach, with a completion date of 2007.

'Today, over five years on, the property market has changed significantly. Property values are increasing month by month, so even if a seller is offered their asking price they can be tempted to drop out of the sale as their property has increased in value. Buying through a master developer offers a low risk of non-delivery; smaller developers, especially in the current market, have been known to miss scheduled completion dates – or even fail to get the development under way. Another benefit of buying off-plan from a master developer is that the price is fixed and non-negotiable. Historically, there was also a discount for off-plan properties, compared to buying a ready-built property, but today this is not always true.

'Buying a property at JBR was relatively straightforward, although the paperwork took a bit of getting used to. The process is still very alien compared to the UK, as the property market in Dubai is really only six to seven years old, but now professional safeguards are being developed each year. Most documents are non-negotiable, as during this present property boom, developers are in a position where they have more buyers than units to sell. So the average buyer wouldn't think of consulting a lawyer to assist them, but lawyers can add value – especially where the buyer is inexperienced in this market. Today, our purchase at JBR has quadrupled in value in just five years, so I'm pleased that we had the foresight to invest in Dubai early, well before the boom.'

One drawback of off-plan purchasing is that it often means committing to a dream, not a reality – without a tangible bricks-and-mortar product to assess. Signing a down-payment away on the basis of developer's plans can be a daunting prospect for the uninitiated. Glossy brochures, of course, can promise a lot but ultimately deliver less – in 2004 and 2005 there were several reports of foreign buyers being unhappy with the specifications and finish of their completed properties. On the upside, buying at pre-construction phase can give purchasers considerable control in terms of design. It can also provide buyers with advantageous lower (or discounted) early-entry pricing.

Another major consideration is that few youthful property sectors can boast such a regulated real estate framework as Dubai. Unlike many embryonic markets, 'off-plan' isn't a byword for reckless risk-taking. In 2008, Dubai remains an opportunity that global investors trust – primarily because of the mathematics of demand. With so many people moving to Dubai each month, new housing remains at a premium. More than 125,000 properties will be required in the next two years to meet demand, according to a report by international estate agents Knight Frank. Almost all of this will be sold off-plan, despite an increase in the demand for completed stock. Such is Dubai's potential that more than 180 million dirhams of foreign investment is expected by 2010. Since early 2006, sterling has gained nearly 12 per cent against the dirham – an advantageous situation for UK buyers making staged payments for off-plan purchases, as the final cost of the property will be less than expected a year earlier.

Payments

A series of payments are spread over the construction period. The schedule depends upon the developer but in the vast majority of cases payment must be finalised before completion. You will normally be required to pay instalments of between 15 and 20 per cent every few months. Costs depend on the size and type of the property purchased, but typical financing structures offered by Dubai-based developers involve the following:

- **10 per cent deposit payable on signing.**
- **10 per cent payable after 30 days.**
- **Five staged payments at set construction milestones.**
- **20 per cent final payment upon completion.**

Construction Delays

As with any embryonic property market, Dubai remains susceptible to risk, especially given the sheer volume of the construction projects that are under way. As of April 2007, the number of infrastructure projects in GCC countries topped 2,000, according to a report by Lehman Brothers, with an estimated

US$1.3 trillion earmarked for projects to 2012. The core of these ventures is in Dubai and Abu Dhabi, with projects under way to the tune of US$300 million. In 2006 the government of Dubai confirmed a 15-year plan of infrastructure investment of US$130 billion. As of January 2006, the UAE had US$35.6 billion worth of construction projects running, according to a report by Abu Dhabi National Exhibitions. Much of this building work centred in Dubai. Reports by the Dubai Chamber of Commerce suggest that more than 6,000 construction companies were active in Dubai during 2005 alone, according to the Dubai Chamber of Commerce and Industry.

This simultaneous construction on such a vast scale in Dubai has made delays on scheduled completion inevitable. Much like China and the USA, the industry is exposed to the fluctuating costs of construction materials. Shortages of steel on the worldwide market have also hampered construction schedules. Like other expanding nations, Dubai is under pressure from a sharp rise in cement prices and restricted supplies, according to *Gulf News* reports. Cement product manufacturers have increased prices by up to 20 per cent since the start of 2007, with demand continuing to outstrip supply. In 2006, Dubai also experienced its first major labour dispute. Yet when, compared to other developed nations, the emirate's building process is faster than most Western countries. Labour costs remain low and the quality of workmanship exceptionally high – setting Dubai apart from many other emerging real estate markets.

Given the potential threat of delays, many buyers have been inclined to take a conservative view rather than err on the optimistic side when it comes to completion dates. Rescheduled delivery schedules have become increasingly common. In the short term, restriction in supply is driving prices higher, while soaring energy costs threaten to impact project costs. Some developers have resigned themselves to readjusting rental income calculations – a frustration for investors, but a symptom of a market that is yet to fully come of age.

Top Tips for Buying Off-plan

- Be sure to visit the site to establish exactly where it is before handing over any cash. Ask lots of questions about the plot and the build. Work through a checklist and take some photos. Never rely solely on a developer's plans.

- Establish what deposit is due and the exact payment terms (these are usually made in stages during the life of the construction project). Check the status of the development (is it on time or already experiencing delays?). Build times are usually 12–18 months, but it is important to establish what, if anything, may have an impact on the date of final completion.

- Check how well the site is managed. If part of the development is already occupied, speak to residents to get a feel for the quality of the workmanship and customer care.

Case Study: Matt McNeill and Nikki Wright

Matt, 27, from Cheshire, and his fiancée Nikki, 32, live in Fulham.

'As CEO and founder of two software companies, I first became aware of Dubai when I was sent details of the Dubai Internet City's tax incentives. The deal was a good one, offering software companies zero per cent corporation tax for 50 years to set up there. The fact that there is also no personal tax in Dubai was a real temptation. So, we travelled out for a holiday in March 2006 and I took some time out to visit Dubai Internet City to find out more. It all looked promising, but there was a huge waiting list as it seemed everyone wanted to start a business in Dubai. Over the course of that year, I returned for more meetings – there was a real buzz about the place, and it wasn't long before we started to look at properties on the internet with a view to buying.

'Basically, Dubai offers Nikki and me the chance to buy a much bigger property for our money – we can get a two-bedroom apartment the size of our three-storey house for less than the price of a one-bed shoebox in Fulham. Dubai's higher quality of living and year-round sunshine also really appeals – we are prepared to take the risk of a move abroad, so we thought "why not?"'

'At first our main priority was a view, as but after seeing many properties and looking at plans in sales centres we realised that the size of the apartment, its location and internal finish was much more important. We liked Dubai Marina best as an area, as it's close to the beach, the water and Internet City. With around 200 towers being built there, we soon had property details coming out of our ears! It all got very confusing. Luckily, we met a really good estate agent, called Ian Hollingdale, who helped us no end – we definitely owe him a drink.

'Properties sell out fast in Dubai and we were a bit late at cottoning onto the Dubai real estate boom; all the apartments we liked at Bayside Residence on the Marina had already been bought direct from plan. Eventually Ian found an apartment on the secondary market that sounded ideal, but as we were due to fly back to the UK that night we weren't able to follow them up. However, when we got home we did some more homework and decided to go for it – we paid a lump sum to the apartment owner and entered into a contract direct with the builder, Trident. This set out all the instalments due for the remainder of the construction period. A disappointment for us was the delayed delivery of the apartment, as the build schedule kept being put back. On the bright side, this gave us more time to pay for it – in total, the amount due was £260,000 and we were able to fund this using savings and our regular income without a mortgage. In April 2008, we visited Dubai to take a look at our almost-finished apartment – and, for the first time, standing next to the building, it felt as if our dreams were approaching reality. Fingers crossed, we should take delivery of our apartment in a couple of months, so we are already planning our next trip. We were staggered to learn that the property has doubled in value – but we aren't investors and just want to make it our home in the sun.'

- Clarify exactly when the site amenities are scheduled for completion. You may not want to wait five years for the pool, restaurants, golf course, etc. to open after the last house is built. Also consider the location of the development. How far is the nearest airport, hospital, shop or beach? These factors will have an impact on the rental potential of the property (and will affect annual yields) as well as being crucial to its future value.

- Ascertain the basis for any claims made regarding the property's rental potential. Fact, not fiction should form the bedrock of your financial calculations, so be sure to scrutinise the local market to double-check all yields quoted in publicity material or by the agent or development. Some properties are sold with rental guarantees, usually a fixed period programme over one or two years. These should also be checked against the state of the market to ensure you are obtaining the going rate for maximum yields.

- Avoid solicitors recommended by the agent or developer. Find a reputable (bilingual) independent lawyer who fully understands the off-plan sector.

Resale Properties

Sales of existing properties (resales) are becoming a growing part of the UAE's property sector as more and more buildings are completed. Now that Dubai is a real estate 'free for all', many of the available off-plan sales are made to serious investors; many entire developments are sold out within hours, often to large-scale investor-buyers. Those who manage to purchase at early-entry stage are extremely fortuitous. Dubai's resale sector is therefore now an established secondary market, and many purchasers will find that buying pre-owned is a viable alternative way of snapping up a home.

After an initial flurry, the real estate market experienced a lull in 2004 before springing back to life in early 2005. Today, few signs of dormancy are evident as more and more people relocate to the city – all of them requiring a place to live. Due to supply shortages, the resale market has much of the fervour and intensity of a primary market. Many foreign buyers, more used to purchasing actual bricks and mortar than on the basis of a model or a blueprint, are actually more comfortable with the concept of resale.

In Dubai, however, this *still* can mean the property has yet to be built! Indeed, a significant number of properties are sold multiple times prior to construction being completed (you may hear the term 'flipping') – and in Dubai this is a simple process. The developer re-issues the **property sales agreement** (PSA) in the name of the new owner. At this point a **transfer tax** is charged (at around 7 per cent) and borne by the seller. A **resale clause** may now stipulate that 30 per cent of the value must have been paid before resale is allowed.

The Process of Buying a Resale Property

Buying a property in any foreign country is a complicated process, especially when the Arabic language, culture and red tape are wholly different from that at home. In Dubai, the buying process is quite unlike in the UK. Seeking **independent legal advice** is imperative for those unfamiliar with the nuances of the system – even if they have bought abroad before. Dubai's property procedures have been implemented relatively recently, as foreign ownership wasn't permitted until 2002. Consequently, the system is subject to a handful of unfathomable 'quirks' that will undoubtedly be ironed-out over time, but remain an issue of puzzlement. However, generally speaking, the process of buying property in the UAE will provide few headaches, other than those caused by seemingly endless reams of red tape.

Typically the process is as follows:

- **View the property and make an offer** (signing nothing until a lawyer is engaged).

- **Seek financial advice**, if funding the purchase with a **mortgage** (be sure to seek professional advice, as opting for the wrong loan product is an expensive mistake). You'll need to obtain a **'homebuyer's valuation'** to confirm the market price and any premium on the property.

- **Instruct a lawyer** to check out the lease and title and negotiate clauses. You will also be advised on the options of a **Reservation Contract** (a short-term order to hold the property for a small non-returnable deposit); an **Offer to Buy** (a formal written document drafted by your lawyers that, once accepted by the seller, can become a legally binding commitment); or a **Preliminary/ Promissory Purchase Contract** (a legally binding contract that leads to a formal contract of sale). To avoid a conflict of interest it is advisable to seek an independent lawyer, other than that recommended by the estate agent selling the property.

- **Instruct a surveyor** to check the property out structurally (advisable, even on new properties, to assess the quality of the build).

- Arrange for **Power of Attorney** to complete the purchase in the event that the seller and purchaser are unable to sign the **Final Purchase Contract/Deed of Sale (Title Deed)** in person.

- Make a local **will** and amend existing ones.

In the UAE, there is **no cooling-off period** when you buy a property. Once you have signed the Preliminary/Promissory Purchase Contract (or Developer's Contract) – that's it, you're committed. Only in exceptional cases, as may be detailed in the contract, is release from agreement possible. It is therefore crucial that the terms of the purchase are thoroughly understood before signing on the dotted line.

Note that all properties must have a **Habitation Certificate** to permit occupation as a dwelling – ensure your lawyer checks this.

Apart from the usual buying considerations (location, price, etc.), in Dubai the following issue deserves consideration: the **inheritance of property** is subject to certain forms of legal ownership, as ascertained by counsel with professional independent legal advisors. There are many ways to purchase and own the property to deal with this issue, as your legal representation will point out.

- in your own name alone.
- in your name and in the name of your co-purchaser(s).
- wholly or partly in your children's names or in the name of somebody whom you would like (eventually!) to inherit the property from you.
- in the name of a limited company, whether English, Arab or 'off-shore'.
- via an investment fund (REIT, PUT, etc.).
- via an investment club .
- via a trust.

Contacts

- **International Law Partnership (Solicitors & International Lawyers)**, Holborn Hall, 193–7 High Holborn, London WC1V 7BD, **t** (020) 7420 0400, **info@LawOverseas.com, www.LawOverseas.com**. Provides a full international service using UK lawyers in the UAE for 0.5 per cent of the value of the property, with a minimum of £750/€1,125/$1,425 (scaled reduction in fees for properties over £500,000/€750,000/$950,000).
- **International Bar Association (IBA), www.ibanet.org**. Operates a Middle Eastern office in partnership with the Dubai International Financial Centre.

Sample Prices

The following are correct at the time of writing (September 2008).

- A spacious family villa with four bedrooms has a typical price tag of around £375,000 in a master-planned Jumeirah community complete with shops, restaurants and leisure facilities.
- Budget for around £90,000 for a two-bedroom luxury apartment at The Cube Condo Residence, Dubai Sports City.
- Expect to pay around £125,000 for a two-bedroom fractional ownership apart-hotel at the Red Residence development in Dubai Sports City (restricted to 30 days' use per year).
- Studio flats start at £67,000 on the Persian International City development, complete with terrace.

The Cost of Buying and Selling Property

Fees to lawyers, surveyors and the lands department amount to around 5 per cent of the value of the property. Other than that, the following additional points should be noted:

- **A deposit of 10–15 per cent of the value of the property is required.**

- **Fees for estate agents are normally paid by the seller of properties in Dubai, although this can be split or passed onto the buyer.**

- **If borrowing money to fund the purchase, you'll need a valid life insurance policy.**

- **Mortgage-lenders (see pp.105–14) typically charge a processing fee of 1.25 per cent of the loan.**

- **There are no government taxes, such as stamp duty or transfer tax, payable when you purchase properties in Dubai.**

- **Capital gains tax on Dubai property sold for profit does not apply.**

- **Once yours, the property will incur an annual service charge if located on a complex, to cover maintenance, refuse collections and landscaping. The charge will vary according to each individual development. Check the cost of this before committing to a purchase.**

Mortgages: Funding the Dream

Now that new home finance providers have entered Dubai's expanding mortgage market, the mortgage sector is offering a broader range of products to non-nationals as lending values soar. *See* p.94.

Prior to 2005, getting a mortgage in Dubai was nigh-on impossible. Loans were elusive at best, difficult to obtain, and expensive at worst. Financing was only offered by the major developers in conjunction with domestic lenders. The criteria were often prohibitive to non-nationals, so for many foreign purchasers of real estate the only real funding alternative was equity release. Today, the mortgage market is open to foreigners, with the value of mortgages up 170 per cent in 2006 on the previous year to AED 40.59 billion, according to figures from the Dubai Land Department. Islamic mortgage financier Tamweel predicts that the total cumulative value of mortgages could rise to more than AED 100 billion by 2010. The absence of mature mortgage products such as interest-only mortgages and hybrid variable-rate mortgages places Dubai's mortgage sector in the position of being ripe for further expansion, fuelled by the implementation of the long-awaited Dubai Property Law in March 2006.

More than 14 financial providers currently service the non-Gulf Cooperation Council mortgage market in Dubai, including foreign lenders HSBC, Lloyds TSB,

Standard Chartered and Barclays. New contenders are likely to enter the market in the medium term – a move that will challenge the dominance of the sector's major mortgage providers, Amlak and Tamweel. Following the 2007 merger between Emirates Bank International (EBI) and the National Bank of Dubai (NBD) to create one of the Middle East's largest banks, with assets of AED 165 billion, other banks are rumoured to be considering similar consolidation moves; the UAE has about 50 local and foreign banks and is considered an 'over banked' country. Fresh impetus is certainly good news for non-UAE borrowers, who are sure to benefit from a more competitive mortgage culture, even in a market bolstered by low interest rates.

Products on the Market

Lending criteria vary across Dubai's key mortgage providers and the following data is subject to the fluctuations of the market. Rates alter and products are continually updated, so time-sensitive information should always be verified with individual lenders via the website and contact details listed.

Abu Dhabi Commercial Bank (ADCB)

• **t + 971 (0)2 621 0090, www.adcb.com.**

Although the ADCB focuses on commercial construction financing, it does also provide home loans for residential property. Much of its strength lies in supporting investment buyers, and ADCB loans fund a large number of purchases specifically for rental income. It also finances building on residential plots. Although funding criteria vary, the following can be used as a guide:

• **Repayment periods of up to 25 years.**

• **A mortgage amount of up to 90 per cent of the property value, subject to a satisfactory valuation report by ADCB-approved inspectors.**

• **Financing offered on properties sold by Nakheel, Damac, Rose Tower 1, Sharjah, Emaar, Union Properties, Dubai Properties, Al Dar and Areef.**

• **A choice of flexible and fixed rate options.**

Amlak

• **t + 971 (0)4 366 1505, www.amlakfinance.com.**

Amlak offers a range of Shari'a-compliant Islamic financial products. The company is publicly listed and specialises in fixed and variable property finance products. Their main products are as follows:

• *Ijara* **(variable rate). This lease product involves Amlak purchasing the asset and leasing it back to the 'buyer' over a specific period of time. The title is only transferable once Amlak has recovered its payments in full. A** minimum down-payment of 10 per cent is required. Rates apply on a sliding scale for UAE nationals and a fixed variable rate for foreign residents.

• *Istisna'a* (fixed-rate construction finance). This contract relates to a property under construction. It legally obliges the builder or developer to hand over the asset to the buyer on completion. Fixed rates on a reducing balance are offered on tenures of 5–15 years at different rates to UAE residents and non-UAE nationals.

• *Murabaha* (fixed rate). This involves Amlak purchasing the property from the vendor on behalf of the buyer. The company then sells the asset to the buyer for an agreed profit. A 5–15-year tenure applies (restricted to Emaar's Emirate Hills plot finance for tenures between seven and 15 years).

The following criteria apply to Amlak lending:

• Loans of 90 per cent of the property value are available to UAE nationals.

• Loans of 70 per cent of the property value are available for foreign buyers.

• Maximum tenure of 15 years for non-UAE nationals.

• The loan amount is dependent on individual assessment of income and status, with variable and fixed rate finance available.

• Mortgages offered on properties sold by Emaar, JBR, Al Fattan, Nakheel and Palm Developments.

• A mandatory insurance policy is required against natural peril and damage through AMAN Insurance at 0.03 per cent per annum of the property price (or AED 300 per year).

• Applicants must be over 21 years of age.

• The debt is to be settled by the age of 60 (65 for the self-employed).

Barclays

• t + 971 (0)4 362 6888, **www.barclays.ae**.

UK banking group Barclays entered the Dubai mortgage market in May 2006, with the launch of a range of mortgages available in four different currencies – UAE dirhams, pounds sterling, euros and US dollars. The mortgages are targeted at three distinct consumers: owner-occupiers looking to buy a completed home; off-plan buyers for homes planned or under construction; and landlords purchasing buy-to-let properties. The bank promises 24-hour loan approval, subject to terms and conditions being met. The following conditions apply:

• A minimum mortgage of AED 500,000; a maximum of AED 7.5 million.

• Loans of 70–80 per cent offered on variable interest rates.

• 20-year terms for villas and townhouses and 15 years for apartments on properties sold at Marina Heights Tower, JBR, Nakheel, Green Community, Emaar Villas & Townhouses (but not apartments).

- For sterling, dollar and euro mortgages, borrowers are expected to have an income source in the same currency.
- Both residents and non-residents are eligible.

Dubai Islamic Bank (DIB)

- **t + 971 (0)4 211 7400, www.alislami.co.ae.**

Dubai Islamic Bank (DIB) won the Best Islamic Bank Award at the Banker Middle East Awards in 2007 and since its launch in 1975 has established a reputation for combining traditional Islamic values with the innovation of modern banking. It has successfully introduced a number of new Islamic financial products to the Dubai property market, including loans under *Istisna'a*, *Musharakah* and *Murabaha* contracts (*see* 'Amlak', pp.106–107).

> - ***Musharakah.*** This is an agreement whereby the customer and the bank agree to combine financial resources to undertake any type of business venture; profits and losses are shared in proportion to the respective capital contributions. In a diminishing *Musharakah*, the bank's share in the equity is diminished each year through partial return of capital.

As the UAE's leading provider of real estate finance, Dubai Islamic Bank plays a major role in supporting infrastructure and real estate developments, ranging from construction of road networks and bridges to commercial property, residential estates, and high-rise buildings. Lending criteria on its property financing vary according to status and product parameters, but the following is generally required:

- Applicants should be aged 21 years or over.
- Salaried applicants should be a maximum of 55 years old on repayment.
- Loans of up to 80 per cent of the market value are available, subject to a valuation undertaken by Dubai Islamic Bank.
- A maximum tenure applies for non-nationals (12–15 years).
- Loans are subject to a minimum down-payment of 20 per cent.
- Property and life insurance are required.

Emirates Islamic Bank (EIB)

- **t + 971 (0)4 316 0330, www.emiratesislamicbank.ae.**

Since its formation in 2004, Emirates Islamic Bank (EIB) has made positive inroads into the real estate market. In 2006 it added Nakheel to its partnerships with Emaar and Tameer and now offers three unique home finance products. The **SmartHome** home finance scheme is a fixed rate loan, the **HomeLease** is a floating rate finance product, while **HomeInvest** caters to those borrowers who wish to unlock the value of their property through refinancing. Each is fully

Shari'a-compliant under *Murabaha, Ijara,* and *Musharakah-Ijara* contracts, respectively. A key commercial focus for EIB's home financing operation is the Falconcity of Wonders development in Dubailand, a falcon-shaped tourist and recreational city designed to resemble the national emblem of the UAE.

The following terms apply:

Smart Home

- An instalment period of up to 15 years.
- A minimum down-payment of 25 per cent.

HomeLease

- An instalment period of up to 20 years.
- Fixed or variable rate options.
- A minimum down-payment of 25 per cent.

HomeInvest

- An instalment period of up to 20 years.
- Fixed or variable rate options.
- 75 per cent loans available.

HSBC

- **t** + 971 (0)4 329 1725/1348, **www.uae.hsbc.com.**

HSBC has assets in excess of US$1.8 billion and is one of the world's largest banking and financial services organisations. In the UAE, it offers home loans for non-residents for the purchase of a property either directly, or via re-sale at selected developments only. The loan amount is based on the valuation or purchase price of the property (whichever is lower) with a loan-to-value ratio dependent on development and status. Property valuations must be conducted by an HSBC-approved specialist (for a non-refundable fee of AED 2,500–4,000).

The following lending criteria apply:

- **Loans of up to 80 per cent of the value for completed properties.**
- **Loans of up to 70 per cent for re-mortgage.**
- **Loans of up to 70 per cent for properties under construction.**
- **25-year borrowing term for those aged up to 60 at the end of the term.**
- **Borrowers are required to open an HSBC bank account in the UAE.**
- **Home loan protection policy and buildings insurance are required.**
- **A non-refundable application processing fee of AED 2,500 is payable.**

Joint and single borrower loans are available, and loan amounts are based on 40 per cent of the net disposable income of the primary borrower's total guaranteed salary and fixed allowances, after tax and other deductions, plus 50 per cent of the income of the secondary applicant. Tenure periods run up to 15 years for apartments and up to 20 years for villas and townhouses. Deposits vary according to development and must be met by the borrowers prior to any HSBC funds being advanced. The bank offers variable rate products for both resales and pre-construction lending.

Selected developments are currently restricted to Emaar villas and townhouses as well as completed and under-construction properties at the following: The Palm, Jumeirah; The Palm, Jebel Ali; The Palm, Deira; Jumeirah Islands; Marina Heights Towers; Jumeirah Village; Jumeirah Beach Residence; The Falcon Tower at Jumeirah Lakes Towers; The Flamingo Tower at Jumeirah Lakes Towers; The Lost City; and Green Community.

Lloyds TSB

- **t + 971 (0)4 342 2000, www.lloydstsb.ae.**

Lloyds TSB Dubai offers finance for non-resident UK expatriates with a Lloyds TSB account. All documentation is managed in house, so the service benefits from an absence of legal fees. Associated products include building insurance, life assurance, home contents insurance and mortgage insurance. Loans are offered to those purchasing homes on selected developments only.

The following terms apply:

- **A minimum deposit of 20 per cent.**
- **Loans of up to 80 per cent of the value of the property are available.**
- **Maximum repayment terms of 15 years.**
- **Variable-rate, straight repayment mortgage.**
- **Special lower rate of 6 per cent offered for phase 2 of Green Community.**
- **0.5 per cent arrangement fee.**
- **Penalty-free early repayment and lump sum reduction.**
- **Stage payment is offered for homes under construction.**

Financing is available on properties sold by Emaar, Nakheel, Jumeirah Beach Residence (Dubai Properties), Green Community and UPTOWN Mirdiff (Union Properties) only.

Mashreqbank

- **t + 971 (0)4 217 4800, www.mashreqbank.com/uae.**

Self-styled 'progressive' finance house Al Mashreqbank offers a wide range of home finance products. Loans apply to specific developments only and carry the following conditions:

- **The maximum age of the borrower is 60 years old on loan maturity (65 for self-employed applicants).**

- **A minimum age for applicants of 21 years.**
- **Repayment terms of up to 20 years.**
- **Mandatory property and life insurance required.**

Loans of up to AED 3 million are available on properties on the following developments only: The Palm, Jumeirah, The Palm, Jebel Ali, and Jumeirah Islands (Nakheel); all Emaar projects; Jumeirah Beach Residence (Dubai Properties); Gold Crest Views (GIGA); Palladium, Belvedere, Liberty House and Four Towers (ETA Star); Al Seef Tower I and II (Deeyar); Marina Park (Global Realty); Marina Tower (Reef Real Estate); Ocean Heights, Lake Terrace, The Waves, Marina Terrace, 1 Tower at Lago Vista, and 3 Towers at Crescent (DAMAC); Golden Mile, Fairmount Palm Residence and Laguna Tower (IFA Hotels & Resorts); Indigo Tower (JPIL); Al Shera Tower (Bin Lahej Real Estate); Waterfront, Marinascape, Bayside, Trident Grand Residence (Trident International); Gold Crest Views II and Gold Crest Executive (ETA Star GIGA); 23 Marina (Hircon); Metro Tower and Wadi Tower (City of Arabia); Arabian Heights (Benaa Development); and Lakeside Residence (Al Manal Development).

National Bank of Abu Dhabi (NBAD)

- **t + 971 (0)4 343 3311, www.nbad.com.**

The NBAD is the largest bank in the UAE and also boasts the distinction of being the first UAE bank to have been granted a full Swiss banking licence. The following terms apply:

- **Loans up to the value of AED 5 million.**
- **Terms of 25 years for UAE nationals and foreign buyers.**
- **Financing available on residential property only.**
- **Attractive interest on reducing balances.**
- **Free current and savings account.**
- **Free for life credit card.**
- **Free internet banking and telephone banking.**

National Bank of Dubai (NBD)

- **t + 971 (0)4 310 0222, www.nbd.com.**

The bank was established in 1963 and is involved in virtually every sector of the Dubai business community. It entered the mortgage market in early 2005, launching its **Home Loan** package to both UAE residents and non-residents. The Home Loan package was designed to give the Dubai mortgage industry a 'shake-up', and incentives offered to applicants included the chance to win AED 1 million. In 2007 the NBD merged with Emirates Bank International (EBI) to become one of the Middle East's most formidable banking forces. In the same year it announced the launch of **NBD Office Loans** – a new mortgage product available to finance the individual purchase of commercial property in Dubai.

Lending is subject to income and status but is offered on the following basis for properties sold by Emaar, Nakheel, JBR and Dubai Properties:

- **Finance of up to AED 4 million is available calculated as multiples of salary for 60 months, or 80 per cent of the property valuation (by the Land Department), whichever is lower.**
- **15-year terms for expatriates and 12 years for non-residents.**
- **Repayment break of up to 24 months available.**
- **Borrowers are given free current and savings accounts, a 'free for life' credit card and free internet and telephone banking.**

In 2006, the National Bank of Dubai announced a special 'zero interest' financial product in conjunction with Dubai Properties for apartments purchased in Tower H in the Executive Towers project. The following lending criteria apply:

- **A minimum-down payment of 15 per cent.**
- **Finance is available at up to 85 per cent of the purchase price.**
- **Loans offered up to 70 times monthly salary/income (up to AED 4 million).**
- **Flexible repayment periods of up to 20 years from the date of first disbursement.**
- **The applicant's age should not exceed 65 on the date of final repayment.**

RAK Bank

- **t + 971 (0)4 213 0000, www.rakbank.ae.**

RAK Bank offers conventional mortgage finance with a variable interest rate that is subject to annual review. It lends against specified projects built by three approved developers only – Nakheel, Emaar and Dubai Properties – with the following stipulations:

- **Loans are available at up to 80 per cent of the value of the property to a maximum sum of AED 5 million.**
- **Applicants should be a minimum of 21 years old.**
- **The maximum age upon maturity is 65 years.**
- **A maximum tenure of 20 years for a non-national, and 25 years for a national.**
- **Single borrowers should earn a minimum gross salary of AED 5,000 per month.**
- **A loan-processing fee of 1.25 per cent of the loan amount applies, payable only upon approval of the loan.**

Union National

- **t + 971 (0)4 223 2266, www.unb.co.ae.**

One of the UAE's leading domestic banks, the Union National was established in 1982, and is supported by an extensive network of branches in 49 locations across all the emirates. It is jointly owned by the governments of Abu Dhabi and Dubai. Financing is available on properties sold by Emaar, Nakheel, JBR and Damac. Lending criteria vary, but are generally the following:

- **Flexible mortgages available to UAE nationals and foreigners.**
- **Maximum term for non-nationals 20 years.**
- **Loans arranged on a reducing balance basis.**
- **Minimum down payment 10 per cent.**
- **Maximum loan AED 5 million.**
- **Early repayment penalties apply.**

Standard Chartered

t + 971 (0)4 352 0455, www.standardchartered.com/ae.

Standard Chartered launched its mortgage services in the UAE in 2004 and offers loans for off-plan and resale properties for both personal use and buy-to-let in Dubai. Refinance options are also available to the bank's customers. A range of Shari'a-compliant mortgages tailored to specific customer needs will be launched in 2007.

Applicants must comply with the following criteria:

- **Be residents of the UAE.**
- **Be at least 23 years old, and no more than 70 years old.**
- **Have a minimum net income of AED 8,000 per month.**
- **If salaried, have been in their current job for a minimum of six months. Self-employed applicants must have at least three years' experience in the same line of business, including but not limited to one year's experience in the UAE.**

Standard Chartered offers mortgages for all properties developed by Emaar, Dubai Properties and Union Properties. A processing fee of 1 per cent is charged for the loan, of which part is collected on approval as an arrangement fee.

Tamweel

t + 971 (0)4 295 2259, www.tamweel.ae.

As the largest provider of home finance in the UAE, Tamweel benefits from the legacy of two notable organisations, the Dubai Islamic Bank (the world's first

Islamic bank) and Istithmar, a UAE-based investment company owned by the government that includes a number of Dubai's large commercial entities. Tamweel offers a wide range of home loans, including the **Home Builder**, the **Home Owner**, **Rent-to-Own** and **Lease-to-Own**, at fixed or variable rates. Each Tamweel product is Shari'a-compliant. Tamweel also offers the *Yusr*, which is the world's first Shari'a-compliant adjustable repayment mortgage.

Managing Currency Exchange

Dubai's dirham is linked strongly with the US dollar, and the current economic climate is ideal for Britons to spend their sterling on homes in Dubai, as they will benefit from exceptional rates of exchange. When the dollar slumped to take the British pound back above US$2, this presented an excellent opportunity to lock in AED purchases.

Moneycorp's Ten Top Tips

Foreign exchange specialist Moneycorp suggests the following top tips for purchase abroad and managing the currency market.

• **Do your research.** Even before you start looking for property abroad, it is advisable to see your lawyer first. There are a number of preliminary issues that can best be discussed in the relative calm before you find the house of your dreams. These include ownership of the property, mortgage finance and structuring the purchase to minimise taxes and costs.

• **Choose a reputable estate agent.** Estate agents in most countries abroad must be professionally qualified and hold a licence to practice. Check that the estate agent has the required paperwork to verify its licence. This will ensure that you are covered by the legislation and codes of conduct to which the agent must adhere as well as by any insurance and bond.

• Just as you would in the UK, **make sure you obtain a survey** or have the property inspected before you enter into a purchase agreement.

• **Research your mortgage requirements and the options available to you thoroughly.** Weigh up the pros and cons of having a mortgage by a UK lender versus one with by a local bank or lender near to the property you are purchasing.

• When buying a property abroad you will inevitably need to transfer a sterling sum of money into a foreign account to pay for your property. Exchange rates change constantly and fluctuations in excess of 10 per cent can occur, even over a short space of time. This means that costs can change significantly, especially for purchases that take time to complete, such as the purchase of property. A **specialist currency dealer** will normally offer you a better rate of exchange than that of a high street bank. It can also offer a range of services that will help protect you from adverse currency movements.

For example, in May 2002, when Dubai opened up to international invest-ment, the dirham traded at 5.365 to the pound, meaning that property with a price tag of AED 2,000,000 would have cost £372,786.58. The recent 26-year-high US dollar exchange rate saw it rise to US$2 against the pound, with dirham exchange rates hitting similar record highs. A property of the same AED value now costs £274,725.27 – nearly £100,000 less. Since early 2006, sterling has gained nearly 12 per cent against the dirham. This has been highly advanta-geous for UK buyers making stage payments for off-plan purchases, as the final cost of the property is less than expected a year ago.

If you are paying for your Dubai property from a UK bank account, however, then every time you send a payment to Dubai, you will face two costs. The first is the price of the dirhams. This, of course, depends on the exchange rate used to convert your sterling. The second cost is the charges that will be made by your UK and UAE banks to transfer the funds – which can be substantial.

- **Beware: if you ask your bank to transfer the money you should expect them to charge you for doing so**. The local bank may also make a substantial charge for receiving the money. A reputable currency specialist can often reduce these charges substantially and should offer to pay any receiving bank charges for you.

- **Use a currency dealer to your advantage**. At Moneycorp, we offer a very pro-active and personalised service to our clients, using our expertise and long experience to monitor exchange rates on their behalf to help achieve the best possible rate of exchange.

- You can agree to buy your foreign exchange currency for delivery within a period of anything up to two years and fix the exchange rate at the time of the agreement. This is called '**forward buying**' and it will help you secure an exchange rate at an advantageous level, removing the risk of adverse currency movements that could lead to the sterling value of your overseas property increasing between the time of signing the contract and actual payment.

- If you need to make regular overseas payments, such as mortgage repay-ments, you should speak to a currency specialist about **setting up a payment plan**. This will remove the worry caused by exchange rate fluctuations when making currency payments, and the transfer fees will only be at a fraction of the cost charged by your bank.

- **Knowledge is power**. Every world currency has its own personality, so it is beneficial to understand the factors that could influence a currency fluctuation during the period that you intend to transfer funds. Your awareness of the currency market, coupled with the expertise of your currency trader, will help you decide the most advantageous time to make a transfer and to help your money go further.

There are steps that you can take to control both of these charges. As far as the exchange rate is concerned, you should be receiving the so-called 'commercial rate', not the tourist rate published in the papers. Rates vary from second to second and so it is difficult to get alternative quotes. By the time you phone the second organisation, the first rate has changed!

Bearing in mind the cost of conversion and transmission of currency, it is better to make **fewer rather than more payments**. You will therefore have to work out carefully whether, taking into account loss of interest on the funds transferred but bank charges saved, you are best sending money monthly, quarterly or every six months.

There are various organisations that can convert your sterling into dirhams. Your bank is unlikely to give you the best exchange rate. **Specialist currency dealers** will normally better the bank's rate, perhaps significantly. If you decide to use a currency dealer you must deal with one that is reputable. Using a foreign exchange specialist to transfer your funds can save you money on the exchange rate when buying abroad, but also, management of currency transactions is a crucial tool, as timing can directly impact the value of a stake or return. Managing these currency fluctuations can be highly advantageous, and a growing number of brokers offer a specialised service for real estate transactions in Dubai.

Renting or Letting a Property

Renting a Home

Until freehold reform in 2002, a significant portion of Dubai's 1.2-million population relied on the house rental market. Today, despite the wealth of property available for purchase, the rental pool is still a sector much in demand. This is due in part to the transient nature of expatriate careers and the flexibility of accommodation required by contract staff, and also to Dubai's rapidly expanding population, fuelled by economic growth and a demand for overseas workers to fill a gap in skill-sets. Another burgeoning rental market is that of holiday villas, and many of Dubai's master-planned resort communities have focused on the needs of vacationers in light of forecasts that predict tourism figures will reach 60 million by 2010.

Most **rental agreements** require a minimum of a 12-month commitment by the tenant. It also involves obtaining employer **references** as well as proving residency and financial means. Although the practice of charging a full year's rent upfront is less common now, some Dubai landlords may still request it. However, as this is now prohibitively expensive due to rising rental rates, a growing number of individuals and agencies now offer more flexible terms.

Case Study: Bill Kennedy

'As the senior vice president of global construction consultancy Hill International I'm primarily responsible for operational management of the Dubai, Kuwait, Saudi Arabia and Bahrain claims group offices. I'm also in charge of client-focused business development in Dubai and MENA. I've been based in Dubai for the last three and a half years. I used to rent a place in Umm Suqeim for 160,000 dirhams a year but it went up to 180,000 before the landlord tried to raise it to 390,000 – so I decided it was a good time to buy.

'I purchased a four-bedroom single-storey home in Green Community West for 4.21 million dirhams. It's a 4,200 sq ft property on 10,800 sq ft plot which will eventually be part of a 350-villa development with three pools and several fitness centres that include a gym, spa, squash courts and tennis. Moving into a new house has been a nightmare, though I've no regrets. What's also horrendous is the rising cost of living. Although there's an extremely high standard of living for those who can afford it, Dubai is tough for those who can't – and some labourers here earn as little as 1,000 dirhams per month.

'What's great about Dubai? Well, there are huge business opportunities and the weather is good, although there's a bit too much air pollution at the moment. There are also some superb restaurants and bars here – Dubai has a real buzz to it. Socially, I am an active member of the Caledonian Society and help promote all things Scottish here, from a St Andrew's Ball and Burns Supper to the Chieftain's Ball and Hogmanay. I'm all set to enjoy another few years in Dubai until it's time for me retire, then I'm hoping to return to Penang.'

Finding rental accommodation requires shopping around, as completed housing stock in Dubai is currently in short supply. In 2009–2010, a considerable number of large-scale apartment and villa projects are scheduled for completion, so the situation will be markedly eased. Analysts agree that, while the population continues to expand at current rates, any eventual oversupply of property will be absorbed.

Renting a property through a **property management agency** incurs a commission of around 5 per cent. It is also common to pay a refundable **security deposit** when renting – usually at least one month's rent.

Letting a Property

Those who decide to purchase property in Dubai may decide to enter the rental market as landlords. Not only can this generate a rental stream of upwards of £15,000 per annum on a two-bedroom apartment in Dubai Marina, but it can also help strengthen ties in the emirate for those keen to stay long-term. Although rents in Dubai have come under scrutiny since the city's real estate explosion, the cost of renting a home has actually risen, not fallen. Two-bedroom apartment properties that yield over £1,200 per month would set a purchaser back around £167,000 to buy. Villas in Dubai that typically generated £16,000 in 2003 are now realising a return upward of £23,000. Similarly, one-bedroom apartments that may have generated £5,000 per annum are now commanding rental yields at over £13,000. Indeed, the Dubai property continues to demonstrate resilience, delivering capital returns to investors more quickly than even the most optimistic might imagine. Today, rental yields of 10 per cent per annum remain realistic, with guaranteed 2- and 3-year deals from developers at 7–8 per cent being the norm.

Property Management Agencies

For renters, and property-owner/letters who prefer not to self-manage, Dubai's vast number of established property management agencies can make life simple. Buyers who decide to let out their properties will find that the developer often offers this service. Renters in Dubai rarely deal with a private landlord as almost all properties, whether apartments or villas, are let through specialist agencies. Services vary, but many agencies take care of everything, from both the landlord and the tenant's perspective, from preparing the property for occupation and securing a suitable tenant to making sure it is properly maintained and all bills paid and rents collected.

Property management agents understand the needs of absentee landlords and are skilled at identifying potential problems. For the property owner, this reduces the likelihood of any unforeseen events threatening your investment. For the tenant, it means a well-equipped home that meets Dubai's exacting standards, let by an agent with their eye on the ball. The very best agents in Dubai have invested in sophisticated IT systems to manage their rental portfolios and are able to produce all manner of reports, for tenant and owner. This may include inventory reports, tenancy agreements, payment schedules, inspection reports and monthly statements, usually issued by email or fax.

Property owners will need to supply the managing agent with the following:

- **Completion certificate of payments.**
- **A map of the property and details of the development.**
- **The full address of the property.**
- **A detailed floor plan.**
- **A DEWA (Dubai Electricity and Water Authority) account number.**
- **A key to access the unit.**

The owner's obligation is to provide a property that is both clean and habitable. Once the management agency has secured a suitable tenant, a fee (typically 1,000 dirhams) is due on the signing of the tenancy agreement. Other fees apply in relation to ongoing property management (and can depend on the package chosen). Rates vary, but generally relate to a percentage of the overall rental, typically at 10 per cent.

For this the management company undertakes to do the following:

- **Advise the landlord on legal obligations.**
- **Appraise the property for maximum yield.**
- **Advertise the property for rental.**
- **Conduct accompanied viewings.**
- **Check the references of potential tenants.**
- **Prepare rental contracts.**
- **Collect a deposit from the tenant.**
- **Manage rental collection.**
- **Prepare an inventory.**
- **Manage the tenant into the property.**
- **Oversee utility accounts in the tenant's name.**
- **Conduct regular property inspections.**
- **Administer bills and service charges.**
- **Transfer monies to the owner.**
- **Ensure regular reporting on matters of finance and services.**
- **Manage tradesmen regarding repairs and general maintenance.**
- **Carry out a final inspection at the end of the tenancy.**
- **Manage damages caused by tenants.**
- **Find replacement tenants to ensure continuity of occupation and rental income.**

Most agents also offer a **caretaking service for empty properties** via a standard package that includes regular inspections, general cleaning, and pool and garden maintenance. Rates vary but range from 300–350 dirhams per month. The service is usually subject to an agent being in receipt of adequate funds for 3–6 months in advance.

Furniture and Fittings

Dubai's style-conscious expatriates have set a high standard as a bottom line. Most agents employ a décor specialist to hand-pick furniture and furnishings with attention paid to durability, practicality and style. With expectations high, furniture is tailored to meet specific budgets, suit individual requirements, or provide standard room sets. The cost of this is borne by the property-owner. The following cost brackets are a guide.

Studio Unit / One-bedroom Apartment
Average price for package: 32,000 – 42,000 dirhams.

Bedroom
- 1 x mattress and base 180cm x 200cm
- 2 x bedside tables
- 2 x lamps and shades
- pictures

Dining room
- 1 x dining table with 4 chairs
- pictures

Lounge
- 1 x sofa bed (2-seater) + 1 x casual chair
- 1 x coffee table
- pictures

Kitchen
- cooker
- fridge/freezer
- washing machine
- microwave
- utensils
- cooking equipment
- crockery
- cutlery
- toaster
- iron and kettle

Soft furnishings
- curtains and blinds for living room, bedroom, dining room, bathroom
- 1 x matching quilted bedcover, towels, bedding

Two-bedroom Apartment
Average price for package: 53,000 – 70,000 dirhams.

Bedrooms
- 2 x mattress and base 180cm x 200cm
- 4 x bedside tables

- 2 x dressing table / chest of drawers
- 4 x lamps and shades
- pictures

Dining room

- 1 x dining table with 6 chairs
- 1 x chest of drawers
- pictures

Lounge

- 1 x lounge suite (3 + 2 + 1 or 2 + 2)
- 1 x coffee table
- 2 x side tables
- lamps
- pictures

Kitchen

- same as 1-bedroom property (4 people)

Soft furnishings

- curtains and blinds for living room, bedroom, dining room, bathroom
- 2 x matching quilted bedcovers, towels, bedding

Four-bedroom Villa

Average price for package: 80,000–90,000 dirhams.

Living room

- 1 x sofa set 3 + 2 + 1
- 1 x coffee table
- 2 x side tables
- lamps and pictures
- 1 x wall unit

Dining room

- 1 x dining table with 8 chairs
- 1 x buffet/side table
- lamp and pictures

Kitchen

- same as 2-bedroom (8 people)

Family/Living room

- lounge suite (3 + 2 + 1 or 2 + 2)
- 1 x TV cabinet
- 1 x coffee table
- 1 x side table
- lamps and pictures

Maid's room

- 1 x single mattress and base

Bedrooms

- 4 x mattresses and base units 180cm x 200cm
- 8 x bedside tables
- 2 x dressing table/chest of drawers
- 2 x casual chairs
- 8 x lamps and shades
- pictures

Terrace

- 1 x garden table and 6–8 chairs

Soft furnishings

- curtains and blinds for living room, bedrooms, dining room, bathrooms, kitchen, maid's room
- 4 x matching quilted bedcovers, towels, bedding

Extras (at cost)

- TV, stereo and DVD players

First Steps

06

Getting to Dubai

Unless you plan to arrive by cruise ship, the only viable way to travel to Dubai is by plane. *See* **Red Tape**, pp.140–41, for information on customs declarations.

By Air

Prior to 1990, **Dubai International Airport (DXB)** was primarily used by passengers in transit. Today, around 28.78 million people pass through its terminals each year, with more than 6.3 million arriving on holiday. More than 60 million passengers are expected to touch down by 2010. To keep pace, Dubai has invested heavily in its airport infrastructure, adding the Sheikh Rashid Terminal in 2001 to absorb extra airport traffic and investing US$4.1 billion in a further phase of expansion due for completion by 2009. A brand new Terminal 3 and Concourse 2 will be exclusively for Emirates Airline and is slated to open by the end of 2008. A mega-cargo terminal is being constructed in phases and is due to be fully complete by 2018. The airport also intends to become the world's most user-friendly airport for special needs tourists: in 2006 it introduced 20 immigration counters for disabled travellers, three new car parking areas and a special route through the airport for visitors with special needs.

In May 2006, the Dubai government announced the construction of the world's biggest airport and city (almost twice the size of Hong Kong Island) in Jebel Ali at a cost of US$33 billion. At the time of writing, work is well under way on what is known as the **Dubai World Central Airport (Al Maktoum International Airport, JXB)**. Six 4.5km runways have been designed to accommodate the double-decker Airbus A380, while the terminal will be capable of handling 120 million passengers – almost double London Heathrow's current handling capacity. The airport will also deal with 12 million tons of cargo compared to Heathrow's current 1.3 million capacity. Dubai World Central Airport will be 10 times larger than Dubai International Airport; in terms of capacity, it is unlikely to require expansion until 2050. The project is expected to be fully operational by 2017.

The region's airlines have been quick to seize the opportunities promised by increased levels of tourism in Dubai. Direct flights from the UK are frequent and inexpensive thanks to a much increased number of airlines in the mix. In 2006, Virgin launched services between Heathrow and Dubai, triggering a price war on the Dubai–London route, with some competitors slashing fares by as much as 40 per cent. The number of flights from the UK continues to increase, with a new direct service from Newcastle launched by Emirates at the end of 2007. An extra flight was launched by Aer Lingus in mid-2007 from Dublin to the emirate – bringing the total number offered by the Irish airline to four a week. A growing number of regional airports in the UK are also adding Dubai to their routes, including Manchester, Glasgow, Edinburgh, Cardiff and Birmingham.

Budget for around £330, more around major holidays such as Easter and Christmas, when it is essential to book well ahead. The flight from London Heathrow (LHR) to Dubai International Airport (DXB) takes around seven hours.

- Dubai International Airport, **www.dubaiairport.com**.

Airlines

- Aer Lingus, Ireland **t** 0818 365 000, UK **t** 0870 876 5000, **www.aerlingus.com**.
- Aeroflot, **t** (020) 7355 2233, Dubai **t** 04 222 2245, **www.aeroflot.co.uk**.
- Air Astana, **t** (01293) 596622/(020) 7303 1253/1201, **www.airastana.com**.
- Air China, **t** (020) 7744 0800, **www.air-china.co.uk**.
- Air France, **t** 0871 66 33 777, Dubai **t** 04 294 5899, **www.airfrance.co.uk**.
- Air India, **t** (020) 8560 9996, Dubai **t** 04 227 6787, **www.airindia.com**.
- Alitalia, **t** 0870 225 5000, Dubai **t** 04 228 4656, **www.alitalia.com**.
- Austrian Airlines, **t** 08701 24 26 25, Dubai **t** 04 294 5675, **www.aua.com**.
- British Airways, **t** 0844 493 0787, Dubai **t** 04 307 5555, **www.ba.com**.
- Cathay Pacific, **t** (020) 8834 8888, Dubai **t** 04 294 5550, **www.cathaypacific.com**.
- Cyprus Airways, **t** (020) 8359 1333, Dubai **t** 04 221 5325, **www.cyprusairways.com**.
- EgyptAir, **t** (020) 8759 1520/8759 3635, Dubai **t** 04 228 9444, **www.egyptair.com.eg**.
- Emirates, **t** 0844 800 2777, Dubai **t** 04 295 3333, **www.emirates.com**.
- Ethiopian Airlines, **t** (020) 8745 4235, Dubai **t** 04 223 7987, **www.ethiopianairlines.com**.
- Finnair, **t** 0870 241 4411, **www.finnair.com**.
- Gulf Air, **t** 0844 493 1717, Dubai **t** 04 271 3222, **www.gulfair.com**.
- IranAir, **t** (020) 7409 0971/7493 8618, Dubai **t** 04 295 1106, **www.iranair.co.uk**.
- JAT Airways, **t** (020) 7629 2007/7629 6500, **www.jat.com**.
- Kenya Airways, **t** (020) 8283 1818, Dubai **t** 04 295 7236, **www.kenya-airways.com**.
- KLM Royal Dutch Airlines, **t** 0871 222 7474, Dubai **t** 04 800 4744, **www.klm.com**.
- Korean Air, **t** 0800 413 000, **www.koreanair.com**.
- Kuwait Airways, **t** (020) 8745 7772/3/4/5/6, Dubai **t** 04 228 1106, **www.kuwait-airways.com**.

- Lufthansa, **t** 0871 945 9747, Dubai **t** 04 343 2121, **www.lufthansa.com.**
- Olympic Airlines, **t** (020) 8745 7339, **www.olympicairlines.com.**
- Qatar Airways, **t** (020) 7399 2577/2579, Dubai **t** 04 221 4448, **www.qatarairways.com.**
- Royal Brunei, **t** (020) 7584 6660, Dubai **t** 04 351 4111, **www.bruneiair.com.**
- SAS, **t** 0870 607 2772, **www.flysas.com.**
- Saudi Arabian Airlines, **t** (020) 7798 9898, **www.saudiairlines.com.**
- South African Airways, **t** 0871 722 1111, Dubai **t** 04 397 0766, **www.flysaa.com.**
- Sri Lankan Airlines, **t** (020) 8538 2001, Dubai **t** 04 295 0011, **www.srilankan.lk.**
- Swiss, **t** 0845 601 0956, Dubai **t** 04 228 3151, **www.swiss.com.**
- Thai Airways, **t** 0870 606 0911, Dubai **t** 04 268 1701, **www.thaiair.com.**
- Tunis Air, **t** (020) 7437 6236, Dubai **t** 04 221 1176, **www.tunisair.com.**
- Turkish Airlines, **t** (020) 7766 9300, Dubai **t** 04 211 2528, **www.thy.com.**
- Virgin Atlantic, **t** 0870 380 2007, **www.virgin-atlantic.com.**

By Sea

Dubai's sophisticated ports, Jebel Ali and Port Rashid, are among the leading container ports in the world. In 2007 around 77,838 passengers used marine transportation, with more than 170 shipping lines serving the ports of Dubai. Dubai's **Cruise Terminal** was officially inaugurated by His Highness General Sheikh Mohammed bin Rashid Al Maktoum, Crown Prince of Dubai, in 2001 at the state-of-the-art Port Rashid complex. However, Dubai has receiving cruise ships since the mid-1990s (*see* **Dubai Today**, p.31). Among recent newcomers, Crystal Cruises have deployed *Crystal Serenity* and *Crystal Symphony* on round-trip sailings to Cape Town, Istanbul, Singapore and Rome. *Queen Mary II* has also been welcomed.

- Dubai Cruise Terminal, **www.dubaitourism.co.ae.**
- Jebel Ali Port, **www.dpa.co.ae.**
- Port Rashid, **www.dpa.co.ae.**

By Rail

Reports by *Gulf News* suggest that the UAE is also considering blueprints for a 700km-long nationwide rail network that would link Abu Dhabi with Dubai, Sharjah, Ras Al Khaimah and Fujairah in the east and with Ruwais and Ghowaifait in the west. The first phase would be for a cargo and container network, followed by a passenger project in the second phase.

From Merchant Vessel to Champagne Cruise

Dubai's age-old boat-building industry once served traders plying their wares along the Persian Gulf. Today it ferries tourists along the Creek in the style of ancient seafarers.

From ancient times until the mid-1960s, the Arabian wooden dhow (boat) carried cargoes of dates, spices, incense and fish to trade along the Persian Gulf. Using only sails as a means of propulsion, the dhows journeyed south with the monsoon in winter or early spring and back again to Arabia in late spring or early summer. Commercial seafaring became an important part of establishing the port now known as a Dubai, and the dhow was crucial to this prosperity. Boats ranged from crude sewn-constructed wooden rafts held together with coconut fibres to sophisticated, hand-carved, beautiful vessels complete with lateen rigging of slanting, triangular sails. Today, dhow boats play an important role in Dubai's popular river cruises, which fuse some ancient touches with Arabian-themed kitsch. To the tourist they are synonymous with champagne dinner cruises: an elegant mode of water-transit along the Dubai Creek on a backdrop of city sights. Dubai still has a modern and traditional fishing industry, while dhow-building retains a presence, albeit small. Old docks and boatyards can still be found just a few kilometres from the centre of the city, providing a glimpse of a trade that has been carried out for hundreds of years. For a glimpse of Dubai's fishing-village roots, wander around the Jaddaf district and watch local craftsman hand-carving dhows.

Dhow-racing has cultural and historical significance in Dubai and still takes place today, especially on government holidays such as the UAE National Day on December 2nd. Three different racing categories offer places to 60ft, 43ft and 22ft dhows. A larger dhow may have a crew of approximately 30, while smaller dhows have crews typically ranging around 12. More than 80 traditional boats take to the clear blue waters, adhering to age-old tradition with hulls of polished teak and billowing white canvas sails.

Travel Health

A successful government immunisation programme, the provision of clean water and high standards of cleanliness in hotels and restaurants virtually guarantee you a sickness-free visit to the UAE. However, despite this, travellers should remain vigilant, as most reported visitor-illnesses are easily avoided. Most involve sickness from food that has been left lying around in the heat for too long; if a buffet appears to be several hours old, it pays to eat elsewhere.

Always pack sufficient high-factor **sun-cream**, as burning badly is a real risk in Dubai's searing heat. Although this is sold locally, prices are exorbitant and supplies can run low in high season. Although many medical centres and pharmacies offer most over-the-counter medications, there are some exceptions.

Before You Go

Numerous websites provide travel health advice and information. Make sure the sites you use offer advice from a qualified doctor. The National Travel Health Network and Centre (**www.nathnac.org**) is funded by the Department of Health (UK) and provides professional advice and up-to-date information on vaccines and illness worldwide. The Center for Disease Control and Prevention (USA) (**www.cdc.gov/travel**) gives advice on clinics, vaccines and outbreak warnings. The International Society of Travel Medicine, **www.istm.org**, provides a worldwide online clinic directory. You can also try **www.tripprep.com**.

Vaccinations

Although the UAE doesn't require any immunisations to visit, it is wise to check if you are travelling from a health-risk area. Outbreaks of localised infections can happen overnight in any area of the world, so it is always worth asking a trained travel health professional what the situation is on the ground.

Malaria

Intensive fumigation and spraying programmes have rid most UAE towns and cities of mosquitoes. This means malaria is not considered a risk, so anti-malarial tablets are rarely prescribed. Visitors planning day-trips further afield may find mosquitoes more of a problem, especially when camping near the mountains or walking in the date groves at sunset. As a precaution, pack adequate insect repellent and consult a travel clinic before your trip.

Health Insurance

As with all travel, health insurance for your trip to the UAE is a must to cover all eventualities. *See* **Living in Dubai**, pp.162–4.

Flying and Health

The seven-hour flight from the UK to Dubai is unlikely to cause most healthy travellers problems, but there is no substitute for good old-fashioned common sense when it comes to in-flight health.

Deep Vein Thrombosis (DVT)

Although relatively rare, there is an increased risk of deep vein thrombosis if you fly for longer than eight hours. If you have a long-haul flight ahead, consider taking medical advice from your GP before you leave to check you are not in a high-risk category. DVT occurs when blood clots that form naturally in an immobilised body get stuck in the lungs. Travellers should not be alarmed, as clots form regularly in the body without causing a problem. However, some people, such as cancer and heart disease sufferers and the elderly, are considered at higher risk of DVT than others. If you think you are high-risk, make sure you get your doctor's permission to fly.

In general, anyone on a long-haul flight should move about the plane regularly throughout the flight, stretch their legs at regular intervals and rotate their ankles frequently, avoid heavy sedatives such as alcohol or sleeping pills, and drink plenty of water and/or fruit juice. You can also try socks that have been designed to reduce the risk of DVT (**www.donttravelwithoutit.com** or **www. legshealth.com**) or ask your GP if you can take an aspirin before flying.

Jet Lag

The world is divided into 24 time zones. The Greenwich meridian (an imaginary line which passes through Greenwich, in London, and is used to measure longitude) is the base. The time changes, backwards or forwards, by one hour for every 15 degrees travelled in either direction from the Greenwich meridian.

Jet lag occurs when the body clock is disrupted by crossing a number of time zones, and is a common condition that sometimes occurs when you are flying long distances. Deep in your brain there is a 24-hour master clock governing every aspect of the body's functioning. Called the circadian clock (from *circ*, about, and *diem*, day), it synchronises the following internal systems so they function smoothly with each other and in relation to the external world.

- **sleep and wake cycle.**
- **levels of alertness.**
- **performance.**
- **mood.**
- **hormone levels.**
- **digestion.**
- **body temperature.**

Light is one of the primary cues that the clock uses. Travelling confuses the body clock because it has to adjust to a new time and new patterns of light and activity. To make matters worse, not all internal body functions adjust at the same rate. So your sleep/wake cycle may adjust more quickly than your temperature. Your digestion may be on yet another schedule. Confusing the clock like this causes the mental and physical upset we call jet lag.

Though the body clock has difficulty adjusting to time zone travel, it prefers flying in an east-to-west direction. This is because, although we live on a 24-hour day, the natural rhythm of our clock is programmed to operate on a day that is longer than 24 hours. So our internal clock can naturally extend our day, but it finds it very difficult to reduce the hours in our day. When flying west you are adding hours and going in the natural direction of your internal clock. For example, flying westward from London to New York involves extending your day by five hours, while the eastward flight from New York to London results in shrinkage of five hours.

Although jet lag may be problematic for people who have to fly frequently, or who are travelling to an important meeting or event, it does not cause any serious, or long-term, health problems. Most people find that jet lag symptoms pass within a few days.

Managing Jet Lag

Anyone can get jet lag, regardless of how frequently they travel by plane, although it is more common in those who are over 50 years of age, and it is relatively rare in children and babies. Jet lag is not always inevitable when you are flying long distances, and there are ways that you can help prevent the condition from occurring. The following advice is provided courtesy of British Airways and NHS Direct.

Before You Travel

- **Change your sleep routine.** Try to adapt to your new sleeping pattern a few days before you are due to travel. If you are travelling east, try going to bed an hour earlier than your usual time. If you are travelling west, trying going to bed an hour later.

- **Get enough sleep.** It is important that you get enough sleep before you are due to travel. Flying when you have not had enough sleep can make jet lag worse.

- **Keep calm.** Airports can be stressful places. Try and keep as calm and relaxed as possible, because being stressed can make jet lag worse.

During the Flight

- **Drink plenty of fluids.** Ideally, you should also ensure that you are well hydrated before and after your flight.

- **Avoid alcohol.** It can make the symptoms of jet lag worse.

- **Keep active.** Make sure that you keep active if you are flying long distances. Walk around the cabin occasionally, and regularly stretch your arms and legs when you are sitting down.

- **Change your watch.** When you board the plane, you may find it helpful to adjust your watch so that it matches the time of your destination. This will help you to adjust more quickly to your new time zone.

- **Get some sleep.** If it is night time at your destination while you are on your flight, try and get some sleep. Some people find using ear plugs, or eye masks, helpful.

When You Arrive

- **Get into your new routine.** Try to get used to your new routine as soon as possible. This means eating meals and sleeping at the correct times for your new time zone, and not the time you would normally be eating and sleeping back home.

- **Avoid napping.** Try not to nap as soon as you arrive at your destination. You may be tired from a long flight, but try to stay active until it is the correct time for you to sleep. This will help your body adjust more quickly.

- **Spend time outdoors.** Try to spend as much time outdoors as you can. Natural light is a very effective way of getting your body to adjust to a new routine.

Melatonin

Melatonin is a hormone which your body releases in the evening. It is a way of telling your brain that it is time for your body to sleep. Some jet lag remedies contain melatonin and aim to help you sleep at night when your body is finding it hard to adjust to the new time zone. There is currently inconclusive evidence as to how effective melatonin supplements are. Although some people find them helpful, they are not currently licensed to prevent jet lag in the UK. If you are thinking about taking a jet lag remedy containing melatonin, it is important that you talk to your GP first, who will be able to advise you about whether it is suitable for you to take.

The UAE has a banned substance list that can be mystifying on occasions. In 2008, a traveller from Britain was arrested for drug possession after a jet lag remedy containing melatonin was found in his luggage. Such over-the-counter medications are sold in Dubai but can still arouse suspicion. Any visitor found with traces of banned substances is likely to face the threat of a four-year prison sentence in the United Arab Emirates, so it is worth seeking professional advice prior to travelling with a bag full of pills.

On the Spot

Healthcare

In all instances, local medical procedures, including the use of sterilised needles and the provision of blood transfusions, are very reliable, as long as you have insurance that will pay. See **Living in Dubai**, pp.162–4.

Sunburn

Western visitors are often ill-prepared for the sheer ferocity of the intense UAE sunshine. Heatstroke is a real threat year-round, as is heat exhaustion, so it is

Case Study: Martin Thomas

'I moved to the UAE three years ago with my wife to take up a senior role in Dubai for one of the richest men in the country – in the world, actually. My job, as group director of strategy and planning, ensured I had direct contact with the chairman. This meant a lot socially, affording me huge amounts of kudos and access, but I had precious little actual power to *do* anything – which is perfectly normal in Dubai. I never did have a proper job description, and was appointed on a whim by the chairman. It was all pretty exciting, but none of the rest of the executive team had any real idea of what I was there to do.

'I was promised a decent accommodation package, and when I arrived on my 4.30am flight I was met by a car at the airport and whisked off to the company's first hotel. This was my home for a month or so till my apartment was ready; this was attached to the hotel, right next door to head office. My entire commute was a six-minute walk – including locking the apartment door and waiting for the lift. However, when the apartment was ready to move into, it was something of a disappointment – as were many aspects of what was actually delivered versus what had been promised. Rather than the two-bedroom accommodation we'd requested, there was just one bedroom, so visitors were a problem. And, although the apartment initially came fully-serviced, with full access to all the hotel's facilities, this ceased after just a few months. Worst of all, it overlooked the hotel's noisy air-conditioning equipment. We were also close to an English pub and a Tex-Mex bar – two of the best-known haunts of prostitutes in the country. Cockroaches also found their way into the apartment, disturbed by building work nearby – so we soon knew the pest control guy better than we did our housemaid.

'My senior status meant that other people took care of the paperwork for me and Yvonne on arrival. Blood tests were taken, visas applied for and granted, a

crucial to pack adequate sunglasses, hats and high-factor sun creams, especially for children. It is tempting to lie in the sun, especially in the tropics where you might picture yourself lying under a palm tree sipping something exotic. However, the incidence of skin cancer due to sun exposure is rising. UV rays from sunlight trigger DNA cell change which can initiate melanoma, a malignant skin tumour now responsible for around three-quarters of all skin cancer deaths. Fair-skinned people are more susceptible than dark-skinned, but everyone should take precautions and avoid excessive sun exposure. It is advisable to avoid the midday sun, apply a sunscreen with sun protection factor (SPF) of 15 or higher with both ultraviolet A (UVA; wavelength 315–400 nm) and ultraviolet B (UVB; wavelength 280–315 nm) protection as well as wearing a wide-brimmed hat and sunglasses. Reapply cream regularly, and especially after swimming. Babies and children are at great risk from the sun and should be covered with long-sleeved swimsuits, high-factor sun cream and wide-brimmed hats whenever they are outside.

bank account set up and credit cards arranged, phone and internet and satellite TV installed, cleaners arranged, a driving licence acquired – someone arranged it all, presented me with forms to sign and stuff eventually happened.

'For the first couple of years here we lived the executive expat lifestyle. I occasionally got to "substitute" for the chairman at events, so got to be treated like royalty at the Dubai World Cup or the Carreras Concert held by DIFC, for example. But I didn't do much work of substance. Projects would be cut off unfinished or ideas floated and abandoned. It was a classic case of what the European expats refer to as 'trophy management' – a grand title, but with nothing to do except drink, shop and play golf. That's OK, if your pride can stand it. Mine couldn't. So we decided to up-sticks to move to the neighbouring emirate of Sharjah, where I now enjoy a hardworking freelance career.

'On a positive note, good food is incredibly cheap in Dubai and the choices are endless. Every hotel, street and mall is full of eateries, from local fast food (*shawarma*) to Japanese, dim sum, Lebanese, Georgian, Persian, Russian, German, McDonald's, Pizza Hut or any other chain you can think of. There are also coffee shops, tea shops, shisha bars, French pâtisseries and delis. The list goes on.

'Even the tiny back-street places that we Europeans get so nervous about are scrupulously clean and incredibly friendly. Most expats miss out on these back-street joints as they stick to the hotels and malls – it's easy to stay only among your own kind – especially in Dubai. Living in Dubai can be like living in London or LA if you want it to – and almost as expensive too. But if you do that, you miss so much. You really can't beat enjoying a cup of Turkish coffee with a bunch of elderly Indians for endless gossip on a backdrop of Dubai's hustling cityscape – it makes all the aggravation of work just disappear, and is the "real" UAE.'

Heatstroke is caused by excessive sun exposure; drinking alcohol or taking strenuous exercise in the sun are also factors. Symptoms include dizziness, nausea, headache, unclear vision, confusion and unreasonable behaviour. If you suffer heatstroke, get out of the sun immediately. Drinking plenty of fluids, keeping cool with wet towels and resting for at least 24 hours can treat mild cases. You may also find after-sun creams or aloe vera gel a soothing comfort to burned skin. For severe sunstroke seek medical attention immediately as you will need rehydration. Remember, it is just as crucial to wear sunscreen at high altitudes (mountain) or on rivers and at sea, where snow and water reflects ultraviolet light whatever the air temperature.

Traveller's Diarrhoea (TD)

Around 60 per cent of the world's travellers get TD at some point on their journey, so do not be shocked if it happens to you. Opinion is divided about TD:

some argue that it comes from contaminated food and water, others believe it is simply caused by a change in diet. It's wise to stick to bottled (or boiled) water, avoid eating from dirty-looking street stalls, and avoid cooked food that has been sitting around for a while. Beware of salads that may not have been washed or, worse still, washed in dirty water.

TD is unpleasant, with symptoms that vary in severity from person to person. In general symptoms settle within 48 hours, but it is imperative you replace lost fluids, salts and sugars, as dehydration can be quick, and very serious. Take re-hydration sachets mixed with bottled or cool boiled water and avoid food for 24–48 hours. Don't drink alcohol or caffeine for several days, as these can dehydrate you and cause cramping. If you experience diarrhoea for longer than 48 hours, seek medical attention, just in case you have something more serious.

Some travel clinics (e.g. the Hospital for Tropical Diseases, **www.thehtd.org**) sell very effective antibiotic treatments for TD.

Fungal Infections

Fungal infections are common in hot, humid climates where they thrive on moisture. They usually flare up in crevices of the body that sweat in the heat, in particular the groin area and between the toes. However, fungal infections are not serious and respond well to antifungal creams. Wear loose-fitting clothing in natural fabrics and if possible expose the area to air as much as possible.

Women's Health

Cystitis and other urinary tract and bladder infections are extremely common in female travellers, especially those on long haul trips and/or on a budget. Spending hours on old buses, sleeping in less than sanitary conditions and not getting the chance to wash properly for long periods all help to raise the risk.

Such infections can be extremely uncomfortable and cause a painful burning sensation while urinating. To make things worse, it will make you feel as though you constantly need the toilet, even when you do not. It is vital to drink plenty of water, which will help wash out the infection. Over-the-counter medicines can help. If symptoms persist, seek medical attention, as the infection can be dangerous if it spreads to the kidneys.

Like fungal infections, vaginal yeast infections such as thrush are also common, but react well to over-the-counter treatment. Buy creams or pessaries before you leave and have them in your first-aid kit just in case. Some people recommend applying fresh yoghurt to the area; it could help with the itchiness.

In rural areas it may be difficult to buy tampons, so, if these are your preferred method of period care, bring some from home.

You'll find female-friendly hotels, accessories, travel tours and health tips on a web directory for discerning women travellers: **www.safetravel4women.com**.

Red Tape

07

Everything involved in settling into Dubai life seems to involve mountains of paperwork. Dealing with red tape in the UAE is not a super-fast process and, given the sheer volume of non-nationals in Dubai, the Immigration and Naturalisation Department offices are often jam-packed with people waving bits of paper. Many millions of visas and permits are issued here to keep pace with the massive influx of visitors and residents. Even on a so-called quiet day, you can expect to encounter long queues of confused people attempting to navigate a muddle of perplexing documents. What makes the red tape even more difficult to master is that it can often change overnight.

Since 2007, UAE residents also now need to apply for an ID card, *see* p.138.

Essential Documentation

Many of the documents required for visa and residence applications need to be certified, notarised and attested **prior to arrival in the country** – an important factor to consider when planning a move. Always photocopy every document, several times. Different papers are asked for in every instance. The following are essential to have with you during your initial settling in stage:

- **passport (must have at least six months' validity and two unused pages).**
- **birth certificate.**
- **marriage certificate (and divorce papers if applicable).**
- **driving licence.**
- **education certificates (for every member of your family).**
- **professional membership cards and certificates.**

Those setting up a business in Dubai should bring every document relating to the company, from the audited accounts of the parent company and board of directors' resolution to the parent company's memorandum of association and main certificate of incorporation.

In the event that an important document is misplaced or stolen, the police should be notified immediately in person. A report will be issued if the document isn't recovered within 48-hours. This can then be used when applying for a replacement document. Meanwhile, should anyone attempt to use the original, the police are alerted by an electronic flagging system.

Visas, Permits and Other Paperwork

Except for citizens of GCC countries (Bahrain, Oman, Qatar, Saudi Arabia, Kuwait and the UAE) and a few other specified countries, everyone entering Dubai needs a **visa** for even a short visit or temporary period. Arrangements change, however, so always be sure to check with your local UAE consulate.

Visitors are issued with their **tourist visa** or limited-term **visit visa** by the Immigration and Naturalisation Department (IND), and should apply for these at IND offices abroad, unless they are staying fewer than 30 days and are eligible for a visa on arrival, *see* below. A visit visa is a single-entry permit only – once the duration has expired, you must leave the country or face an incremental per-day fine.

Those keen to stay longer will need to obtain permission in the form of a **residence permit**. To apply for a residence permit you'll need to have a job, unless your spouse is already resident and working in Dubai.

The Ministry for Labour and Social Affairs is closely linked to the Immigration and Naturalisation Department, as many of the eligibility rules are intertwined. Prior approval should always be sought before entering the country as a **new employee**. Those who arrive on a tourist visa or visit visa are not allowed to work in Dubai; however a potential employer can apply for a work and residence visa on your behalf (*see* 'Sponsorship', p.139).

Visas

Transit Visa (96-hour)

This short-term transit permit allows a stay of up to 96 hours in the country. It is non-renewable and wholly dependent on certain criteria. It is issued free. Only airlines may grant this visa, in the event that a flight is cancelled or delayed. It allows for an extended time to be spent in Dubai and is issued at the airport, under the airline's sponsorship.

Transit Visa (14-day)

This so-called 'visa for a mission' (Entry Service Permit) is non-renewable and permits stays of up to 14 days. A fee is charged for issue. It is primarily used by business travellers. Spouses are also eligible to accompany the applicant. Prerequisites include a return flight ticket and a valid passport. The visitor should also belong to a professional employment category. GCC nationals and those from exempt countries do not need to apply for this visa.

Visa on Arrival

This free-of-charge visa is granted to passport-holders who are visiting only for tourist purposes and have no intention of engaging in work, either paid or unpaid. The visa is stamped into the passport on arrival at Dubai Airport and lasts **up to 30 days**. Only those from 32 **specified countries** are eligible: Andorra, Australia, Austria, Belgium, Brunei, Canada, Denmark, Finland, France, Germany, Greece, Hong Kong, Iceland, Ireland, Italy, Japan, Liechtenstein, Luxembourg, Malaysia, Monaco, Netherlands, Norway, Portugal, San Marino, Singapore, South Korea, Spain, Sweden, Switzerland, UK, USA, the Vatican.

Tourist Visa

A tourist visa is issued for a visit of **up to 30 days**. It is non-renewable and carries a fee. This visa applies to nationalities not covered by the 'visa on arrival'. Applicants should be sponsored by a hotel or tour company, who will apply on your behalf.

You'll need to send documents in advance of your trip to the sponsor, who will then send out a copy of the visa (you'll need this to board your flight). Passports should have at least three months longer to run than the visa expiry date. The original visa is available for collection at the Immigration Desk at Dubai Airport. Hotel-sponsored applicants may only stay at the specific sposoring hotel for the duration of their visit.

Visit Visa

A visit visa is issued for a stay of **up to 60 days**. In certain circumstances, it can be extended for a further 30 days, depending on circumstances and status. A fee is charged for issue. It is only issued to those who are attending a job interview or who have an appointment or meeting with a company in Dubai, or those who intend to visit family or friends. Family sponsors of this visa applicant will need to earn a certain level of minimum income.

Residence Permits

This permit allows residency in the UAE for a standard **three-year** period. Permit-holders can come and go freely without restriction, although the permit will expire should they stay out of the country for longer than six months.

This is one of the most document-heavy of permits in the UAE administrative system. You'll need copies of *every* major document when dealing with the Immigration Department (including receipts). You'll also need a Ministry of Health Medical Card. Those sponsored by a company (*see* p.139) should obtain a Labour Card from the Ministry of Labour.

Student residence permits are restricted to a one-year initial period, as are those for people engaged in **domestic help**. GCC nationals are exempt.

Applicants should be over 19 years of age and under 60 years (those aged 60 or over will need to prove that they have a high-ranking position, a specialised skill or a unique qualification). As an employee of a Dubai-based company, you

ID Cards

The all-singing all-dancing ID card was launched in 2007 as a UAE-wide initiative and is a mandatory requirement for nationals and expatriates alike. Not only does it assign each person a unique ID number, it is also multi-purpose, combining the functions of health card and driving licence. It is issued for a fee that varies dependent on your status and the period of residence applied for.

Case Study: Carole and David Brewer

'We decided to buy an apartment in Dubai as a holiday home as we both wanted somewhere to escape to for at least 12 weeks a year. We bought a three-bedroom apartment in The Point as an off-plan purchase in 2006 through UK-based Select Property after trawling the internet. The Point appealed to us because it is situated on the Marina and we both love to be near the waterfront and the beach. Our apartment is located just opposite the Marina Yacht Club and offers fantastic access to the sea and wonderful views. Many of our neighbours are also British, so it is easy to make friends in the sun. I'm a part-time teacher and David owns his own business. Our plan is to spend more time here – it helps to have the option of residency permits for the future.'

will be able to sponsor your own family, as long as you can meet certain key requirements. You will also be able to sponsor a maid. Prerequisites include a certain minimum level of income. Only immediate family qualify, including the sponsor's parents. Daughters should be unmarried and sons under 18 years of age. To sponsor a maid, you'll also need to provide an air fare home to the home country at least once every two years, meet certain salary requirements and offer housing, electricity and air-conditioning.

Residence permits are complicated, and become even more so when sponsored daughters get married, sons pass 18 years of age, or a wife becomes pregnant. These are just some of the many factors that can require a daunting mountain of paperwork to be completed. Dubai's Ministry of the Interior, Naturalisation and Residency has set up a partnership department with DNATA to help demystify the red tape puzzle. The service costs a small fee, but guarantees speedy assistance and straightforward guidance through the bureaucratic minefield. Visit the DNATA Travel Shop near the Clock Tower in Deira with all the paperwork you can muster – and keep your fingers crossed.

In all cases, official residence applications should be initiated as soon as possible after entering Dubai, as all paperwork must be complete before the entry visa expires. On approval, a residence permit is added into your passport.

Sponsorship

A sponsor can be a company or individual that takes legal responsibility for your entry into the UAE. Sponsorship carries with it no financial implications as an individual but, as a future employer, it requires overseeing all aspects of the entry process. A sponsor will usually apply for your visit visa or residence permit at the Immigration and Naturalisation Office in Dubai.

In business, sponsorship is also an important concept, as most commercial entities require a sponsor in order to set up outside a Free Zone. Company sponsorship allows individuals to work only for the company they are sponsored by.

Fees and the e-Dirham Card

Many charges apply to every aspect of paperwork processing, from nominal sums for obtaining special departmental envelopes to more significant fees applied to official verification and screening.

Introduced by the Ministry of Finance and Industry to dispense with the need for cash payments for many government documents and procedures, the e-Dirham Card is a prepaid electronic payment system designed to ease red tape. Cards are protected by a PIN number and come with all the protection of a credit card, such as a special 24/7 security hotline in the event of loss, misuse or theft. To qualify for an e-Dirham Card, you'll need to have a valid residence permit (as an individual) or a valid trade licence (as a company). They can be obtained from member banks, where a credit is applied to the card balance. To apply, you'll need cash payment or a bank transfer and a passport photograph.

Company-sponsored applicants from **Free Zone**-status companies and **government-related organisations** follow a different set of procedures from those sponsored by **private sector organisations**. The private sector is much more red-tape heavy and follows very different rules; employees of Free Zone and public sectors do not need Ministry of Labour approval.

Arrival and Customs

Entry into the UAE does not require a **health certificate** unless a visitor has travelled through a cholera or yellow fever zone in the 14 days prior to arrival.

Other than the usual airport laws relating to safety and security, officials at Dubai International Airport enforce strict controls regarding certain items regarded as **non-Islamic**. Serious consequences result from any person being found in possession of the following:

- firearms.
- pornography.
- religious material.
- antiquities.
- medications (even some prescription items without a GP's note).
- counterfeit goods (such as CDs, DVDs and computer software).

The following **personal possessions** are allowed entry without customs duty:

- gifts worth less than 3,000 dirhams.
- up to 400 cigarettes, 50 cigars or 500 grams of tobacco, as long as passengers are over 18 years of age.

- up to 4 litres of alcoholic beverages, or 2 cartons of beer, each consisting of 24 cans not exceeding 355ml for each can or its equivalent; passengers must be aged over 18.
- cameras and video recorders (and appropriate tapes, films and accessories).
- projectors for displaying slides and films (including accessories and reasonable quantities of slides and films).
- telescopes.
- portable music equipment.
- radio systems, combined broadcasting apparatus, CD and DVD players with reasonable quantities of discs.
- mobile telephones.
- portable TV sets.
- portable typing sets.
- computers, including laptops.
- portable calculators.
- baby carriages.
- disabled wheeled chairs and cars.
- sports equipment.
- cash, currency and traveller's cheques with a value under AED 40,000 (passengers must be aged over 18).

Exemptions are subject to the following conditions and controls:

- **Luggage and gift items must be of a personal nature and must not be carried in commercial quantities.**
- **The passenger must not be a customs officer, trader or a member of the respective conveyance crew.**
- **Age restrictions must be strictly adhered to in relation to the carriage of tobacco products, alcohol and currency.**

Customs tariffs or **duties** are applicable to quantities and values in excess of these exemptions. Where no customs duty is paid, excess quantities will be impounded for 30 days – or until the prescribed duty is paid. After the impoundment period has elapsed, the goods may be sold at public auction.

Cash amounts that exceed AED 40,000 must be declared on arrival. Equivalent currencies and traveller's cheques over this value also must be declared, using a declaration form.

There are separate customs regulations relating to the declaration of quantities and values of, and the charges and procedures for importing, goods for **commercial purposes**.

Customs Declaration Glossary

In a bid to make declaration paperwork easier to complete, Dubai Customs has created a simple glossary of terms and procedures. The list below conforms with regional and international laws, legislations and agreements.

• **Importation:** The act of bringing or causing any goods to be brought into the country's customs territory.

• **Importer's code:** A code issued by the Customs Administration to the Company for their customs transactional clearing.

• **Temporary admission:** The customs procedure under which certain goods can be brought into a customs territory conditionally relieved from payment of import duties and taxes; such goods must be imported for a specific purpose and must be re-exported unchanged within a specified period.

• **Customs office:** The customs administrative unit competent for the perform-ance of customs formalities, and the premises of other areas approved for that purpose by the competent authorities.

• **Customs territory:** The territory in which the customs law applies in full.

• **Declarant:** Any natural or legal person who makes a customs declaration or in whose name such a declaration is made.

• **Harmonised system:** Sets out in a systemised form coding, designations and description of goods including their payable customs duties.

• **Representative card:** A card issued by customs administration authorising a person to clear customs transactions.

• **Certificate of origin:** A specific document identifying the goods, in which the authority or body empowered to issue it certifies that the goods to which the certificate relates originate in a specific country.

• **Delivery order:** A permit from the agent, shipper or port authority for the release of goods.

• **Packing list:** Detailed list showing description, quantity and weight of goods.

• **Goods owner:** Any natural or legal person whose name is contained in the delivery order issued by the carrier.

• **Goods:** Any natural material or agricultural, animal, industrial or intellectual produce mentioned in the tariff nomenclature or may be classified under a tariff heading thereof.

• **Examination of goods:** The physical examination of goods by the customs to satisfy themselves that nature, origin, condition, quantity and value of goods are in accordance with the particulars furnished in the goods declaration.

• **Prohibited goods:** Any goods the import, export or movement of which is prohibited under the provisions of any law, notice, order or system issued by a legally authorised agency.

- **Restricted goods:** Those goods the import, export or movement of which is restricted under a system issued by a legally authorised agency.

- **Customs declaration:** The declaration being submitted according to the customs approved form wherein the importer indicates the customs procedures applicable to the goods and describes the details, which the customs requires to be declared for the purposes of applying such procedure.

- **Manifest:** The document containing a full description of the goods carried on the various means of transport.

- **Transhipment:** The customs procedure under which goods are transferred under customs control from the importing means of transport to the exporting means of transport within the area of one customs office.

- **Temporary export:** The exportation of goods outside the country for the purposes of completing their processing or repairs; these shall be re-imported and relieved from customs duties and taxes.

- **Goods in transit:** The exported goods, which are allowed to transit the territories of the country to a third country.

- **Customs value:** The actual value of goods based on the principal basis for evaluating the goods for customs purposes provided for in the law.

- **Customs duties:** The duties laid down in the customs tariff to which goods are liable on entry or leaving the customs territory.

- **Customs formalities:** All the operations, which must be carried out by the persons concerned and by the customs in order to comply with customs law.

- **Customs clearing:** The accomplishment of the customs formalities necessary to allow goods to enter home use, to be exported or to be placed under another customs procedure.

- **Security:** The procedure, which ensures to the satisfaction of the customs that an obligation to the customs will be fulfilled.

- **Free Zone:** A part of the country's territories in which commercial or industrial activities are exercised under the respective laws of the country. Any goods entering that zone are considered to be outside the customs zone and shall not be subject to the usual customs control and procedures.

- **Customs warehouse:** A place authorised by customs authorities for storage of goods on which payment of duties is deferred until the goods are removed.

- **Dual channel system:** A system for customs control allowing passengers on their arrival to declare the accompanied items and goods through selecting either the red or green channel.

- **Personal effects:** All articles new or used, which a passenger may reasonably require for his or her personal use during the journey taking into account all the circumstances of the journey, but excluding any goods imported or exported for commercial purposes.

• **Postal items:** Letter-post and parcels, as described in Acts of the Universal Postal Union currently in force, when carried by or for postal services.

• **Release of goods:** Action by the customs to permit goods undergoing clearance to be placed at the disposal of the persons concerned.

Taxation

Tax Residence in the UK

There are some basic points of UK taxation law that you should understand. In the UK there are two tests that will help determine where you pay tax. They assess your domicile and your residence.

Your **domicile** is the place that is your real home, the place where you have your roots. For most people it is the place where they were born. You can change your domicile but it is often not easy to do so. Changes in domicile can have far-reaching tax consequences and can be a useful tax reduction tool.

Residence falls into two categories. There is a test of simple residence – actually living here rather than staying temporarily – and of ordinary residence.

People are generally treated as **resident** in the UK if they spend 183 or more days a year in the UK. Visitors are also treated as resident if they come to the UK regularly and spend significant time here. If they spend, on average over a period of four or more years, more than three months here per year they will be treated as tax resident. People can continue to be **ordinarily resident** in the UK even after they have stopped actually being resident here.

The most important thing to understand is that, once you have been ordinarily resident in the UK, the simple fact of going overseas will not automatically bring that residence to an end. If you leave this country in order to take up permanent residence elsewhere then, by concession, HM Revenue & Customs will treat you as ceasing to be resident on the day following your departure; but it will not treat you as ceasing to be ordinarily resident if, after leaving, you spend an average of 91 or more days a year in this country over any four-year period. In other words, it doesn't want you to escape too easily!

Taxes Payable in the UK

The significance of these residence rules is that you will continue to be liable for some UK taxes for as long as you are either ordinarily resident or domiciled in the UK. Put far too simply, if you leave the UK to live in Dubai:

> • **You will continue to have to pay tax in the UK on any capital gains you make anywhere in the world for as long as you are ordinarily resident and domiciled in the UK.**

- You will continue to be liable for UK inheritance tax on all of your assets located anywhere in the world for as long as you remain domiciled in the UK.

- You will always pay UK income tax (Schedule A) on income arising from land and buildings in the UK, wherever your domicile, residence or ordinary residence.

- You will pay UK income tax (Schedule D) as follows:

  - income from 'self-employed' work carried out in the UK (Cases I and II) – normally taxed in the UK in all cases if income arises there.

  - income from interest, annuities or other annual payments from the UK (Case III) – normally taxed in the UK if income arises there and you are ordinarily resident in the UK.

  - income from investments and businesses outside the UK (Cases IV and V) – normally only taxed in the UK if you are UK-domiciled and -resident or ordinarily resident in the UK.

  - income from government pensions (fire, police, army, civil servant, etc.) – taxed in the UK in all cases.

  - sundry profits not otherwise taxable (Case VI) arising out of land or building in the UK – always taxed in the UK.

- You will pay income tax on any income earned from salaried employment in the UK (Schedule E) only in respect of earnings from duties performed in the UK unless you are resident and ordinarily resident in the UK – in which case you will usually pay tax in the UK on your worldwide earnings.

If you are only buying a holiday home or investment property in Dubai and will remain primarily resident in the UK, your tax position in the UK will not change very much. You will have to declare any income you make from your foreign property as part of your UK tax declaration. On the disposal of the property, you must disclose the profit made to HM Revenue and Customs.

If, however, you are going to live and work in Dubai for a significant period of time, then you will cease to be ordinarily resident in the UK and your tax position will change. Changes to your domicile should be considered separately.

Residence in Dubai

*Thanks to **Steve Travis** of the **Fry Group**'s International Division (The Fry Group, **t** (01903) 231545, **www.thefrygroup.co.uk**) for the following section.*

When looking at the taxation implications of emigration to Dubai, it is important to consider that normal UK rules for achieving non-resident status still apply. Just because you are moving to Dubai, it does not mean that the UK rules are somehow different. In addition, whilst the Revenue's guidance (booklet IR20 (**www.hmrc.gov.uk/pdfs/ir20.pdf**) is useful, the Revenue is looking increasingly at why people leave the UK and, if for non-employment reasons, they can some-times also ask for evidence of a 'clear and distinct break' from the UK. Suffice it to say that advice is needed! The following points are important to consider:

- **Tell HMRC you are going, using Form P85. Often, departing expatriates are entitled to some form of tax refund for the year of departure.**

- **You will be exempt from tax on non-UK-sourced income whilst non-resident in the UK, and from capital gains tax on your worldwide assets if you remain non-resident for at least five complete tax years. In most cases the exemption begins from 6th April following the date of departure.**

- **UK-sourced income remains taxable in the UK; however in most cases you will continue to be entitled to full UK personal allowances.**

- **Lots of expats let their UK homes while abroad. The profit counts as taxable income in the UK, though the UK personal allowance is available to absorb that. Profit is very broadly defined as gross rental income less 'allowable deductions'. 'Allowable deductions' are generally expenses incurred in the running of the rental (agent's fees, utility bills, etc.) but may also include mortgage interest on the property.**

- **Rental agents are required to withhold income tax at 20 per cent from the rental income they manage, unless the taxpayer is in the UK's non-resident landlord (NRL) scheme. Joining this scheme is highly recommended, though often results in the need to submit an annual tax return.**

- **Departing the UK often has no impact at all on inheritance tax. If the taxpayer is domiciled in the UK (a concept entirely distinct from residence) UK IHT will apply to their worldwide assets regardless of how long they are absent from the UK. It is possible to change your domicile and to eliminate UK IHT on non-UK assets, though some very strict conditions must be met.**

- **There is no double tax treaty with Dubai and no local taxation to speak of. There is also no reciprocal agreement for social security purposes. Those not of pensionable age are advised to make voluntary contributions in the UK.**

- **More and more people are buying real estate in Dubai, and often a local will is needed that is compliant with Shari'a law. If UK domicile is retained, a UK will should also be drawn up to govern assets outside Dubai.**

Financial Planning: Relocating to Dubai, and Returning

Anyone looking to relocate to Dubai, and also when planning to return, should consider the following important issues from a financial planning point of view.

While **overseas income and earnings are tax-free**, do not be dazzled by this fact: the actual **cost of living** in Dubai has increased significantly. This should be allowed for when negotiating any package of employment benefits.

Knowing with certainty how long you will be based in Dubai is unusual. Therefore, it can wise to avoid committing to long-term savings or pension commitments locally that may prove costly if circumstances change. Building a varied portfolio may be more prudent, as it offers flexibility enough to adapt to a change in residency position. Four further tips are:

- Assuming an eventual return to the UK, it is worthwhile maximising UK tax-sheltered investments in the year of departure, especially pensions and ISAs. An individual who makes contrbutions to a personal pension in the year of their departure can continue to make gross contributions of £3,600 a year for five more tax years, and pension tax relief is provided at source.

- Consider that the local currency – the dirham – is pegged to the US dollar, and this will have implications for the savings approach to be adopted.

- Hold and accumulate cash deposits offshore. UK deposit accounts can – depending on circumstances – increase one's UK tax liability. This is because UK deposit interest is still counted as UK-sourced income.

- If you hold any offshore deposits with significant accrued interest, make sure you close these accounts before returning to the UK. By concession,

The Cost of Living

Even a tax-free Dubai salary can be stretched by the price of everyday essentials. Local food is inexpensive, good quality and tasty but often overlooked in favour of the city's chi-chi gourmet culinary joints. Other high-priced luxuries include alcohol. Utilities and running costs are generally comparable with Europe. Expect a heavy mark-up on imported food items.

- Average two-day business trip (excluding flights): 3,740 dirhams.
- Taxi journey (10km): 25 dirhams.
- Wash, cut and blow-dry (women) in top salon: 120 dirhams.
- Monthly rental on a modest one-bed furnished apartment: 6,170 dirhams.
- Services of a cleaner (1 hour): 25 dirhams.
- Average utility bills (per month): 500 dirhams.
- Internet connection (per month): 180 dirhams.
- Three-course dinner at a top restaurant (for 4 people): 1,500–3,000 dirhams.
- Bottle of house wine (restaurant): 150 dirhams.
- Bottle of house wine (off-licence): 40 dirhams.
- Pint of beer: 20 dirhams.
- Carton of cigarettes: 40 dirhams.
- Round of golf (18 holes): 450 dirhams.
- Nightclub entrance: 75 dirhams.
- Cinema ticket: 30 dirhams.

Exchange rates at Sept 2008: US$1 = AED 3.67/AED 1 = US$0.27 (pegged); £1 = AED 6.42/AED 1 = £0.16. See **www.xe.com/ucc** for the latest rates.

HMRC allows the individual to 'split' the tax year of return for tax purposes, and ceasing the offshore interest source before return draws a line in the sand as to what interest has been earned and when.

And finally: there is of course no substitute for individual advice.

Taxing Issues

'It pays to research the tax implications of living and working in Dubai,' says Leonie Kerswill at PricewaterhouseCoopers LLP. 'There are many who, tempted by the tax-free salary packages and attractive lifestyles, choose Dubai as a place to work, and the majority will try and negotiate local packages so that housing and schooling for children are included. But employees should be cautious. While the employment income and other benefits under local arrangements are tax-free, there may well be less obvious costs. For example, employment law is less favourable to the employee than in the UK, and individuals could lose rights to maternity or paternity leave, compensation for loss of office and redundancy protection. Employees on local packages generally cannot stay in UK pension plans, which means they lose continuity of service.

'Inflation is quite high in Dubai, and this, combined with the fact that many local packages are negotiated and paid in dollars, means that contracts agreed on local terms may well become unattractive after only a couple of years.

'However, there's no getting away from the fact that Dubai remains a hot spot for expats, and, to try and combat some of the above issues and concerns, many employers are looking at arrangements which try to ensure that employees are left in no worse a position in net income terms than had they stayed in the UK.

'Talking of the UK, assuming you're going to be non-resident following a move to Dubai, then before you leave, think about the following:

- If you let your house while away, register as a non-resident landlord (NRL) so you receive rental income gross. Any income tax due on rental profits will then be collected via the completion of a UK self-assessment tax return.

- Review your pension arrangements, and consider whether you should be making some alternative retirement savings arrangements.

- If you have assets with in-built capital gains that you are planning to sell, and you are going to be away for at least five complete tax years, wait until you have left before you sell. Conversely, assets showing losses should be sold before you leave, to ensure that the loss realised will be available against any future gains.

- Check that no UK tax charges will be triggered on your departure from the UK (e.g. on previous reliefs claimed such as the enterprise investment scheme relief, capital gains tax holdover relief).

- Arrange for your UK bank or building society interest to be paid gross by completing a 'not ordinarily resident' declaration form R105.'

Living in Dubai

As the UAE's commercial and tourism capital, Dubai is globally regarded as one of the world's most sophisticated, futuristic and cosmopolitan cities: a modern phenomenon that balances Arab traditions with architectural ambition and empire-building thrust. Few nations on the planet boast such a fascinating mix of cultural and ethnic diversity, due largely to one of the most rapid rates of non-native population growth on the planet. Ultra-progressive 21st-century economic energy blends with ancient Arabia in this unique city of contrasts where dazzling skyscrapers rub shoulders with domed coral-roofed mosques in an East-meets-West fusion.

This hybrid of influences in Dubai has also permeated many aspects of daily life in the city, from the richly exotic Arab heritage still evident in the eclectic souks to the miles of immaculate white-sand beaches and international restaurants, clubs and cafés. Dubai's 100,000-plus community of Western expatriates also delights in a subtropical climate that brings with it major lifestyle benefits, such as pool parties, water sports and golf under year-round sunny blue skies. Dubai's clean sandy beaches, craggy mountains and lush green PGA-standard fairways offer plenty of respite from the urban humidity of the city hub. Yet few forays can compete with the timeless majesty of the desert, where shifting sands and towering dunes can provide the eye-popping unworldly grandeur of an intergalactic jaunt.

However Dubai isn't an idyllic land blessed with rose-tinted perfection and, as with any big decision, those considering relocation should approach it with open eyes. An essential part of planning any move is conducting plenty of research – and Dubai is no exception. There simply is no substitute for honest assessment, so be prepared to make a warts-and-all checklist. Key considerations when weighing up pros and cons include cost-of-living comparisons, salary packages, housing, schooling, medical care, transport, safety, crime and communication. Ask around for the opinions of others and talk to those who have moved to Dubai before you, and accept that, unlike the tax-free wages on offer, not everything in Dubai is an attractive proposition. For such a progressive modern nation, Dubai has a shocking environmental record, with man-made islands that have caused untold damage to the ocean's delicate ecosystem. Coral reefs, sea grasses, and oyster beds that were once part of protected marine lands lie choked under a barrage of dredged up sea sand while building rubble from new construction deluges the city with a smog of dust. Dubai has yet to implement an effective recycling programme, and boasts more gas-guzzling SUVs than fuel-efficient vehicles. Roads are gridlocked with fume-spewing cars, while residential zones roar with 24-hour air-conditioning. The issue of road safety is also a growing national concern – Dubai's accident statistics make grim reading in a nation where speeding, tailgating and erratic behind-the-wheel behaviour is the norm.

Yet by far the majority of Dubai's burgeoning expatriate community makes allowances for these irritations. After all, they reason, every city has its annoyances – yet few offer the temptations of a sunshine lifestyle with tax-free benefits and impeccable first-class standards.

Learning the Language

Mastering Arabic is not easy. Not only are words often tricky to pick up but they can also be near-impossible to pronounce. The fact that Dubai is so cosmopolitan also acts as a disincentive to would-be Arabic speakers: English is so widely spoken that many residents will never require a single word of the local language. However, those who do make the effort to learn a few basic phrases with be viewed with great respect – and warm smiles. It can also serve to enrich the Dubai cultural experience and is a great way to make new friends.

A number of **language schools** offer Arabic courses and tuition at beginner, intermediate and advanced levels. Many are offered in both day and after-work sessions, often with language support classes that are run online. Some of the most established include the following:

- **El Ewla Language Academy, t** 391 1640, **www.elewla.com**.
- **Berlitz, t** 344 0034, **www.berlitz.com**.
- **Polygot Language Institute, t** 222 3429, **www.polygot.ae**.

Pronunciation

a as in 'had'
e as in 'bet'
i as in 'hit'
u as in 'put'

Basic Words and Phrases

hello *salaam* or *marhaba*
response to above *marhabtayn*

peace be upon you *salaamu alaykom*
response to above *wa alaykom is salaam*

good morning *sabah il-khayr*
response to above *sabah in-nuwr*

good evening *masa il-khayr*
response to above *masa in-nuwr*

goodbye *ma is-salaama*

What is your name? *sho Ismak?* (m) / *sho Ismek?* (f)
My name is... *Ismiy...*

I don't speak Arabic *Ana ma ba'aref ahkee Arabee*
I speak Arabic a little *Baa'ref Arabee showayya*

how are you? *keef halak?* (m) / *keef halek?* (f)
response to above (= 'thanks God') *Al-Hamdolillah*
response to above (= 'fine') *kowayyes* (m) / *kowayyesah* (f)

hopefully *Inshalla*

thank you *shukran*
thanks indeed *shukran jazilan*
response to above (= 'you're welcome') *afwan / ahlan wa sahlan*
excuse me? (as question) *laww smaht* (m) / *laww smahti* (f)
excuse me! (= 'sorry!') *afwan*
pardon me *samehni* (m) / *samehini* (f)
sorry *aasif*
if you please *min fadlak* (m) / *min fadlik* (f)
help me *sa'adni* (m) / *sa'adini* (f)
congratulations *mabrook / tahanina*
wait *istanna*
hurry up *besora'a*
go away *emshi*

yes *na'am/aaywa*
no *la'a*

I/me *ana*
you *inta* (m) / *inti* (f)
he *howwa*
she *heyya*
we *ehna*
they *homm*

I want *biddi*
we want *bidna*
do you want? *beddak* (m) / *beddek* (f)
how much? *bekam? / addesh?*
this *hada*
that *hadak*
these *hadol*
how much is this? *bekam hada? / addesh hada?*
what is this? *sho hada?*
expensive *ghali*
too much *kteer*
beautiful *jameel / helow*

nice *lateef*

right *yameen*
left *shemal*
straight *doghree*

downtown *wast el-balad*
street *share'a*
hotel *fondoq*
museum *mathaf*
mall *souq*
restaurant *mat'am*
hospital *mustashfa*
toilet / WC *hammam*
doctor *tabeeb*
police *shorta*
passport *el-jawaz*
identity *haweyya*

car *seyyara*
taxi *taxi ojrah*
bus *bas*
aeroplane *teyyara*
train *qetar*

tea *shai*
coffee *ahwe*
food *akel*
juice *aaseer*
hubbly-bubbly water pipe *nargile*
sugar *sokkar*
without sugar *bdoun sokkar*
milk *haleeb*
the bill *el-hesab*
invoice *fatora*

Removal and Shipping

A large number of international shipping companies specialise in forwarding goods to Dubai – from virtually anywhere in the world. Choose from a comprehensive door-to-door service including packing, or simply arrange for goods to be transported to Dubai Airport or Jebel Ali Port for collection, where they can then be cleared for customs and dispatched to a local address. Costs vary dramatically, so be sure to shop around for a few comparison quotes before signing on the dotted line.

Deciding what to ship and what to leave behind is a very personal choice, of course, but one that requires careful planning. Will you really want an Axminster carpet when tiled floors are all the rage in the searing heat of Dubai? Similarly, winter duvets may be surplus to requirements. Other furnishings can be bought relatively cheaply locally, with many noticeboards offering second-hand appliances, so it doesn't always make economic sense to cart your worldly goods halfway across the world. If in doubt, put it in storage or sell it on.

Most used personal effects can be imported into Dubai without incurring fees or taxes (*see* **Red Tape**, pp.140–44). Many specialists, such as the Removal Group, offer a weekly shipping service to Dubai and also an air freight service, with part-load and full container load service to all areas of the emirate. A team of dedicated agents unload and unpack all items upon arrival into the country, making sure customs clearance is a smooth process for the ultimate 'peace of mind' removal package. Self-storage is also popular. For more details contact:

- The Removal Group, **www.removalgroup.com.**
- European Van Lines, **www.evl.co.uk.**
- Self Storage Dubai, **www.storagedubai.com.**
- Over's International, **www.overs.co.uk.**

Transporting Pets

Assuming your pets are healthy and their inoculations up-to-date, it is more than possible to take your pets with you to Dubai – but there are several hurdles for owners to overcome. Pets brought into the UAE must be imported as cargo (not as accompanying baggage) and can only travel after an **import permit** has been obtained. To apply, you'll need a document from your veterinary surgeon proving that your pet has been vaccinated against rabies. This should be signed and stamped by the vet between 12 months and 30 days prior to travel. You'll also need a good health certificate from the country of departure, and the pet will need to be microchipped. Dangerous breeds of dog, such as pit bulls and Neapolitan mastiffs (and cross breeds of these breeds) are banned. Travel boxes must meet International Air Transport Authority guidelines. The import permit will cost AED 200 and is valid for one month. It is payable by e-card (*see* p.140).

Animals brought into the UAE without the proper documents are quarantined until authorisation is obtained for release.

Once in the UAE, your pet will need to be **vaccinated** against rabies on an annual basis. In Dubai this means obtaining a red identification disc from Dubai Municipality, where the jab incurs an AED 50 charge. In addition to rabies, dog-owners should also consider vaccinating against hepatitis, distemper, leptospirosis and parvovirus. Cats should also be inoculated against two types of cat flu as well as panleukopenia.

To transport pets out of Dubai, an **export permit** should be obtained from the Ministry of Agriculture and Fisheries at least five days before travel. You'll need a copy of your passport and residence permit too. A government vet will examine the animal before checking all necessary export documentation, including a signed and stamped document from your vet showing the animal has been vaccinated against rabies between 12 months and 30 days prior to travel. Pets should also be microchipped. An AED 100 fee is payable by e-card.

The UAE, including Dubai, is one of the non-EU listed countries that falls under the **PETS** travel scheme (often referred to as 'Pet Passports"). This means that dogs, cats and ferrets are permitted to return to the UK from the UAE without entering quarantine. Before you leave for Dubai, see **www.defra.gov.uk/ animalh/quarantine/pets/index.htm** to check that you have complied with all the requirements – once you have left the UK, it's too late!

The **British Veterinary Centre** in Abu Dhabi is an excellent source of advice on pet import and export. A country-by-country guide provides an up-to-date breakdown of requirements; visit **www.britvet.com**.

The UAE has a significant problem with stray cats and dogs, so it is important to always keep your pet under control.

Specialist Pet and Animal Services

- **Dubai Kennels and Cattery, t** 285 1646, **info@dkc.ae**, **www.dkc.ae**.
- **Pet Land Resort (Cattery and Kennels), t** 347 5022.
- **Modern Veterinary Clinic, t** 395 3131.
- **European Veterinary Centre, t** 343 9591.
- **Feline Friends (Animal Rescue Charity), t** 347 4611.
- **Creature Comforts (Pet-sitting), t** 050 695 9480.
- **Pet Partner (Pet-sitting), t** 050 774 2239.
- **Shampooch Mobile Pet Grooming, t** 344 9868.
- **The Doghouse (Grooming), t** 347 1807.
- **Paws Canine Training Centre, t** 050 784 5350.

Utilities and Public Services

Electricity, Water and Sewerage

Electricity and water, along with sewerage, are all provided by the **Dubai Electricity and Water Authority (DEWA), www.dewa.gov.ae**.

Electricity is supplied at 220/240 volts and 50 cycles using a three-pin British system, so US appliances will require an adaptor.

In order to get the utilities connected to your apartment or villa, you will need to visit the DEWA office in person with a tenancy contract and a refundable deposit of AED 1,000 (apartment) or AED 2,000 (villa).

Property utilities are billed each month according to usage. Expect bills to amount to around AED 350–650 per month, depending on the size of your property. In 2008, DEWA announced the introduction of a new tariff system that raised prices for those who consume the most energy – the first increase since 1998. The hike in prices does not affect those with moderate consumption of electricity and water (around 80 per cent of Dubai residents) and, controversially, only applies to non-UAE nationals. DEWA figures suggest that Dubai's average individual consumption of 20,000 kilowatt hours a year and 130 gallons of water a day is higher than the United States, United Kingdom and Singapore combined.

Although the **tap water** is good enough to drink, most expatriates order bulk orders of mineral water. Dubai's local brands are nice-tasting and come in five-litre bottles for home-sited water coolers. Expect to pay around 30 dirhams for a bottle, with a refill likely to cost about 7 dirhams.

Sewerage is managed by municipal contractors or DEWA offices, via a mains sewer or septic tank.

Gas

Dubai's gas supply is via individual canisters, as there is no mains supply. Gas is the popular cooking method, however, so bottles can be delivered 24/7. Within half an hour of a telephone order, a delivery van will turn up with a replacement.

There are three sizes of canister, with connections and refills available from a number of gas suppliers city-wide. Expect to pay around AED 300 for a canister, with refills at 60 dirhams.

Some of the largest gas supply companies include **Honest Gas Hands**, **t** 285 6586; and **New City Gas Distributors**, **t** 351 8282.

Rubbish Disposal and Recycling

Dubai's consumer-orientated society is responsible for some of the highest levels of per capita household waste on the planet. Estimates suggest that each household generates over 1,000kg per annum – a staggering amount, and a figure that is rising as the population swells. Thankfully, municipal departments offer a highly efficient waste collection service and are, slowly, cottoning on to the importance of recycling.

Domestic waste bins are emptied into large skip-style dumpsters on the corner of each street for frequent collection. If this isn't the case (say, in a brand new development) simply call **t** 206 4234 to arrange collection.

A rising number of recycling points can cope with glass bottles, tin cans and paper, while residents in Emaar developments can benefit from Earth Watch's impressive recycling collection service (**t** 050 347 4576).

Telephone and the Internet

Since the deregulation of the UAE's telecommunications sector, consumers in Dubai have had a great deal more choice. Telecommunications between the UAE and the outside world are generally good, with residential telephone lines, mobile services and internet connections readily available city-wide. Every Dubai resident seems to have a mobile phone permanently pressed to their ear, and pay-as-you-go services are just as common as contract packages.

Almost all of Dubai benefits from high-speed internet connections based on DSL technology, although access to some sites is restricted in line with the UAE's censorship policies. Expect to pay around AED 200 for installation, with monthly rental at around AED 20.

The main telecommunications suppliers **Etisalat** and **du** offer a constantly changing array of deals, discounts and special packages on internet, landline phones and mobiles, so it pays to keep an eye on promotional offers. Bills are issued monthly and can be settled online or by telephone banking. Some of Dubai's major developers already have assigned telecommunications providers, such as Emaar and Nahkeel who both favour du.

- Etisalat, **t** 101, **www.etisalat.ae.**
- du, **t** 369 9988, **www.du.ae.**

To sign up for anything, you'll need a copy of your passport, residence permit and tenancy contract. Installing a landline takes around three days, while a SIM card for a mobile can be arranged on the spot.

Calling the UAE

To dial a landline number within the UAE from outside, you dial the country code 971, then the local code (Dubai 04) without the initial zero, then the seven-digit number.

To dial a mobile number from within the UAE, dial 050 and then the number. If you are dialling a mobile phone number anywhere in the UAE from outside the UAE, dial the country code 971, then 50 and then the mobile number.

Public Phones

Public telephones in Dubai take both coins and pre-paid phone cards. You'll find them dotted around the city in malls, shopping centres, petrol stations and

Operator Services

Service	English	Arabic
Directory enquiries	181	181
Call bookings and enquiries	151	151
Fault reporting	171	171
Clock/time enquiries	140	141
Operator assistance	100	100
Phograms/telegrams	130	131

UAE Local Dialling Codes

Emirate	Code	Emirate	Code
Abu Dhabi	02	Kalba	09
Ajman	06	Khor Fakkan	09
Al Ain	02	Masafi	09
Aweer	04	Ras Al Khaimah	07
Dubai	04	Sharjah	06
Fujairah	09	Umm Al Quwain	06
Jebel Ali	04		

on street corners. Phone cards are available from bookstores, grocery stores or Etisalat or du offices. They are issued in denominations of AED 25 upwards.

Internet Cafés

Internet cafés come and go, but the following are some of Dubai's most established. Services vary, from a comprehensive technology suite to more rudimentary set-ups. Expect to pay around AED 3 per hour.

- Al Jalssa Internet Café, Al Ain Centre, Bur Dubai, t 351 4617, *open 9am–1am.*

- Al Matrix.com Café, Metropolitan Hotel, Sheikh Zayed Road, t 343 0000, *open 10am–12am.*

- C@fe Net, Al Sharafi Centre, Karama, t 396 9111, open 9am–1am.

- Citi Dot Com, The Lobby, Atrium Centre, Bank Street, Bur Dubai, t 359 3434, *open 9am–2am.*

- Digital Office, Moosa Tower I, Sheikh Zayed Road, t 332 8880, *open 24hrs.*

- E-mail Internet Café, Al Attar Centre, Karama, t 335 6353, *open 8.30am–3am.*

- F1 (Formula One) Net Café, Palm Strip Shopping Mall, Jumeirah Beach Road, t 345 1232, *open 10am–10pm.*

- Online@thetowers, Emirates Towers Boulevard, Sheikh Zayed Road, t 330 0000, *open 8am–12am.*

- Star Net Café, Karama Centre, Karama, t 3340881, *open 8am–1.30am.*

- WorldNet Internet Café, Holiday Centre, Sheikh Zayed Road, 1st Floor, **t** 332 2913, *open 10am–11pm.*
- World Systems Computer, Khalid bin Al Waleed Road, Bur Dubai, **t** 393 9997, *open 9am–2am.*

Post and Courier Services

Once Dubai's streets are finally assigned names, it plans to implement a home delivery postal system. However, until that day comes, mail is despatched to **PO boxes** via the Central Post Office.

To apply for a PO box you'll need to pay an annual fee of around AED 150. You'll also need to complete an application form and present your passport. Once approved, you will be issued with a set of keys and assigned a box office number. In the event that a registered letter or parcel arrives for you, Dubai's postal provider **Empost** will notify you in writing. Other than that, you'll need to check your box every few days to see if anything has arrived.

Most people use **registered post** as standard, as it is more reliable than regular mail and offers the added benefit of a tracking number along with delivery guarantees. Empost also provides a **courier service** for local and international deliveries, all of which can be tracked and insured against loss. Other courier companies serving the UAE include DHL, UPA, TNT and FedEx.

Dubai's **post office** buildings are generally open between 8am and 5pm, Saturday to Thursday. Some of the city's main Emarat **petrol stations** also incorporate postal services, usually on a 24-hour basis. These include Safa Park, Al Gahoud, Al Wasl Road and Al Diyafah Street. Each sells stamps and dispatches letters and parcels.

Post Offices

- **Dubai Central Post Office, t** 337 1500.
- **Jumeirah Post Office, t** 337 1500.
- **Mumtaz Speed Post, t** 337 1243.

Television, Satellite and Cable Services

See Chapter 03, **Dubai Today**, p.46.

Money and Banking

For all its sophisticated consumerism, Dubai remains very much a cash culture, although credit cards and debit payments are now accepted without a frown. The **dirham** (Dhs, also referred to as the Arab Emirate dirham, AED) is the local currency. Each paper denomination is specified clearly in English and Arabic, with brown-coloured 5s, green 10s, pale blue 20s, purple 50s, pink 100s, blue 500s and a brown-mauve 1,000s. The dirham is broken up into 100 fils. Coinage is in Arabic only but comes in just three regularly used silver-coloured denominations: 1 dirham, 50 fils and 25 fils. The 1, 5 and 10 fils coins are rarely used in everyday life; the common practice of 'rounding up' to multiples of 25 fils can also be muddling when you're new to Dubai and trying to get to grips with what's what. Rather confusingly, some older versions of the most recent coinage remain in circulation. For further information visit **www.centralbank.ae** – the website of the Central Bank and an excellent source of information on all things money-related, from what each coin looks like to the banknotes that are currently valid.

Since 1980, the dirham has been pegged to the US dollar at a mid-rate of US$1 to AED 3.6725. However, the UAE is widely expected to consider following Kuwait's lead in deregulating its currency from the dollar, but only if supported by other Arab nations. Also under discussion is a move to a single GCC currency – once on the cards with a target of 2010, but now unlikely to happen until at least 2015.

The UAE has about 50 local and foreign banks. All local and international banks are strictly governed by the **UAE Central Bank**, and an ever-growing number of organisations is entering a disciplined and well-ordered market. Recent mergers to create so-called 'mega-banks' have led to speculation that others may consider similar moves of consolidation. Fresh impetus is certainly good news for non-UAE borrowers, who are sure to benefit from a more competitive financial culture.

Tipping

Dubai has an established tipping culture, with gratuities commonly shared between staff – it is virtually impossible to single out an individual on the basis of good service. Adding 10–12.5 per cent is standard – and much appreciated by most hospitality workers. However, be sure to check restaurant bills, as the practice of including a service charge has crept into Dubai's accepted norm.

Hotel workers, such as bell boys, chambermaids and room service, should be paid a gratuity of around 5 dirhams. Windscreen washers at petrol stations should be tipped about 2–3 dirhams. Taxi drivers will be grateful for a 'rounded up' fare, although this is not compulsory – so if he's driven erratically, been rude or less than helpful, just pay what's on the meter.

Banks and Bank Accounts

Newcomers to Dubai will find opening an account relatively straightforward. With just a few exceptions, you'll need to prove residency and provide the usual documentation of passport and proof of employment. Standard banking hours are 8am–1pm (or 2pm in some cases), Saturday to Thursday. Almost every bank provides **ATMs** that accept a wide range of cards (not just those of the issuing bank) and a large number of cashpoints dotted throughout the city, especially around shopping malls, petrol forecourts, hotels and supermarkets.

The following are some of the biggest banking organisations:

- ABN AMRO Bank, **t** 351 2200, **www.abnamro.ae.**
- Abu Dhabi Commercial Bank, **t** 295 8888, **www.adcb.com.**
- Arab Bank, **t** 295 0845, **www.arabbank.com.**
- Bank of Sharjah, **t** 282 7278, **www.bankofsharjah.com.**
- Barclays Bank, **t** 362 67000, **www.barclays.co.uk.**
- BNP Paribas, **t** 222 52000, **www.bnparibas.ae.**
- Citibank (Middle East), **t** 324 5000, **www.citibank.com/ae.**
- Dubai Islamic Bank, **t** 295 9999, **www.alislami.ae.**
- Emirates Bank International, **t** 225 6256, **www.emiratesbank.ae.**
- Habib Bank AG Zurich, **t** 221 4535, **www.habibbank.com.**
- HSBC Bank Middle East, **t** 800 4722, **www.uae.hsbc.com.**
- Lloyds TSB Bank, **t** 342 2000, **www.lloydstsb.ae.**
- Mashreqbank, **t** 217 4800, **www.mashreqbank.com.**
- National Bank of Abu Dhabi, **t** 267 9993, **www.nbad.com.**
- National Bank of Dubai, **t** 222 2111, **www.nbd.com.**
- RAK Bank, **t** 224 8000, **www.rakbank.ae.**
- Standard Chartered Bank (Middle East), **t** 352 0455, **www.standardchartered.com.**
- Union National Bank, **t** 800 2600, **www.unb.co.ae.**

Credit Cards

Very few small retailers will entertain the idea of credit cards, and even some of the larger shops make it obvious that they'd much prefer to do business in cash. However, almost every commercial entity is set up to accept payment by credit card, although the cards they accept are restricted to major companies such as American Express, MasterCard and Visa. Don't be surprised if some retailers add a charge for credit card payment; it's a practice that is dying out (and illegal) but applying an extra 5 per cent for 'processing' can be something you will encounter.

Currency Exchange Offices

See also **Buying a Property**, pp.114–16.

Dubai is blessed with dozens of *bureaux de change* and, in many instances, the rate of exchange offered if better than in the banks. Shop around for the best deals and you'll find plenty of friendly outlets more than keen to do business. Most are clustered around the shopping malls and souks and are open 8.30–1.30 and 4.30–8.30. Some of the most established outlets as follows:

- Al Fardan Exchange, **t** 351 3535, **www.alfardangroup.com.**
- First Gulf Exchange, **t** 351 5777, **www.fgb.ae.**
- Al Ghurair Exchange, **t** 222 2955, **www.alghurairexchange.com.**
- Wall Street Exchange Centre, **t** 800 4871, **www.wallstreet-corp.com.**

Health and Emergencies

State Healthcare

State healthcare in Dubai is operated by the **Dubai Health Authority (DHA**, **www.dha. gov.ae**), a new body created to replace the 30-year-old Department of Health and Medical Services (DoHMS, **www.dohms.gov.ae**). This provides medical care for all UAE nationals, visitors and resident expatriates, although most expatriates opt for private healthcare via a health insurance plan. Both public and private hospitals, clinics and medical centres offer high-quality health and dental care, from emergency services to treatment for routine ailments, repeat prescriptions and jabs; the added benefits of private care include English-speaking staff, shorter waiting lists and more home comforts.

Emergency medical attention is free in the UAE, regardless of nationality or status or whether you hold a health card. The Dubai Hospital is one of the Middle East's most respected medical facilities and boasts an impressive ER wing.The main emergency hospital is Rashid, where a state-of-the-art A&E department is slick, efficient and well-run. Be warned, however: ambulance response times aren't as super-fast as they could be, as paramedic services are relatively new. Expect an ambulance to take around 35 minutes to arrive following an emergency call-out compared to eight minutes in the UK.

- Rashid, **t** 337 4000, **www.dha.gov.ae.**
- Dubai Hospital, **t** 271 4444, **www.dha.gov.ae.**
- Al Maktoum, **t** 222 1211, **www.dha.gov.ae.**

- Al Baraha (aka Kuwait Hospital), **t** 271 0000, **www.dha.gov.ae**.
- Al Wasl, **t** 324 1111, **www.dha.gov.ae**.

For **non-urgent healthcare**, UAE residents seeking treatment need a **health card**, for which a fee is paid. Dubai's new **e-Health card** was launched in 2006 and combines four services: a medical fitness certificate, residency permit, e-Gate and health card. This 'one stop shop' electronic card entitles residents to low-cost medical treatment at public hospitals and clinics. Simply pick up an application form from any public hospital and submit with the correct documents to your local health centre with an AED 300 fee. Processing is supposed to take 24 hours, but can be a few days.

Pharmacies are located on practically every street corner, and are well stocked with a mix of top-name brands and generic drugs. Personnel, however, are untrained and should not be relied on for medical advice.

Private Healthcare

Private hospitals and clinics are of an exceptional standard in Dubai, although the experience borders on consumerism, such is the emphasis on cost and ability to pay. It pays to have good health insurance in Dubai, but be sure to check the policy, as not all private hospitals and clinics are covered.

Some of the best private hospitals include:

- Al Zahra, **t** 331 5000, **www.alzahra.com**.
- Welcare Hospital, **t** 282 7788, **www.welcarehospital.com**.
- American Hospital, **t** 336 7777, **www.ahdubai.com**.
- Medic Polyclinic, **t** 355 4111.

Dubai is also home to the mega-development **Dubai Health City**. The UAE is expected to receive 11.2 million medical tourists by 2010, much of them in Dubai.

- Dubai Healthcare City, **www.dhcc.ae**.
- Dubai Health News, **www.dubaihealthnews.com**.

Health Insurance

Hot on the heels of Abu Dhabi's ruling that all employers must provide health insurance for their full-time employees and dependants, Dubai has made its own decree in 2008: to provide government employees and their dependants with health insurance with immediate effect. Government employees, including all expatriate residents as well as UAE nationals, will now have access to a range of healthcare services and facilities for the first time.

Those sourcing health insurance will find that the level of cover varies dramatically, with dental care and medical screening often exempt. Some of the most established companies in Dubai's health insurance sector include the following:

- Alliance Insurance, **t** 605 1111, **www.alliance-uae.com.**
- AXA Insurance, **t** 800 4845, **www.axa-gulf.com.**
- Mednet, **t** 800 4882, **www.mednet-uae.com.**
- National General Insurance, **t** 222 2772, **www.ngi.ae.**
- Nextcare, **t** 286 9311, **www.nextcare.co.ae.**

Maternity Services

Pre-natal care, pregnancy, labour and post-natal care are very different in Dubai from in the UK. For a start, some hospitals may not permit husbands and male family members to be present in the labour ward or pre-natal clinic. All state-operated hospitals also levy a charge for expatriate births, with different costs depending on the package you choose. Some of the best maternity deals include pre-natal care, delivery and post-natal care for mother and baby – although it is important to remember that all prices quoted are for a 'standard' service. Should you need additional medical services (such as a C-section delivery), additional charges will apply. Many medical insurance policies include a clause that covers pregnancy, with many stipulating a qualifying period of 12 months' premiums paid before conception.

Dubai's best maternity hospitals include the Dubai Hospital, Al Zahra, Al Wasl, Medlink and Welcare – where gynaecology and obstetrics are also first class.

Dentists and Orthodontists

Some of the world's finest dental practitioners now operate in Dubai, and the standard of dentistry is extremely high. Services range from cleaning and check-ups to major orthodontist surgery. Residents with a health card are entitled to dentistry at their assigned hospital. Expect to pay around AED 50 for a filling and up to AED 4,000 for major dental work in clinics where English-speaking staff are the norm.

- **Modern Dental Clinic, t** 228 2784.
- **Swedish Dental Clinic, t** 223 1297.
- **British Dental Clinic, t** 342 1318.
- **American Dental Clinic, t** 344 0668.

Opticians and Ophthalmologists

You'll find an optician in every Dubai shopping centre, from small independent outlets to major ophthalmologist chains. Standards are very high, with a wide range of services from eye tests to contact lenses and eyewear sales. Some of Dubai's most notable practitioners include the following:

- Barakat Optical, **t** 329 1913.
- Gulf Eye Centre, **t** 329 1977.
- Atlanta Vision Clinic, **t** 348 6233.

Therapy and Counselling

As the number of expatriates grows in Dubai, so do the number of psychological counselling services, family therapy groups, workshops, couples' counselling, psychiatric services and support groups. The challenges of living abroad, in a foreign culture and demanding working environment away from family and friends can take its toll on frazzled nerves. Homesickness can lead to marital difficulties, while stress can come from culture shock.

The following organisations offer practical support and counselling services:

- **Health Call, t** 363 5343.
- **Dr Roughly McCarthy Psychology Clinic, t** 394 6122.
- **British Medical Consulting Centre, t** 344 2633.
- **Dubai Community Health Centre, t** 395 3939.

Weight Loss and Nutrition

Should Dubai's legendary Champagne brunches and mile-long gastronomic buffets begin to take their toll on the waistline, help isn't hard to find. More and more slimming clubs, weight management centres and nutritionists are springing up across the city. Some provide comprehensive dietary advice and meal plans while others involve exercise and fitness. The most established in Dubai include the following:

- **8 Weeks to a New You, t** 050 559 2852, **http://8weeks.net**.
- **Good Habits, t** 344 9692.
- **Right Bite, t** 351 4453.
- **Shapes Weight-loss Club, t** 367 2137.

Alternative Health

You'll find a good range of homeopathic, spiritual, holistic and herbal therapists in Dubai, from crystal healers to acupuncturists. Ailments that respond well to alternative health therapies include colds, coughs, influenza, vomiting, diarrhoea, dysentery, colic, tonsillitis, bronchitis, breathlessness, measles, mumps, dentition problems, sinusitis, ear infections, gastroenteritis, acidity, excess wind, headaches, recurrent urinary infections, joint pain, pimples, corns, warts, psoriasis, eczema and allergies. Treatments include aromatherapy, healing meditation, reflexology, massage and reiki.

Spas and Wellbeing

Dubai is well-positioned to become a leading spa destination and is on target to be the top choice for wellness vacations in the world by 2010, according to a study by Alpha Tours. Dubai and the UAE have invested heavily in a range of dazzling upscale spa facilities that are being globally acclaimed for their excellence, from city-slicker retreats and day spas to beachfront pampering palaces. A large number of Dubai's leading hotel spas carry a prestigious reputation that can give the luxurious facilities in such spa-centric destinations as Thailand and Arizona, USA a run for their money.

What makes them so special? It's hard to quantify, but it certainly helps that each has been spared no expense. Then there is the availability of exquisite products for therapies, such as lemongrass scrubs and mango and sea salt wraps. Dubai's mix of different nationalities also influences the therapies found in the city's spa menus, from the finest Indonesian wellness disciplines to Swedish massage and Japanese health rituals. Many of Dubai's spa therapists hail from Singapore, the Philippines and Indonesia, where touch therapies are part of ancient culture. So, while prices may be on the steep side, treatments are generally world-class.

Highlights include the Balinese-inspired **Spa at the Ritz Carlton** (**www.ritzcarlton.com/resort/dubai**), where traditional *bureh* is used in its signature body treatment amid stunning Indonesian décor. The heady aromas of treatment ingredients fill the air, including ginger and almond oils, rice powder and freshly grated ginger and mashed cucumber. Don't miss out on a kneading Balinese massage for the ultimate body rejuvenation – it uses deep thumb-strokes to work the pressure points and relieve stress and strains.

- Essentials Aromatherapy Centre, **t** 344 8776.
- Art of Living (Healing Meditation), **t** 344 9660.
- GMCKS Pranic Energy Healing Centre, **t** 336 0885.
- Holistic Healing Medical Centre, **t** 348 7172.
- Bliss Reflexology, **t** 286 9444.
- Dubai Herbal & Treatment Centre, **t** 335 1200.
- The Healing Zone, **t** 394 0604.
- Herbalplan Ayurvedic Centre, **t** 321 2553.
- House of Chi and House of Healing, **t** 397 4446.

Social Services, Welfare and Pensions

In 1999, the **General Authority for Pensions and Social Security (GAPSS, www.uae.gov.ae)** was established with the sole aim of providing better

Located on the entire 18th floor of the iconic Burj Al Arab hotel, the **Assawan Spa (www.burj-al-arab.com)** boasts one of the most luxurious addresses in the city. Dubai's spas comply with local Islamic laws that decree that male clients must have male therapists and female clients female therapists. As Muslim women are not traditionally allowed to mix with men who are not their husbands, most spas also have designated 'women only' areas. At the Assawan Spa, the left-hand side of the Arab-designed facility is specifically for men, while women use the right-hand side. A cool white marble interior is one of Dubai's most decadent, while therapies use Middle Eastern incense and spices.

For a spa sanctuary away from the mêlée of the city, head to the ultra-chic desert resort of Al Maha, a Bedouin-tent style luxury encampment set amid amber-coloured rolling sand dunes. Only the finest top-notch styling has been used to create an Arabian setting at the **Timeless Spa at the Al Maha (www.al-maha.com)**, where only the Hajar Mountains distract from the R&R. The theme here is serenity, and a sleepy peacefulness prevails, ensuring guests benefit from the isolated setting. Drawing on traditional Arab influences, the resort fuses European touches with Middle Eastern décor. Individually designed suites echo conventional Bedouin architecture and feature contemporary modern comforts along with unique artwork, hand-crafted furniture and Persian rugs. Spa therapies include such treats as a Desert Sand-Herb Rasoul Scrub.

Each year, Dubai's **Summer Surprises Festival** offers spa treatments via an arrangement between 25 of the finest spas in Dubai as part of its 65-day programme. Visitors and residents can take advantage of the special price promotion between the period mid-June to mid-August. The initiative is designed to showcase Dubai's spa sector to further boost wellbeing tourism.

pension and social security insurance and benefits to all nationals in the UAE's public and private sectors. All aspects of social services, welfare and pensions come under the control of GAPSS, from the management and administration of pensions to the development of social security rules and laws. In recent years, reforms have been made to cover nationals other than those who work in government departments via a new scheme that extends to the public sector. Nationals are now entitled to pensions from the age of 60. The Federal National Council also approved new legislation regulating social security benefits, allowing widows and divorced women, the disabled, the elderly, orphans, single daughters, married students, relatives of a jailed dependent, estranged wives and insolvents access to social security benefits. Under the law, all widowed and divorced national women who are married to foreigners are also eligible for social security benefits. The Social Security Committee will also consider application from national women whose foreign husbands are unable to earn a living for reasons beyond his control – or if his income is less than that considered necessary to run a home (AED 5,000).

However, there are **no social security provisions for foreigners** in the UAE, who must prove the means to support themselves in order to stay in the country.

At present, there are also **no contributory state pension schemes** in Dubai. Most international companies operate their own corporate pension schemes, generally with the option of making lump sum payments or regular contributions. Other than that, expatriates making contributions towards a state pension scheme in their home countries are advised to continue with these for as long as possible – take financial advice (*see* p.147).

At the time of writing, the whole issue of retirement and pension provision is a hot topic in the UAE's expatriate communities. Newspaper reports suggest that the government is planning to bring expatriates under the national pension scheme. The proposed 'Pension Savings' draft law is currently being studied by the General Authority for Pensions and Social Security (GAPSS), and aims to include all expatriates working in the public and private sectors, according to senior government officials. As it stands, pensions in the private sector are provided through an end-of-service payment (gratuity) relative to the employee's length of service calculated on the basis of basic salary. A whole raft of proposals covers all expats in the country's public or private sectors. The study includes various pension proposals and mechanisms including the collection of the pension amount by an entity other than the employers, through monthly subscriptions to be cut from their salaries. So far, feedback from the expat community has been positive, although some concerns remain regarding the implementation of a mandatory pension system.

Shopping

Dubai's soaring tourism figures are driven largely by its readiness to introduce initiatives to continually bolster visitor attractions. One of the most famous is the **Dubai Shopping Festival**, an annual month-long event that attracts around three million visitors and generates a total spend of in excess of US$160 million. During the festival, dozens of stores and boutiques offer special discounts, deals and offers on a wide range of goods, from top designer clothing brands to the latest gadgets, cars and electronics. Almost every price is slashed, be it couture from Paris or Milan, hi-tech electronics from Japan or a piece of silver Bedouin jewellery – with a host of catwalk shows and special events that pull in crowds.

No Dubai shopping experience is complete without sampling the hubbub of the city's souks, where old market traditions and haggling bazaar traders ensure plenty of colour and bustle. Traditionally, Dubai is renowned for its gold, jewellery, carpets, perfumes, copper coffeepots, textiles, spices and pearls as well as local handicrafts and fragrances at the **Gold Souk**, **Perfume Souk** and **Spice Souk** – each well worth a visit. Visit **www.dubaigoldsouk.com**.

The Spice is Right

As a region, the Arabian Gulf is rich in spice trade history with an Indo-Arabic spice trade route many centuries old. Today, Dubai remains an important spice hub and boasts an incredible spice souk, where an exotic rainbow of seasonings deluges every sensory organ from ramshackle huts and stalls. The Dubai Spice Souk is the market for fresh Arabic spices and is a cornucopia of rich fragrances and heady aromas: cloves, cardamom, cinnamon, chillies, saffron, cumin, garam masala, coriander, incense, dried fruit and nuts, imported from all over the Middle East. Piled high in large open sacks, the spices spill out over the pavement to form a colourful, painterly splurge.

Dubai's massive influx of migrant workers from all corners of the globe has added numerous Asian, Indian and African ingredients and spices to the mix. Oriental supermarkets now stock five-spice blends, miso and coconut paste alongside traditional Arab seasonings.

Shopping Malls

In recent years, tourism chiefs have bolstered the city's shopper's paradise claims by adding new malls and shopping centres. Today Dubai's 50-plus retail zones offer consumers an incredible array of items at highly attractive tax-free prices. Some items are better value than others so it pays to shop around, especially for handbags, sunglasses and designer shoes. Commercial areas, such as the **Central District**, **Dubai Gates** and the **Forbidden City**, have attracted an impressive range of international investors, traders and retailers.

Dubai Duty Free (www.dubaidutyfree.com) opened for business on December 20th 1983 and achieved first full year sales of US$20 million. In 2007, sales reached US$880 million and had recorded an average of 52,000 sales transactions per day. In addition to being an innovative retail operator, Dubai Duty Free also runs promotions, such as the Finest Surprise Luxury Car draw and the Millennium Millionaire. Dubai Duty Free has won many industry awards, and in April 2000 opened a huge state-of-the-art shopping complex at the centre of the Dubai International Airport's Sheikh Rashid Terminal.

The 50-hectare **Dragon Mart** (www.dragonmart.ae) opened in International City in December 2004 and is built to a colourful dragon design along a 1.4km-long central spine. The dragon's head serves as the main entrance, which is accessible from the Dubai-Hatta road. With 2,000 parking spaces, it serves as a showcase for over 3,000 Chinese companies selling artefacts, clothing and food, and is adorned with lanterns.

One of Dubai's major shopping draws is **Deira City Centre** (www.deiracity centre.com), a central retail hub that boasts around 280 outlets plus numerous big-name restaurant chains. Part of the complex is a huge cinema and entertainment centre, so it's a great place for a family trip keen to turn shopping into a day out. An AED 60 million revamp added 10 extra food outlets to an already massive food court to offer even more culinary choice, from Arab staples such as falafel to exotic Japanese sushi, Thai curries and even English fish 'n' chips.

Part of the biggest urban development in the Middle East, the **Dubai Mall** (**www.thedubaimall.com**) boasts the world's largest shopping and entertainment centres adjoining the tallest building on the planet, Burj Dubai. The Mall opened in the summer of 2008 and features a gold souk, a collection of sophisticated retail outlets and leisure facilities, such as an ice-skating rink, adventure sports and an aquarium. Landscaped gardens and parklands surround the mall, while over 16,000 parking spaces cater for around five million visitors per annum. More than 1,000 stores are sited within over a dozen retail areas.

Dubai's **Mall of the Emirates** (**www.malloftheemirates.com**) also breaks records on a number of levels: it is the largest mall in the world outside North America, plus it includes the largest indoor family entertainment centre in the country and the largest indoor ski dome in the world. There are also two hotels, including a Kempinski, the Dubai Community Arts and Theatre with a 500-seat

Haggling

Haggling is an integral part of Dubai's traditional local culture, where barter has been part-and-parcel of trading since ancient times. For outsiders unused to the rigours of serious negotiation, the prospect of haggling can be daunting. Bartering is time-consuming, requires patience and can be a little embarrassing. However, those prepared to give it a go will also discover that is also a great game to be played, for, in Dubai, it is imperative to remain mindful that the price tag is always grossly inflated – unless, that is, you're in a Carrefour supermarket or McDonald's. It is hardly surprising that some of the most successful barterers on the planet can be found in Dubai's maze of shops and side-street markets. The best have a single focus – to snap up a good deal. They are well aware that the seller doesn't make any money if he makes no sale.

So, what should the buyer do first? Well, to start, try to establish the seller's lowest selling price. This will, of course, coincide with the seller's goal of ascertaining the highest price you're prepared to pay. It also helps if you know the real value of the item – once you are armed with this knowledge you can launch a major assault. It may also help to pooh-pooh the merchandise, especially if there is better quality or greater choice in the immediate vicinity. After all, what is stopping you from buying from the competition? Successful bartering may require both parties to bat prices back and forward over time for upwards of an hour. Buyers with time on their side should go through the full negotiation process and arrive at a price – then leave without flinching. This makes the seller think he has lost you after expending lots of effort on courting your interest. As you disappear out of the door, he may dwell on this lost sale and lament the fact that he didn't clinch the deal. When you eventually return to snap up a bargain, don't be surprised if an extra five per cent is forthcoming.

theatre and art gallery, two mosques and over 70 restaurants. Then there are the shops, of course. Almost every major global brand can be found in the 400 outlets; the largest shops in terms of space include Debenhams, Harvey Nichols, Carrefour and Virgin Megastore. Some well-known designers include: H&M, Guess, Zara, Pepe Jeans, Lacoste and Tommy Hilfiger. A swish Rodeo Drive offers the more exclusive brands, such as DKNY, Ralph Lauren, Burberry and Dolce and Gabbana. A highlight is the mall's indoor ski dome, the largest of its kind, featuring real snow and chair lifts to the top. Other features are a 14-screen cinema, a huge arcade area (Magic Planet) and a food court.

A brand new interchange leads to the **Ibn Battuta Mall (www.ibnbattuta mall.com)**, a project that boasts a 16-outlet sector and food court, retail zoning, and a huge 21-screen Megaplex, including the UAE's first IMAX theatre (21 screens). Since it opened in April 2005, this building – designed to reflect the travels of Arabian adventurer Ibn Battuta – has attracted hundreds of thousands of visitors. Ibn Battuta's 75,000-mile voyage led him on many dangerous and thrilling adventures as he journeyed through Andalusia, Tunisia, Egypt, Persia, India and China – and the main geographical themes of these six regions are very much in evidence in the six distinct shopping areas found at the mall. Wear a pair of comfortable shoes to journey under beautifully decorated ceilings past exotic sculpture, boats and mini displays. More than ten car parks serve this vast shopping extravaganza.

There is something distinctly Manhattan-esque about the ultra-stylish **Dubai Outlet Mall (www.dubaioutletmall.com)**, the first 'outlet' concept in the Middle East. Here, shoppers can make big savings on premium and top fashion brands via year-round special promotions in a setting that boasts a stunning white minimalist décor. Located in Dubailand on Route 66 (Dubai–Al Ain Highway), the mall is home to over 800 of the world's premium and top fashion brands; discounts of between 30 and 90 per cent are commonplace in over 240 stores.

Other malls and shopping centres include:

- **Bur Juman Centre, t** 352 0222.
- **Gold Land, t** 226 2901.
- **Gold & Diamond Park, t** 347 7788.
- **Jumeirah Plaza, t** 349 7111.
- **Lamcy Plaza, t** 335 9999.
- **Mercato, t** 344 4161.
- **Palm Strip Shopping Mall, t** 346 1462.
- **The Beach Centre, t** 344 9045.
- **The Gold Centre, t** 226 5011.
- **The Mall, Crowne Plaza, t** 331 7755.
- **Twin Towers, t** 221 8833.
- **Wafi Shopping Mall, t** 324 4555.

Groceries and Food

Just a few years ago, expatriate residents were served solely by small local supermarkets, fish stalls and food markets. Today they are spoilt for choice by mega-grocery stores and hypermarkets that stock an array of global brands. In theory, local shops offer colour, excitement and exotic regional produce. In practice, only the most adventurous expatriate forgoes the convenience of supermarket shopping for haggling in the heat.

Every one of Dubai's large grocery stores offers frozen, fresh, canned and dried foodstuffs along with delicatessens, bakeries, flower stalls, stationery aisles, electronics and clothing – all under one roof. Given the ordeal of finding a parking space in traffic, these supermarkets also provide the ease of expansive car parks. Many are also open 24 hours a day.

There is just one noticeable absence on the shelves: **alcohol**. Apart from a shop in the arrivals hall of the airport, only two retailers are licensed to sell alcohol across 17 special outlets in Dubai. A&E (African & Eastern) and MMI (Maritime Mecantile International) are names well-known to Dubai expatriates, as these are the companies that operate the city's 'bottle shops'. Most are located next to supermarkets frequented by non-Muslims and are typically innocuous-looking doorways without shop-fronts or window displays. Hours vary, depending on the branch, with some remaining open throughout Ramadan. An alcohol licence is required to purchase even the smallest quantity – simply fill out a form in the outlet (non-Muslims only, over-21s only) and provide proof of residency, income and status. Every application is subject to police validation and is allocated a specified monthly allowance of alcohol. Other goods that are considered to contravene Islamic teachings are also permitted but are subject to a '*haraam*' tax (meaning forbidden). It runs at 30 per cent, so hikes the cost considerably for several items regularly consumed by non-Muslims, such as pork products (bacon, sausages and ham) as well as alcohol.

Price fluctuations occur frequently in Dubai for a number of reasons, notably: price-setting by government associations, seasonal ebbs and flows, oversupply of goods and the strength of the dollar (because the UAE dirham is tied to the US dollar). Political disputes can also cause certain products to be banned (as in the case of Danish-made items after the dispute about cartoons). Dubai is also heavily reliant on the flow of imported goods to the UAE and is therefore particularly vulnerable to shortages and shipment delays.

Some of the most popular supermarkets in Dubai include the following:

- Geant Hypermarket, **www.geant-uae.com.**
- Al Maya, **www.almayagroup.com.**
- Spinneys, **www.spinneys.co.ae.**
- Carrefour UAE, **www.carrefouruae.com.**
- Union Cooperative, **www.ucs.ae.**

- Majid Al Futtaim, **www.majidalfuttaim.com**.
- Lulu Hypermart, **www.luluhypermarket.com**.

Since 2004 **Waitrose** own brands have been sold in Spinneys supermarkets. In 2008, Waitrose opened three supermarkets in Dubai aimed squarely at the British and European expatriate community, its first foray abroad. By 2010, Waitrose plans to open more than 20 stores in the city.

Dubai also has a decent scattering of **7-Elevens** and convenience stores that open early till late or 24 hours. In a bid to compete with the new, larger outlets, many offer free home delivery and credit, helping them to retain local custom.

Everyday Clothing

Well-known British brands in Dubai include **Marks and Spencer**, with nine stores in the UAE, including at Dubai Festival City, Deira, Wafi City Mall Dubai, Sharjah, Abu Dhabi, Bahrain, Kuwait, Qatar, & Muscat. Stores boast a wide range of products including ladieswear, menswear, kidswear, lingerie, beauty, home products and food. Dubai also has its own branches of **Next** and **Debenhams**, with a **Harrods** rumoured to be opening in 2010.

Transport and Infrastructure

Dubai's government has spared no cost in putting in place the infrastructure necessary to accommodate its economic vision. In 2006, it announced a 15-year plan of infrastructure investment of US$130 billion, from brand new multi-lane highways and bridges to state-of-the-art airports and super-fast metro lines. To consolidate its role as a trading and tourist hub and global gateway to the region, Dubai has made a number of large-scale investments. According to a 2007 report by Lehman Brothers, more than 2,000 infrastructure projects are under way in GCC countries, with the core of the estimated US$1.3 trillion earmarked for projects between 2007 and 2012 in Dubai and Abu Dhabi.

In a move to assist pedestrians with special needs, Dubai has announced the introduction of wide-ranging disability aids, including wheelchair-adapted public transport, bleeping street lights, taxis with respirator equipment and specially equipped elevators.

Cars

For most Dubai expatriates, owning a car is essential for getting from A to B. Although the municipality is making positive strives in improving public transport to ease car traffic, these have yet to take effect. So, until the metro is completed in 2010 and the bus system upgraded to temper overcrowding, driving remains the most popular mode of transport – the reason there are over 600,000 private vehicles on the road.

Since 1964, Dubai's road system has grown from just 200km to 9,100km in 2004. Today's 3.1 million daily car journeys are expected to top 13 million by 2020. In readiness, Dubai Municipality has implemented several schemes aimed at lessening traffic congestion including a US$1.9 billion injection of funds into road infrastructure. The goal is to increase public transport use to 30 per cent of commuters from the current 5 per cent over the next 15 years.

Although petrol costs are rising rapidly, fuel remains much cheaper than in other countries, so gas-guzzling SUVs are very much the rage. Gridlocked streets and maniac drivers are a major annoyance for people attempting to cross Dubai during rush hour, so be prepared for lots of unexpected switching of lanes, tooting of horns, sudden stops and terrifying U-turns. In April 2007, the International Association for Human Values (IAHV) formally launched an initiative titled 'Road Alertness Programme' to help reduce accidents on Dubai's busy roads. An initiative by the Dubai Police Traffic Department and Dubai's Road Traffic Authority looks set to lead to better road-crossing facilities for pedestrians, including more crossing points with pedestrian bridges and tunnels. Traffic speed control measures have also been earmarked for implementation by 2009. **Parking** in the city is also under strain, with Dubai's limited spots highly prized and metered.

Drivers should be warned that the police operate a strict zero tolerance policy towards **drinking and driving** – with stiff penalties for those who break the law, including deportation and heavy fines. Should you be involved in a **fatal** accident that is your fault due to drinking, you'll need to pay blood money to the family of the deceased under current UAE law. This stands at AED 200,000. Drivers caught **parking illegally** or using a vehicle without proper **licences** will also incur a fine, unless the state decides imprisonment is more apt. Fines for **speeding** run at around AED 200, while **skipping a red light** will set you back AED 500 – plus a week-long suspension. On a second offence, your car will be confiscated and you may lose your licence. Dangerous driving will also result in a court appearance.

- Dubai Traffic Police, **www.dxbtraffic.gov.ae**.
- Road and Transport Authority, **www.rta.ae**.
- Dubai Municipality, **www.dm.gov.ae**.

Buying a Car

Only people with a residence permit are able to purchase a car, from one of Dubai's many swish dealerships or in the thriving second-hand market. Big American and Japanese brands are particular sought-after, and numerous dazzling showrooms cater well for this market. Cars are relatively low-priced in

Dubai which, coupled with lower fuel costs and maintenance bills, means expatriates are often tempted to splurge on a vehicle they'd be unable to afford at home. Check out the classified adverts in both the *Gulf News* and the *Khaleej Times* for the best car deals, especially second-hand.

Most of the banks and many of the dealerships can organise vehicle **finance**. Once you've bought your car, the dealership will also guide you through the **registration** process. You'll need **insurance** – budget for around 4–7 per cent of the value of the vehicle.

New Car Dealers

- Gargash Motors (Alfa Romeo, Saab), **t** 266 4669, **www.gargashmotors.com**.
- Al Habtoor Motors (Aston Martin, Bentley, Audi), **t** 269 1110, **www.habtoormotors.com**.
- AGMC (BMW, Rolls Royce), **t** 339 1555, **www.bmw-dubai.com**.
- Liberty Automobiles (Hummer), **t** 282 4440, **www.liberty.ae**.
- Al Yousuf Motors (Chevrolet), **t** 339 1555, **www.ayme.ae**.
- Al Tayer (Lincoln, Mercury), **t** 266 6489, **www.altayer.com**.
- Al Naboodah Automobiles (Porsche), **t** 338 6999, **www.naboodah-auto.com**.

Used Car Dealers

- 4x4 Motors, **t** 282 3050, **www.4x4motors.com**.
- Auto Plus, **t** 339 5400, **www.autoplusdubai.com**.
- House of Cars, **t** 343 5060, **www.houseofcarsgroup.com**.
- Off Road Motors, **t** 338 4866, **www.offroad-motors.com**.
- Target Auto, **t** 343 3911, **www.target-auto.com**.

Car Hire

Several companies offer long- and short-term leasing options, from a day or week to monthly or annual hire. Costs include repairs, re-registration and servicing as well as 24-hour assistance and insurance. Prices range from AED 1,500 for a small run-around for a month to around AED 5,000 for a top-of-the-range SUV.

- Autolease Rent-a-Car, **t** 282 6565, **www.autolease-uae.com**.
- Avis, **t** 295 7121, **www.avisuae.com**.
- Diamond Lease, **t** 343 4330, **www.diamondlease.com**.
- FAST Rent-A-Car, **t** 332 8988, **www.fastuae.com**.
- Thrifty Car Rental, **t** 800 4694, **www.thriftyuae.com**.

Buses

Public transport continues to grow at a rate of 20 per cent per annum, with 419 buses facilitating more than 90 million journeys. In 2007, over 87.8 million bus passengers travelled the city-state – up almost three million since 2005. More than 60 bus companies run routes through Dubai's residential and commercial districts. However, while being frequent and air-conditioned, buses are still crowded and often slow as a result.

Dubai's Roads and Transport Authority (RTA) has announced a doubling of the number of buses to around 1,200 to better serve all areas of the city. These will include double-decker vehicles and so-called bendy buses that carry greater passenger numbers. The aim is to increase bus usage to around 30 per cent of commuters, an ambitious 24 per cent rise on current figures. To add greater incentive, Dubai has sanctioned the construction of 800 air-conditioned bus shelters, which also include ATMs and vending machines. An initial roll-out of a couple of hundred shelters will take place by 2009 ahead of the introduction of 1,500 hi-tech buses by 2010.

- **Dubai Roads and Transport Authority, www.rta.ae.**

Taxis

Taxis are an easy way to nip across the city. More than 6,000 metered taxis come under the control of the **Dubai Transport Corporation**. All are operated by English-speaking drivers on a fixed fare structure as part of seven separate companies. Over 99 per cent are beige-coloured, with different coloured roofs: **Cars Taxis** (blue), **Hatta Taxis** (gold), **Metro Taxis** (brown), **City Taxis** (white), **Dubai Taxis** (red), **El Arabia** (green) and **National Taxis** (yellow). All have the same company insignia and are individually numbered.

In 2007, a fleet of 50 **pink cabs** was launched for the exclusive use of female passengers, driven by an all-women team. In addition, three firms are permitted to operate on a non-metered basis – **Dubai Taxi**, **Khalibar Taxi** and **Palestine Taxi**. For these you'll need to negotiate a price before embarking on a journey.

Expect to pay between 3 and 7 dirhams for a cross-town trip, depending on whether you call in the cab, or pick it up, and the length of the journey. Taxis can be flagged down on the street or ordered over the phone using a central number, **t** 208 0808. This highly sophisticated call centre stores customer details in an automated system so, after you've called once, it is possible to book a cab via the telephone keypad. There are also electronic booking machines dotted around town – simply drop a 1 dirham coin into the slot.

Drivers are obliged to accept any fare regardless of distance. However, beware of the taxi driver who is a new arrival to the country with absolutely no local knowledge – a common occurrence in fast-growing Dubai. In the event that your driver gets totally lost, insist that he calls in for assistance.

- Dubai Taxi Authority, **www.dtc.dubai.ae**.
- Dubai Transport Corporation, **www.dubaitransport.gov.ae**.

Crossing Dubai Creek: Water Taxis, Water Buses, Bridges and Tunnels

At the Dubai Creek, a network of **water taxis** – called *abras* – make 15 million trips per annum. In 2007, air-conditioned **water buses** were introduced to passengers traversing the Dubai Creek. The new service will use glass-walled catamarans with seating for 35 passengers, with a 6am–midnight service running every 10 minutes. Dubai's integrated transportation think-tank continues to anticipate significant growth over the next 15 years.

Significant investment is under way to build better **bridges** across Dubai Creek, including a recently opened US$53.6 million third bridge and a twelve-lane fourth bridge at Ras Al Khor. In June 2006, Dubai's Roads and Transport Authority announced two more 12-lane bridges across the creek. One bridge will sport a 100-metre-high tower offering a panoramic view of the city. The Al Shindagha Bridge will be shaped to resemble a majestic gate.

In September 2005, it was announced that a US54.5 million contract had been awarded for the 13.1km extension of Dubai Creek, which will require the removal of six million cubic metres of earth and will ease the congestion of water traffic in the area. It will be 500 metres wide and six metres deep, and will accommo-date pleasure yachts of up to 60 metres in length. Seven air-conditioned pedestrian bridges have also been constructed at various locations. A **tunnel** leading under the Dubai International Financial Centre – designed to be used by service vehicles – should also help to ease congestion in the area. In 2005, Australian-based Maunsel Consultancy was rumoured to have partnered with Dubai Municipality on a proposal to start a fast public water taxi service between Dubai and Sharjah. The proposed route runs between Sharjah and The Palm, Jebel Ali via The Palm, Deira, Dubai Creek and The Palm, Jumeirah.

- **Dubai Roads and Transport Authority, www.rta.ae**.

Metro and Trains

Dubai's eagerly awaited **metro** system will be one of the world's most advanced urban rail systems and is poised to be a catalyst for further tourism, financial and economic growth. In May 2005, a US$4.2 billion contract was signed with **Dubai Rail Link (DURL)**, a consortium of five companies – Japan's Mitsubishi Heavy Industries, Mitsubishi Corporation, Obayashi Corporation, Kajima Corporation and Yapi Markezi of Turkey – to build a high-tech driverless rail transit system. This milestone in the city's history will not only serve as a key connector but will also ease road traffic congestion. Park and ride facilities near terminals and at strategic locations across the city will also promote the ease of its use. The two-phase project will comprise a **Red Line** along Sheikh Zayed Road, on a viaduct, and a **Green Line** built mostly underground. The Red Line (Phase I) is marked for completion in 2009 while the Green Line (Phase II) is scheduled to open in mid-2010. A third, 47km section will provide links to Dubai International Airport and the new airport at Jebel Ali. When completed, Dubai Metro will have a total of 70km of lines, and 42 stations (including 9 underground) and will take an estimated 12 per cent of all the journeys made throughout Dubai.

Reports by *Gulf News* suggest the UAE is also considering blueprints for a 700km-long nationwide **rail network** that would link Abu Dhabi with Dubai, Sharjah, Ras Al Khaimah and Fujairah in the east and with Ruwais and Ghowaifait in the west. The first phase would be for a cargo and container network followed by a passenger project in the second phase.

- **Dubai Metro, www.dubaimetro.eu.**

Crime and the Police

Dubai's low crime rate doesn't negate the need for a healthy degree of caution, especially in crowded streets or beaches. Be aware of your surroundings at all times and never be lax when carrying valuables. Make sure your wallet is safe and take care not to flaunt large amounts of cash to all and sundry. Put anything non-essential and valuable in a secure place well away prying eyes.

Most tourist-related police incidents involve the overconsumption of alcohol or being drunk and disorderly in public – both strict no-nos in Dubai and punishable by prison terms (*see* box). Generally speaking the police apply a tolerant approach and allow everyone a second chance. But be warned, you're unlikely to be treated with any leniency should you attract police attention a second time – so expect the full force of law to bear down.

Dubai's **police force** was established on June 1st, 1956 in Naif Fort, which still operates as a police station. In 1973 the Dubai Police Headquarters moved to its present location in Al Towar area on Al Etihad Street. It was the first Arab police force to apply, DNA testing in criminal investigations, the first to use electronic finger printing, and the first Arab department to implement the 'paperless department' concept. It was also a pioneer in the region in community policing and was the first Arab police force to establish a department devoted to human rights. Numerous **police stations** provide good Dubai-wide coverage, with key contacts listed below.

- **Port Police Station, t 345 9999.**
- **Al Qusais Police Station, t 263 1111.**
- **Hatta Police Station, t 852 1111.**

Know Before You Go

Dubai manages what many other Arab cities fail to achieve: a healthy balance between Western influence and Eastern tradition. However, don't be fooled by its open-minded liberal gloss – Dubai's culture is still very much rooted in Islamic traditions. To forget this is to foolishly disregard the centuries-old beliefs that penetrate the Arabian Peninsula and beyond. Yes, Dubai is a visionary city with a cosmopolitan character, but what it is not is Ibiza or Rio de Janeiro. That it chooses to turn a blind eye to some Western high jinks is purely its prerogative, not a given. Ignore Muslim sensibilities, conventions and laws at your peril – as several Westerners have discovered to their cost.

In February 2008, a Briton was arrested at Dubai International Airport after 0.003g cannabis was found trodden into the sole of his shoe. Keith Andrew Brown was stopped in transit from Ethiopia to London last September. The amount of the drug found on his shoe would not be visible to the naked eye and weighed less than a single grain of sugar. It didn't matter that Brown was not, by Western standards, 'in possession'. That he had drugs about him, almost certainly unwittingly, resulted in his receiving a four-year prison term.

In July 2008, a British couple were arrested after being found drunk and partially clothed apparently having sex on the beach. The couple had been drinking heavily all afternoon at one of Dubai's legendary Friday brunches, where free-flowing champagne is consumed in abundance by a hedonistic Western expatriate crowd. Sex outside marriage is illegal in the UAE, as is being drunk in public, while being immodestly dressed contravenes Dubai's moral code. Michelle Palmer and Vince Accors both face charges of indecent behaviour in public and being drunk in public. Palmer is also likely to be charged with assaulting a police officer, as she tried to hit the arresting officer with her high-heeled shoe before being restrained and taken to a cell. She has already been axed from her highly paid publishing job in Dubai. The couple face up to six years in jail and a hefty fine.

In 2006, the British government launched the **Know Before You Go (KBYG)** campaign for travellers. The aim is to make British visitors to foreign nations aware of local customs and legalities to better prepare them for travel. A strong emphasis is placed on minimising the likelihood of falling foul of the law. In-depth advice is available for every country in the world, updated regularly for all British travellers, from travelling during Ramadan to local customs and traditions and what do to should things go wrong. Visit the British Foreign Office and Commonwealth Office website on **www.fco.gov.uk**.

- Al Rashidiya Police Station, **t** 285 3000.
- Naif Police Station, **t** 228 6999.
- Al Muraqqabat Police Station, **t** 266 0555.
- Jebel Ali Police Station, **t** 881 6111.

- Al Rafa'a Police Station, **t** 393 7777.
- Bur Dubai Police Station, **t** 398 1111.
- Nad Al Sheba Police Station, **t** 336 3535.
- Air Wing Center, **t** 224 4222.
- Al Hamriya Police Sub-station, **t** 266 7306.
- Al Hibbab Police Sub-station, **t** 832 1333.
- Al Faqa Police Sub-station, **t** 03 733 1133.
- Rashid Hospital Police Sub-station, **t** 337 4600.

The government has recently also set up a **Department for Tourist Security**, **t** 800 4438, **www.dubaipolice.gov.ae**. Staffed by multilingual police liaison officers, the force is both approachable and informative. It will handle any tourist-related enquiry, from complaints about rowdy beach behaviour and lost passports to suspicious packages and problems with sexual harassment. To report specific problems on the **beach** there is a hotline: **t** 203 6398.

As in the UK, the **emergency** number for the police is **t** 999 (also for ambulance calls). Fire services can be contacted on **t** 997, as can civil defence forces. Dubai Police also guarantee that in an emergency a police helicopter will be with you within 8 minutes using 999.

UAE Police Headquarters

Abu Dhabi, **t** 02 446 1461.

Dubai, **t** 04 229 2222.

Sharjah, **t** 06 563 1111.

Ajman, **t** 06 743 6000.

Umm Al Quwain, **t** 06 565 6662.

Ras Al Khaimah, **t** 07 233 3888.

Fujairah, **t** 09 237 0000.

Education

Dubai has a wide range of schools to cater for all ages, nationalities and abilities, with private education facilities that are world-class. However, places are extremely sought-after, as the expatriate population continues to burgeon. Increasingly, parents in the emirate report their sheer frustration at Dubai's seemingly impenetrable waiting lists. They also tell of élitist cherry-picking of students based on status, which, combined with 'it's who you know' queue-jumping, can leave many children out in the cold. Fees are payable each time you even apply for a place and join a waiting list, and these costs can mount up when you've several children, or have scattered your net wide in search of a

Case Study: Marc Lawn

'A couple of months ago I accepted the best job opportunity of my life. Today I work with one of the most exciting companies in the world, in a very diverse nation with great prospects, superb weather and a salary that is tax-free. My new employers have been very generous and helpful with relocation budgets and advice. Lower fuel costs have had a positive effect on various elements of the household budget, from the obvious running costs and petrol prices to air-conditioning. Is there a downside? Yes: moving out here with two school-age children has been a nightmare.

'Every school we've approached has an extended waiting list, with some flatly refusing to add more names as they are already so over-subscribed. Others have asked us to reapply in 12 months' time – but just to add a child to a waiting list is £80 per school and that's with no guarantee of successfully obtaining a place. What's unbelievable too is the level of bureaucracy: each school requires a form to be completed that ranges in size from 2 to 17 pages. Each form requires 6 photos of each child, copies of birth certificates and school reports - and that's before they sit an entrance exam at an additional fee of around another £80! Imagine how much this starts to add up when you're approaching 10 schools per child. It really is a parent's worst nightmare, and we've even wondered if it would be easier for the family to split up for twelve months. We're not sure if a home tutor is allowed for schooling in Dubai but, even if we can home-school, the skills shortage across most professional services may make it prohibitively expensive – even if we're able to find someone suitably qualified, in time for the new academic year.

'So, it's a problem that has been more difficult to resolve than I'd expected. For me it won't be a deal-breaker as we'll find a way around it, whether that's being creative with resources or simply deferring my family's relocation for a year while I settle in and sort it out. We're determined to work things out as, other than this, the experience here has been highly positive. However, those thinking of relocating to Dubai with children should be aware that schooling is a major issue – and a major cause of stress.'

school. In 2003, **Knowledge Village** (**www.kv.ae**) was established in Dubai as a hub for learning and training. Today, it has placed the emirate on the map as a destination for learning excellence via a 1km campus of knowledge-based establishments, from school campuses, training centres and learning support.

Generally speaking, you get what you pay for in Dubai when it comes to education, be it kindergarten, primary school, secondary school or high school – or beyond. Almost every **private school** in Dubai offers mixed classes of students from a variety of foreign countries and cultures, although some, of course, are predominantly one nationality. There are American and British curriculum schools and also Arabic, Australian, French, German, Indian, Iranian, Japanese and Russian curriculum-taught classes. You'll need to look beyond the name of the school to establish the content of the curriculum, as many of those with Arabic names operate along English lines – and vice versa.

Theoretically, foreign students are allowed to enrol at **public schools** in the UAE. However, as the qualifications are not recognised in non-Arab nations, few take this route – despite fees of a very reasonable AED 6,000 per year.

Dubai's education system comprises a mix of schools that insist on uniforms and those that don't. A typical school day runs from 7am or 8am to 2pm or 3pm with a standard lunch break. Kindergartens and primary schools usually finish at lunchtime. Almost every academic establishment offers a wide array of extracurricular activities that run into the late afternoon.

Strictly speaking, the UAE Ministry of Education requirements are that students should be segregated according to gender, with teachers the same gender as the class. However, most schools following a Western curriculum run mixed classes. Non-Western curriculum schools usually have two shifts, with girls attending in the mornings and boys attending in the afternoons.

Parental involvement is welcomed in some of the well-established non-profit organisations with active Parent-Teacher Associations. These schools also seem to offer the largest selection of extracurricular activities to students, such as rugby, swimming, Arabic lessons, horse-riding, football and tennis.

To **register** a child, be it a nursery, school or college, you'll need to check with each individual school for specific requirements, as each varies. Generally speaking, the following will be necessary:

- **Passport copies with a valid residence permit.**
- **Birth certificate copies (sometimes with Arabic translation).**
- **8 passport photographs.**
- **Health card (or evidence of medical insurance).**
- **Vaccination card or immunisation record.**
- **School reports from previous schooling.**
- **Letter of recommendation from previous school.**
- **Original transfer certificate from previous school.**
- **Evidence of successful completion of any entrance tests/exams and personal interviews.**

Pre-schooling and Kindergarten

Costs for nurseries in Dubai run to around AED 12,000 per annum for about 4½ hours per day. Children as young as three months are accepted at some kindergartens, although most will stipulate a minimum age of a year. Waiting lists are long, so be prepared to register a child before it has been born in the most popular establishments. Costs run from AED 3,000 to AED 12,000. Some

Case Study: Mark Beer

'I moved to Dubai with my wife, Adriana, in September 1997, when Dubai was still largely unknown. I flew here before accepting the job, with law firm Clyde & Co., and knew, the minute I stepped off the plane, that this was some place. The vision was clear and you could sense the potential immediately – it had a dynamic buzz even then.

'We were in Dubai for four years before we decided to take a break, to Switzerland, to start a family. In terms of taxes and temperatures, we thought Switzerland was a good halfway house between the UAE and the UK. Looking back on it, I think we were still trying to work out in our own minds if Dubai was a mirage or an oasis. We moved back to Dubai soon after our first child, Elena, was born in 2002. We realised that nowhere in the world was better suited to raising children – and since then our family unit has grown and grown. Elena now has three younger brothers, George, 4, Henry, 3, and William, 2 months, and our love for Dubai and the UAE just gets stronger and stronger. In business terms, I am lucky enough to work in the fastest-growing economy in the world, with access to the most exciting high growth markets. As the chairman and CEO of the British Business Group (BBG) – the largest and most active business group in the region – I get to help companies and individuals, with a connection to the UK, get established in Dubai, network and share knowledge. Dubai truly is also an extraordinarily innovative and fast-moving hub, perfectly situated between East and West. We live a wonderful life on good levels of disposable income free from tax, while our children benefit from a first-class education. Weekends are spent as a family camping in Oman, relaxing by the beach or soaking up the atmosphere in the unrivalled spice and gold souks by Dubai's historic creek. Life is a constant adventure.'

nurseries open early and offer breakfast and lunch, while others run summer schools for an extra fee.

- Al Safa Nurseries, t 344 3878, **www.safanurseries.com**.
- Cocoon Nursery, t 394 9394.
- Baby Land Montessori, t 348 6874, **www.babyland.com**.
- Emirates British Nursery, t 348 9996, **www.ebninfo.ae**.
- Kids Cottage Nursery School, t 394 2145, **www.kids-cottage.com**.
- Superkids Nursery, t 288 1949, **www.superkids-nursery.com**.
- Tender Love and Care, t 367 1636, **www.tenderloveandcare.com**.

Primary and Secondary Schools

Children are eligible for primary schooling aged 4½–11 years, while secondary schooling is from 11 years to 18 years. Although the usual application system applies for all students, an **entrance exam** is increasingly common. Schools may also insist on a physical examination and interview.

Most national curriculum syllabuses can be found, from GCSEs and A-levels to the International Baccalaureate. Budget for AED 10,000–30,000 annually for primary schooling, with secondary education likely to cost AED 12,000–60,000 – plus excursion costs, registration and uniform fees.

- American School of Dubai, **t** 344 0824, **www.asdubai.org.**
- Australian International School, **t** 558 9967, **www.ais.ae.**
- Cambridge International School, **t** 282 4646, **www.gemscis-garhoud.com.**
- Dubai British School, **t** 3619 361, **www.dubaibritishschool.ae.**
- Dubai English Speaking School, **t** 337 1457, **www.desdxb.com.**
- Dubai International Academy, **t** 232 5552, **www.disdubai.ae.**
- The English College, **t** 394 3465, **www.englishcollege.ac.ae.**
- Kings' Dubai, **t** 348 3939, **www.kingsdubai.com.**
- Royal Dubai School, **t** 288 6499, **www.royaldubaischool.com.**
- Universal American School Dubai, **t** 232 5222, **www.usadubaiae.com.**
- Westminster School, **t** 298 8333, **www.gemsws-ghusais.com.**

Special Needs

Many of Dubai's mainstream schools have dedicated departments created for children with special needs, such as ADHD and dyslexia. Specialist schools in the city are almost all funded by charitable donations and charge annual fees.

- Al Noor Centre, **t** 394 6088, **www.alnooruae.org.**
- Dubai Centre for Special Needs, **t** 344 0966, **www.dcsneeds.ae.**
- Rashid Paediatric Therapy Centre, **t** 340 0005, **www.rashidc.ae.**

University and Higher Education

Although many expatriate students choose to study at colleges and university in their homeland, a growing number of Dubai educational facilities are offering higher education. Degree and diploma courses tend to focus on management, engineering, business, science and the arts, and are based in Knowledge Village, where there are also a number of postgraduate courses.

- American University, **t** 399 9000, **www.centamed.com.**
- British University, **t** 391 3626, **www.buid.ac.ae.**
- University of Wollongong, **t** 367 2400, **www.uowdubai.ac.ae.**

Working in Dubai

09

'If it's good for business, it is good for Dubai'.

A growing number of foreign investors are enjoying the emirate's sophisticated fast-track business initiatives, from its Free Trade Zones and strategic location to its low-cost work environment. Dubai straddles crucial trade routes, offering easy access to European, Asian, African and Middle Eastern markets. Non-Gulf businesses benefit considerably from a base in the region within a culture of commerce that favours trading with a person who is known and trusted. Dubai continues to attract global commerce via unrivalled taxation incentives and cutting edge technology. One hundred per cent ownership is offered in commercial clusters dedicated to technology and media, finance, logistics and healthcare. Internet City, for example, has attracted such big name players as Microsoft, Dell, Siemens, HP, Oracle and IBM, while media giants such as CNN and Reuters have established a presence in Dubai's Media City.

With rising property costs and leasing fees, the Free Zones are not cheap. However in terms of technical infrastructure and the competitive business opportunities they present, they are unrivalled. Those who arrive in Dubai with a firm job offer, or even just a CV in their hand, will find a nation bursting with opportunity for workers prepared to put in the hours. Private sector careers and business start-ups offer the chance of big-earning potential, and Dubai's Western expat labour force delights in its 'work hard, play hard' ethos.

Business Etiquette

In recent years Dubai's business culture has become so diluted by Western influences that many traditional Arab conventions aren't evident in daily life. However, they do still apply – so, if your business involves interaction with executives from the Gulf region, it will pay to take time to understand the practices of local commerce. Trust and respect combined form the bedrock of any Arab business relationship in a region where introductions are everything. Although foreigners are cut plenty of slack when it comes to Arab business conventions, few potential partnerships can survive a serious *faux pas*, however unintentioned. Indeed, few things are more likely to halt a deal than a lack of sensitivity or basic understanding, so it is worth swotting up on what to avoid. Dubai's many multi- cultural workplaces can also throw up a complex mix of office politics, from different communication styles and management practices to a host of social considerations.

The UAE follows a Muslim **working week** of an eight-hour day, five or six days per week. During Ramadan, this is reduced to six hours a day, although many companies only apply this reduction to their Muslim staff. **Friday** is a day of rest in Muslim countries. The majority of companies in Dubai operate a five-day working week; generally speaking, Thursday or Saturday is taken as a second day off (in the style of a weekend). Many international companies close on a Saturday, as being 'open for business Monday–Thursday' allows better synchronisation of working days with other parts of the world. As a day of prayer, Friday should never be scheduled for meetings or phone calls with Muslim colleagues.

During **Ramadan**, the Islamic month of fasting, Muslims are not permitted to eat, drink or smoke between sunrise and sunset. Muslim hospitality allows that non-Muslims may be invited to eat and drink by their hosts. Foreigners are also permitted to consume food and drink as normal during Ramadan; however, great sensitivity is required (and expected). Gatherings should take place strictly away from the public gaze and food eaten discreetly. Even swigging from a bottle of water is considered offensive to those observing Ramadan. Plan ahead to re-hydrate in private in order to show respect for your host nation – and never offer food, snacks, drinks or cigarettes to Muslims in this period.

Siestas are common practice in the fierce heat of summer in Dubai, usually between 2pm and 5pm. Business meetings, appointments and telephone calls should be mindful of the practice. Business resumes after the temperatures begin to cool at around 4pm and can extend to 7pm. During Ramadan the working day is two hours shorter.

Much like the Ancient Greeks before them, Arabs regard the **number seven** as lucky – so for optimum success it could pay to book meeting room 7, on the 7th floor at Dubai's seven-star hotel.

Despite Dubai's reputation as a liberal, modern super-city, it still adheres to an unspoken **dress code** that is both conservative and modest compared to the West. Even in the heat of the summer, business attire in Dubai should be smart and conventional. Those travelling out of the city for a meeting should also take care to cover up – exposed limbs and shoulders are to be avoided.

In a business meeting with an Arab client or colleague, be sure to allow **plenty of time** for unhurried informal chit-chat. This extended preamble is part of parcel of the business portion of the meeting, so don't be tempted to rush it – or, worse still, dispense with it. In comparison, when it comes to deal-making, this can often be resolved in a very short time.

In Arab circles, to **lose face** is to lose everything, so it is important never to criticise or correct a client or colleague in front of someone else. Shy away from all sensitive topics of conversation and remain mindful of courtesy and respect at all times. Never enter into a heated **political or religious debate** with your hosts – even if it is the 'hot topic' of the day.

Always arrange **private meetings** away from the public glare – and keep business dealings private. Even in the most informal of settings, never sit in a way that causes the **soles of your feet** to point directly at anyone – even accidentally. This is considered highly offensive in Arab culture, so if doubt be sure to plant your feet flat on the ground and avoid the Western practice of crossing legs.

Never drink **alcohol** when doing business over lunch or dinner with an Arab, unless it is offered to you by your host.

While a powerful American-style **handshake** is considered masterful and confident, Arabs care little for this 'pressing the flesh'. Arab handshakes are gentle and are followed by a gesture of sincerity: a touching of the heart by the palm of the right hand. Use the polite greeting of 'Mr' (*Sayed*) or 'Mrs' (*Sayeda*) followed by the person's *first* name. Only shake a woman's hand if she offers it to you; to do otherwise will cause offence. It is standard business practice to offer a **business card** to your Arab clients and colleagues: as a mark of respect, have one side of cards translated into Arabic, and pass this face up.

Time-keeping is tricky in Dubai owing to the city's traffic problems. A running joke that the rush hour in Dubai City starts at midnight and ends at 11.59pm isn't that far-fetched – so allow plenty of time to travel to a meeting, as Dubai's volume of traffic can turn a 20-minute journey into a three-hour slog.

The Labour Market

More than 60,000 people per month move to the UAE to take up employment, and an estimated 10 per cent of this influx is bound for Dubai. In 2005, the emirate's workforce stood at 850,000 – a figure forecast to grow to around 1.75 million by 2015 – with just five per cent of Dubai's national workforce registered as looking for work, though this includes a growing number of women.

Dubai's thriving business community is wholly international. Expatriate workers occupy 99 per cent of jobs in the private sector and 91 per cent in the public sector out of a total 3.1 million employees in the UAE, according to the Dubai Municipality. By 2009 UAE nationals are expected to account for fewer than 8 per cent of the workforce, with fewer than 4 per cent predicted by 2020. In 2008, the UAE was ranked as one of the top ten most preferred destinations of workers, according to a survey carried out by Manpower Middle East, an arm of Manpower Inc. The private sector accounts for more than 52 per cent of the total jobs in the UAE, and average salaries rose by 10.7 per cent in 2008.

Manual labour is primarily supplied by workers from South Asia, with more than a million Indians, half a million Pakistanis, Afghanistanis and Bangladeshis bolstering the UAE's workforce. Foreign domestic workers in private households are generally from Thailand, Sri Lanka and the Philippines. Industries such as IT, finance, telecommunications, the media and pharmaceuticals employ a wide range of graduate professional workers from Europe, America and Australia. The country's considerable hydrocarbon wealth allows the public sector to employ a far greater proportion of the native labour force than in many other countries, while the policy of 'emiratisation' demands that many private companies retain a minimum quota of nationals on the payroll.

Dubai's expatriate residents benefit from political stability, a low crime rate and exceptional healthcare facilities. A strong economy, healthy social climate, first-class recruitment market and tax-free status are also pivotal to its appeal with non-UAE nationals. Competitive amounts of leave and tax-free salaries also ensure that blue-collar workers enjoy considerably more disposable income than many other nations – and the time to enjoy it, despite long working hours. However, manual workers are often given no entitlements and afforded little rights in Dubai working culture where conditions are notoriously bad for labourers and domestic servants. In 2007, 39 building workers died on sites, many as a result of falling due to the inadequate provision of slings and ropes. In the months that followed, the Dubai press highlighted the shady dealings of several leading recruitment agencies, whose dubious practices included poor payment and the confiscation of passports. In 2008, the UAE's Ministry of Labour launched a draft labour law and posted it on a government website for comment. Key topics for discussion included employment policies, emiratisation, regulations for the termination of an employment contract, the employment of women, working hours and holidays.

Salaries

Because the UAE has no personal taxation, net income is usually much greater than in other parts of the world – a major appeal of working in Dubai. However, where, in the past, remuneration packages offered 'extras' over and above basic salary, such as a car provision or allowance, housing provision or allowance, medical cover, education for children and air tickets for home visits, today a salary alone is the norm. This then needs to cover all expenses, although some employers do pay a performance-related bonus and car allowance. Bear in mind that Dubai's cost of living is rising (*see* p.148), and a good deal now might not look so attractive in two years' time.

In addition to a salary, contract workers are awarded an '**indemnity**' based on basic salary excluding any bonuses. This is paid at the end of the contract and can amount to a significant amount of money if you've been working in Dubai for a long time. Indemnity scales usually amount to 15 (in some cases 20) days of basic pay per year of employment for the first three years and thereafter a month's salary per year of employment. Any such bonus or 'exit' pay arrangements for permanent staff are agreed on a per-individual basis.

Salary Comparisons

Median Salary by Job

Project manager, construction	AED 307,809
Civil engineer	AED 118,359
Project manager, IT	AED 200,354
Senior software engineer/developer/programmer	AED 116,485
Business development manager	AED 168,076

Median Salary by Years' Experience

Less than 1 year	AED 87,000
1–4 years	AED 101,072
5–9 years	AED 147,312
10–19 years	AED 220,638
20 years or more	AED 332,244

Median Salary by Employer Type

Government (state and local)	AED 184,932
Company	AED 162,281
Private practice/firm	AED 141,251
Other organisation	AED 121,722
College/university	AED 162,414
Hospital	AED 131,511
Government (federal)	AED 142,925
Non-profit organisation	AED 141,264
Foundation/trust	AED 122,084
Contract	AED 92,312
Franchise	AED 90,000
School/school district	AED 83,008
Self-employed	AED 82,541

Courtesy of Payscale.com

Typical Jobs and Salaries

All the situations below were advertised at the time of writing (2008).

- **Human resources manager, £53,000 + full benefits package.**
- **IT project manager, £120,000 + full benefits package.**
- **Publishing manager, £75,000 + relocation allowance.**
- **Hotel marketing executive, £62,000 + apartment + benefits package.**
- **Senior architect, £80,000 + full benefits package.**
- **Recruitment consultant, £75,000 (engineering sector).**
- **PA to financial services director, £40,000.**

Career Possibilities

Despite easy access to a regional talent pool of around 14 million university-educated workers, Dubai still has an ongoing demand for both highly skilled workers and manual labour. Key areas of recruitment centre on the **construction industry** (especially architects and surveyors); the **financial sector** (from fund managers at the Dubai International Financial Centre (DIFC), the world's newest financial services centre, to financial advisors); the **medical field** (from pharmaceutical specialists and consultants at Dubai Health City to private hospital doctors); to a wide range of disciplines across the **aerospace**, **oil**, **engineering** and **sporting** sectors). **Technology** careers at Internet City;

journalism jobs at Media City and all manner of **consumer sales and service** roles are widely advertised – most require a degree, or professional accreditation, combined with relevant experience.

However, the lion's share of available vacancies arises from Dubai's burgeoning **hospitality** sector. The city-state is one of the world's biggest conference destinations, *see* **Dubai Today**, p.34–6, and tourist hotspots, *see* pp.30–31 – although, other than the upper echelons of management, recruitment tends to be aimed squarely at lower-paid workers from Asia.

Current labour laws in the UAE do not permit **students** on student visas to undertake paid employment in any capacity. However, some universities, such as the UOWD, have internships with a select group of companies based in the Dubai Technology Zone and Media City in the areas of marketing, human resources, information systems and sales.

A Roaring Retail Hub

'It's never been a better time to enter Dubai's booming retail sector,' says Mike Tobin at executive search firm Warren Partners. 'No other nation is capable of competing with Dubai when it comes to offering ambitious retail professionals career potential. Spectacular shopping malls and an enormous assortment of international brands make Dubai the sector's leading destination. Anyone looking to advance their retail careers and expand their networks should look no further than Dubai.

'Many retailers entering Dubai see the emirate as a springboard into the Middle East and India. At the senior level, organisations need people who can deliver a vision and a strategy for growth. For UK retailers, the desire to recruit local talent into their Dubai operations is typically borne out of a need to implement and build on the processes and practices already in place in their domestic operations. So the job of incoming executives will be to train, develop and pass on the parent company skills sets, ensuring a legacy for years to come.

'As well as senior management roles, those in most demand include visual merchandisers, IT experts, and HR and resource professionals, whose skills are needed to execute retailers' strategies. PR, marketing, media and communications consultants are also crucial to allow companies to get their messages across effectively. In terms of softer skills, the individuals that tend to succeed in Dubai are those with outstanding leadership and communication skills, and a natural aptitude for coaching and training. The strongest candidates are also highly culturally adaptive and willing to move around. For the right person, Dubai is a fantastic place to work. Anyone thinking of making the move must research it thoroughly, as the working and living environments are extremely different from those in the UK. However, those that carve out a career here will find a stint in Dubai can be a significant differentiator in the jobs market. This international experience helps individuals stand out in, say, an otherwise crowded UK market – especially in a recessionary climate.'

Teaching

Foreign teachers with good credentials and impeccable English are highly sought-after by private schools in Dubai. Generally speaking, Arab students have high educational aspirations and are enthusiastic about study. They are also well-motivated by their parents who, let's face it, are paying huge fees for good results. Rowdy classes are unheard of, and discipline problems extremely rare. However, the downsides for teachers can be long hours and copious reams of red tape. Another annoyance for teachers is the connections that bind Arab society – an 'Old Boys' Network' that can heavily influence school management issues through family ties.

Most teaching jobs in **private schools** come with a fulsome salary package that often includes health insurance and allowances for transport and utilities. Those teaching the upper echelons of Dubai society may also be offered an accommodation package. A strong and steady flow of teaching jobs come on to the market as the rising levels of expatriate population continue to fuel demand. Some schools have long waiting lists (much to the frustration of parents keen to enrol their children) – a direct result of teacher shortages as schools fight it out to meet their recruitment needs.

Teachers in Dubai are well respected and well rewarded in schools that follow the American and British curriculum and the International Baccalaureate. Many teachers arrive in Dubai to spend a couple of years in the sun teaching children from a broad range of backgrounds. Highly attractive salaries are, of course, very much part of the appeal, especially as they are also tax-free.

Private language schools are also desperately recruiting vast numbers of English-speaking teaching staff. Here, students are a mixture of Dubai nationals and expat workers from Asian countries keen to improve their English. Foreign international language schools, such as Berlitz and Linguarama, have branches in Dubai. Both require teachers to attend their own teacher training courses ahead of leading a class. The British Council recruits English language teachers with a recognised qualification, such as an RSA diploma or PGCE in Teaching English as a Foreign Language (TEFL) and also requires a minimum of two years' teaching experience for most of its positions.

Another huge area of demand is **private English lessons**, a significant source of employment for 'moonlighting' teachers and those keen to work part-time. Private tutoring is an extremely lucrative way to supplement an income during the run-up to the examination season – also once papers have been marked and it is time for those who have failed to retake. Key subjects include English, mathematics, IT and sciences.

Finding a teaching job isn't difficult in Dubai, and can be as easy as simply 'asking around'. However, those looking for something specific should make a direct approach to a school or college of interest. Another option is to seek the services of a reputable Dubai recruitment agency, preferably via word of mouth.

Although Dubai's state schools require English to be taught as a second language, few native English-speakers enter the state system. People with Arabic and English language skills can command sky-high fees as **translators** within the commercial sector; such is the demand within top-end financial institutions and consultancies.

Looking for a Job

You'll find numerous vacancies advertised within the most basic of five-minute **internet** searches. Another source of essential information is the Ministry of Labour, **www.mol.gov.ae**. Dubai's many recruitment agencies range from super-efficient to hopelessly clueless, so be sure to ask around for recommendations. All of Dubai's main **newspapers** carry a job section, with the daily pages in *Gulf News* by far the best. It is also common for job-hunters in Dubai to make direct approaches to specific organizations '**on spec**' to seek out career opportunities. However, in a country where image is everything, you'll need a boxload of hot-looking CVs – so don't be tempted to skimp.

Just a handful of the many of **recruitment agencies** in Dubai are as follows:

- Al Reyami Labour Supply, **t** 885 2193, **www.rlsuaeonline.com**.
- Business Aid Centre, **t** 337 6467, **www.bacme.com**.
- IQ Selection, **t** 324 0886, **www.iqselection.com**.
- Job Track Management Services, **t** 397 7751, **www.jobtrackme.com**.
- SOS Recruitment Consultants, **t** 396 56000, **www.sosrecruitment.com**.
- Talent Consultancy, **t** 335 0999, **www.talentdubai.com**.

Preparing a Winning Résumé

Almost every company in Dubai will ask for a CV as a matter of course – even if you've been headhunted or recommended for a job. Résumés (or CVs) are passed around like business cards throughout the business communities as Dubai's burgeoning hub of HQs and service industries seek much-needed skills.

A CV should be a professional reflection of an individual applying for or looking for an employment. Dubai's ultra-competitive job market demands skilful CV-writing to boost the chance of being invited for interview.

It is important to plan ahead before starting work on a résumé to ensure it really hits the mark. Gather and arrange the **documents, certificates and all the information** that you might need; scan and list all the significant events and data for quick reference; and make notes to highlight **key achievements** worthy of showcasing. This will take time, as recalling your career plan may not happen immediately, but will form the basis of the résumé.

Next you'll need to determine the format of the CV that is right for you and your experience and career. **Reverse chronological format** tends to suit the more conventional business sectors, such as accountancy, academia and law. The **functional format** lends itself to new graduates and 'returners to work' who may lack recent experience but will have other skills to offer. Job-seekers keen to switch careers or who may have broad-based work experience should consider the **combination format**. Each of these layouts requires excellent presentation and clear, concise information in order to yield a positive result. Leave nothing vague or open to interpretation, and be sure to clarify your objectives, using a dedicated section to summarise your goals. This doesn't need to be lengthy, but should detail your most important qualities in relation to the job or company. In short, this is why the company should pick you over another applicant – it is this paragraph which, if worded carefully, can put you to the top of the pile.

Several agencies offer CV preparation services, from a simple typing job to crafting a résumé that's truly the *crème de la crème*. Some, such as **www.careersindubai.com**, offer a downloadable CV formatter.

Reverse Chronological Format

The main benefit of a chronological CV is that it highlights the length of service in each role. This can be a real bonus if your work experience meets an advertised job specification precisely, or if your job titles or employers are relevant – and impressive. It also pinpoints career advancement in a company or a field of work by listing work history, beginning with your most current job.

Other sections may include a job objective; information on your education; a summary of skills; volunteer experiences; memberships of unions and other work-related associations; and community activities. The fact that it is in chronological order ensures that your most recent experience is given priority at the top of the page – so if this doesn't reflect well, or lets you down, this format may not be for you.

One way of addressing such a problem, however, is to add in a job objective and/or your qualifications in a sentence or two before listing your work history. This should be entered according to dates, with job title, employer, and dates of employment for each job clearly stated. It is important to explain exactly what your duties and responsibilities were; what skills you learned; and what you achieved. Next, list your formal education and training with the most recent schooling first – especially if this is a relevant training course.

Functional Résumé Format

What makes a functional résumé appealing to job-hunters keen to change career is that it allows transferable skills that may be used in a new situation to be showcased. Applicants with limited work experience but relevant skills can use the format to identify why they are suited to a particular job or field of work.

Next Stop: Dubai

In an uncertain global economy, there remains an insatiable thirst for senior professionals in Dubai, where the top candidates can choose from many career-enhancing job opportunities. Daniel Griggs, director at international recruitment consultancy Beresford Blake Thomas (BBT, **www.bbt.co.uk**), explains the key steps to take when job-hunting.

'Finding the right role amongst the plethora of possibilities can be daunting. The first questions to ask yourself are "What is my motivation for living in Dubai?" and "What type of job am I seeking?" Some candidates are interested in an attractive lifestyle or the excitement of working on world-class projects; others simply want to experience working abroad. You must then assess your skills and previous experience, as companies require strong credentials. One of the easiest routes for finding the most suitable position is via a reputable employment agency that has local offices in Dubai.

'The full process, from searching for a job to securing a position, normally takes between six and eight weeks. During this period most candidates go through a series of interviews with the agency and with the client. Initially it will be a telephone interview, then possibly a face-to-face interview or a video conference. Meeting the future employer is highly recommended.

'One of the reality checks for many candidates is that salaries and benefits tend not to be as generous as they were ten years ago, mainly because Dubai has developed into a luxury destination. Therefore, roles don't always include packages such as accommodation or transport, or benefits for your spouse. As a tax haven Dubai is a major attraction, but, to escape UK tax demands, make sure you are out of the UK for a full tax year.'

By highlighting major skill areas, the emphasis is placed on your talents not experience alone. Shift the focus away from job titles, dates, or name of employers and concentrate on the job objective and summary of abilities.

Education, memberships and other work-related associations should also be included, but the CV should be ordered to reflect your suitability, showcasing skills and abilities, accomplishments and achievements, areas of competence and proficiency – and then experience.

Ten Tips for a Great CV

- If applying for a specific job, check that you have matched your CV to what the employer has asked for in terms of experience, skills or attributes.

- Use titles and headings that mirror those used in the advertisement or job description. Also match your language and terms to the company style (look on their website or at their prospectus).

- Use a CV style that grabs attention without being kooky, for example using high-quality cream paper rather than standard white.

- Analyse the employer's needs when it comes to the personality of the application. Try to inject this element into your CV by using descriptions in a summary paragraph.

- Cite budgets, figures and statistics to quantify your experience wherever possible, and be sure to demonstrate progress or accomplishments (such as a 50 per cent rise in efficiency or a 30 per cent reduction in wastage) in relation to your role.

- Don't be too wordy, even if your career is long and impressive. Overblown descriptions are a turn-off, so it pays to keep a CV crisp, clear and concise.

- If your experience isn't quite what has been requested, abandon any strict adherence to chronological order in order to highlight your relevant skills, attributes and characteristics.

- A CV should present an image of professionalism that matches the salary and status of the job on offer. Be sure your style, language and goals match the position. It can also pay to use adjectives to convey that you're a doer – a person of action.

- Never sell yourself short; always be positive about every experience. Your CV is a sales tool – an advertisement for you – so be sure to exploit every possible angle that may be relevant.

- Use 'PAR' statements (Problem-Action-Results) to show your achievements in the workplace, from the initial problem that existed to how you approached resolving it, and then the beneficial results to your employer.

- Be sure to check, double-check and proofread to avoid errors in spelling, punctuation and grammar. Ask someone else to read it through in order to ensure that it is easy to follow.

Job Interviews

Dubai's go-getting job market is very much about contacts and opportunities. Huge potential exists in almost every segment of the business community – even if it isn't advertised. Many job offers occur through a person's ability to convince a potential employer that they simply must hire them.

Interviews can be formal or relaxed in style and are often by introduction. However, they all require the interviewee to make a strong, good first impression – an opinion formed within the first few minutes. Being well prepared for an interview is essential, according to **www.careersuae.com**:

- Try to talk to people who have worked or currently work at the company. Note how they dress and behave.

- Research the company by visiting the website to understand its business, target clients, market and direction. Prepare a few relevant questions and memorise the name and title of the person you'll be meeting with.

• Choose clothes that are smart, crisp and professional. Bring CVs, references and letters of recommendation (and work examples if relevant).

• Allow 10 minutes to collect your thoughts ahead of the interview. Stay calm, relaxed, open and positive. Face your interviewer with an easy posture – look him/her in the eye, and be sure to smile. Note the point about handshakes, *see* p.188, and also all the other points of etiquette.

• Keep the good impression going after you leave, by sending a thank-you email or note as a follow up to your interview – it will help ensure the interviewer keeps you in mind.

Employment: Contracts, Terms and Conditions

A standard Dubai contract specifies salary, job title, duties and responsibilities and will outline the detail of your contract period. Often, it will include the reporting structure and performance measures of the organisation along with termination conditions and liabilities connected with the breaking of the contract terms.

Until recently, expatriate contracts were for a **two-year standard term**; however, open-ended contracts are becoming increasingly common. Employers have realised that not stipulating a defined period offers them greater flexibility should the employee prove unsatisfactory. Today, most contracts have a **termination notice period** of between one and three months, or payment in lieu of notice. Many contracts roll on as a **renewable agreement**, with many expatriates staying in their Dubai jobs for a decade or more on an **extended contract** – a situation that has become increasingly the norm.

The phrase '**employment subject to obtaining the necessary permits**' is commonplace in Dubai contracts but is unlikely to present any problems. However, it pays to have already gathered all the documentation you need well ahead of the game to avoid any unnecessary delays. As you start job-seeking in earnest, begin collating birth certificates, exam results, professional memberships and references. A contract can usually be issued within a few days, although the UAE's local labour laws apply whether you hold one or not – so, as an employee, you are afforded protection as a basic legal right.

Medical Examination

A government-controlled medical examination prior to the issue of a work and residence permit is mandatory for all expatriates. The check is standard, and includes a full examination to explore your medical condition. All health considerations are taken into account, from high blood pressure to serious infectious diseases and infirmities, with HIV and AIDS being specific concerns. Anyone proven to be HIV positive will be deported immediately. Tests are conducted again whenever work visas are renewed, usually on a three-year cycle.

Labour Laws

All matters relating to the labour laws in the UAE are governed by Federal Law no.8 (1980), which has undergone some amendments and has some special regulations applicable to Dubai's Free Zones. The law covers all the main aspects of the employer-employee relationship, from conditions of employment, salaries, working hours, holiday entitlement and medical care to benefits and termination of contract. Article 3 of the law applies to all staff and employees in the UAE, both locals and expatriates.

Unions are not permitted in the UAE, and any labour disputes are adjudicated by the Ministry of Labour and Social Affairs, **www.mol.gov.ae**.

Working Hours and Holidays

The working week in Dubai tends to vary between 40 and 48 hours, depending on the particular company's policy, although the retail and hospital trade tend to work slightly longer hours at around nine hours per day. Businesses either work on a straight-shift basis (8.30am–6pm) or operate a split-shift (8am–1pm and 4–7pm). In practice, private companies tend to work for around 45 hours per week, but just 35 hours is common for government employees. Friday is the Muslim rest day and, if your company has a five-day working week, the other day off is usually either Thursday or Saturday. Saturday is the more popular choice for international companies, as taking Thursday off would mean a reduction in the number of operational days in common with much of the rest of the world. Conversely, other companies insist on Thursday, as the school 'weekend' is Thursday and Friday. Summer and winter hours don't vary; however, in the month of Ramadan, the working day is reduced. Legally this should apply to all staff, but many companies only apply it to Muslims, who fast during daylight hours.

While **overtime** may apply to manual labourers and lower-ranking staff, it is rarely available to private sector workers, who are expected to work as the job requires.

There are 10 days' paid **public holidays** per year in the UAE, with employees accruing **two days' holiday entitlement for every month of service** after six months in the first year. After 12 months of service have been completed, an employee gains an entitlement of **30 days paid leave per annum**. This is in addition to public holidays, sick leave and maternity leave for women. There is no paternity leave in the UAE.

Part-time Work and Freelancing

Dubai's job market is not blessed with an abundance of **part-time** opportunities, and those that do crop up tend to be snapped up in a trice. Generally speaking, these tend to be receptionist, secretarial, accounts and clerical roles, with some part-time jobs also offered in sales.

The **freelance** market in Dubai is highly competitive – and doing well (i.e. making money) relies on good connections, not to mention plenty of dogged determination. Freelancers soon become practised at networking in order to fully exploit the potential of the city. In Dubai, who you know is almost as important as how good you are – in certain professional circles, at least.

One notable resource is Dubai Media City's '**Media Business Centre**', where freelancers can work as professionals providing they have the necessary sponsorship and paperwork. You can get a **freelance permit** and 'hot desk' space if you fall under one of the various freelance categories, which includes artists, editors, directors, writers, engineers, producers, photographers/camera operators and techs in the fields of film, TV, music radio or print media. The permit includes a residence visa and access to 10 shared work stations, and allows the use of a shared PO box address and fax line. Freelancers must spend a minimum of three hours per week at the hot desk, but no more than three hours per day. To apply, you'll need a business plan, CV, bank reference letter and a decent portfolio of work samples. At the time of writing, a permit costs AED 5000 security deposit (refundable), AED 5,000 joining fee (a one-off payment), AED 8,000 annual permit fee, AED 4,000 annual membership fee and AED 1,500 annual employee sponsorship fee – no small change. For details, contact Dubai Media City on **t** 391 4555, **www.dubaimediacity.com**.

Setting up a Business

Figures from Dubai's Department of Economic Development (DED) have revealed an explosion of new business start-ups in the emirate, with more than 13,000 private companies becoming licensed to operate in 2006 alone. A report by the DED and the Swiss-based International Institute for Management ranks Dubai 5th out of 61 countries surveyed for ease of doing business. It was polled 3rd for adaptability of government policy to change the economy, and ranked 6th in economic performance.

The Dubai authorities have set out to create a business environment that is well ordered, without being unduly restrictive. As a result, Dubai offers business-operating conditions that are among the most liberal and attractive in the region. The clearest advantage to setting up a business in Dubai is that there are no corporate, personal or withholding taxes. Also, it is possible for legal residency to be obtained by establishing a company in Dubai. Foreign companies must maintain a registered office in Dubai but there is no requirement to live in Dubai once legal residency has been granted, although residents are required to visit every six months.

Currency transfers are also restriction-free, and do not incur taxes. Dubai also does not require EU citizens to report income taxes, investments or earnings in their EU country of origin. Foreign nationals trading as self-employed can take advantage of selling their services via a registered Dubai organisation. Payments are then collected via a confidential Dubai-based bank account, with the net effect that no taxes are paid. Companies do not need to file accounts, and Dubai has no taxation information exchange agreements with other countries. There are no public records kept of the directors and shareholders of a corporation. This city has a confidential and sophisticated banking system, and there's legislation to protect the confidentiality of investors in the country.

Historically, each emirate has followed a separate bureaucratic system to govern the operations of foreign business interests. However, in practice Dubai

Case Study: Joanna Barclay

'Although I was born and raised in London, I decided to uproot and move to Hong Kong in the mid-'90s. I've always enjoyed busy, fast-paced environments and places with entrepreneurial spirit, and so after a successful and fulfilling decade there I looked for a new challenge. By this time, I was a mother with a young child and another on the way.

'With a business partner, I'd run a well-established luxury swimwear and beachwear business in Hong Kong, called **StarBlu.com**. After studying the Dubai market, it was clear it offered a great opportunity. Within a matter of weeks after arriving in Dubai, we commenced our operations – and it was all systems go. Setting up a business was very easy, as we used a company that offered an all-encompassing business package, including a business licence, virtual office and administrative support. Recently, we've been fortunate to open up a boutique on the prestigious Palm Jumeirah – however, this has taken months of paperwork and hard graft to get up and running!

'At that time, Dubai was a city still in relative infancy – but with great vision. It offered a spirit of adventure coupled with a sense that business dreams could become reality, and I was won over by Dubai's stunning beaches, high-standard of living and minimal crime rate. Family life in Dubai is wonderful and we enjoy a wide range of activities with weekends spent in the pool and on the beach. The schools are fantastic and cater for all nationalities and, with Dubai's low crime rate and cleanliness, I feel it's a great city in which to bring my children up. On the negative side, house prices have soared in recent years – doubling since I arrived. However, the pros of living and working in Dubai defiantly outweigh the cons – I'm a five-minute drive from the beach, the Burj Al Arab hotel, the Mall of the Emirates and an indoor ski slope.'

and the other emirates have adhered to the same general administrative process. Foreign companies must adhere to the **Commercial Companies Law (1984)** and are allowed to operate in one of three ways:

- **with a local sponsor.**
- **through a partnership with a UAE national or company.**
- **through a private limited company or public shareholding company.**

Codified legislation was introduced throughout the UAE in 1984. The Commercial Companies Law Federal Law No.8 of 1984, as amended by Federal Law No.13 of 1988) defines each category of business and the obligations of shareholders, and states the required level of UAE-national participation.

In terms of **costs**, a useful online cost-simulation launched by the Dubai government helps you define your budgets. Companies simply enter their trade activity, size and operation at **www.dubaided.gov.ae**, to generate a detailed report of the costs involved in setting up in the city.

The basic requirement for all business activity in Dubai is one of three categories of **licences**: a **commercial licence** that covers all kinds of trading activity; a **professional licence** covering professions, services, craftsmen and artisans; and an **industrial licence** for establishing an industrial or manufacturing activity. The Dubai Economic Department issues these licences, although some categories of business also require approval from certain ministries and other authorities. For example, banks and financial institutions require endorsement from the Central Bank of the UAE, insurance companies and related agencies from the Ministry of Economy and Commerce, manufacturing firms from the Ministry of Finance and Industry, and pharmaceutical and medical product companies from the Ministry of Health. More detailed procedures apply to businesses engaged in oil and gas production and related industries.

Ownership Requirements

In the UAE, 51 per cent participation by UAE nationals is the general requirement for all UAE-established companies except:

- **where the law requires 100 per cent local ownership.**
- **in the Jebel Ali Free Zone.**
- **in activities open to 100 per cent GCC ownership.**
- **where wholly owned GCC companies enter into partnership with UAE nationals.**
- **for foreign companies that register branches or representative offices in Dubai.**
- **in professional or artisan companies, where 100 per cent foreign ownership is permitted.**

The law also defines the requirements in terms of shareholders, directors, minimum capital levels and incorporation procedures and stipulates provisions governing conversion, mergers and dissolution of companies.

All commercial and industrial businesses in Dubai should be **registered** with the **Dubai Chamber of Commerce and Industry**.

The eight categories of company formation as defined by the law are:

- **general partnership company.**
- **partnership-*en-commendam*.**
- **joint venture company.**
- **public shareholding company.**
- **private shareholding company.**
- **limited liability company*.**
- **share partnership company.**
- **branches and representative offices of foreign companies.**

*A limited liability company (LLC) can be floated with a minimum of two and a maximum of 50 people, whose liability is limited to their respective shares in the company's capital. Limited liability companies provide a suitable structure for companies interested in developing a long-term presence in Dubai. The minimum capital requirement for floating a limited liability company is currently AED 300,000, contributed in cash or in kind. Foreign equity in the company may not exceed 49 per cent; the profit and loss distribution can be specified.

Set-up Consultancies

Numerous Dubai-based specialist consultancies offer all-inclusive business set-up packages, tailored to suit companies keen to avoid the hassle of red tape. Services include Free Zone registration, permits, company formation, logo and trademark registration and liquidation, from the legal paperwork and transaction handling to all Dubai's licensing documentation. Most consultancies work on a flat-fee basis and will source the market to meet the specified needs of an individual client, be it a small graphic design company or a major conglomerate with a staff of 500.

Business Premises

In recent years, Dubai's influx of new businesses has seen the value of commercial and retail space in the city hit record levels. At the time of writing, **rental costs** remain at an all-time high, and available units scarce. According to a report in the *Khaleej Times*, rents and purchase prices within the commercial sector will continue to rise as Dubai continues to attract businesses from across the globe. Vacancy rates of around 1 per cent – in addition to pent-up demand from existing businesses and new tenants wishing to upgrade office premises – has allowed rents to rise 40 per cent per year to date on average. A survey by the Dubai Chamber of Commerce and Industry showed that property rents continued to top the list of concerns among businessmen for 2008, with annual commercial rents on Dubai's Shaikh Zayed Road topping US$600 per square metre.

Prices for **freehold office space** have risen 17 per cent per year to date – the result of a prolonged lag in the completion of new commercial supply. Dubai property analysts believe that by the year 2010 the high yield will show a downward trend as the market naturally settles. According to Colliers International, Dubai is less expensive than London, Hong Kong, New York and Tokyo, where average office space prices are more than triple those asked in the emirate.

As might be expected from Dubai's construction sector, high demand for commercial premises is being met with a boom in building projects. Indeed, many of the signature developments combine retail and commercial property with residential accommodation. Dubai's key commercial developments available, under way or planned include The Palm Golden Mile; Festival City; Al Bawadi; the Kingdom of Sheba; Burj Al Alam; Culture Village; The Walk at Jumeirah Beach Residence; Currency House; The One at the TECOM Zone; Dubai Sports City; Dubailand; Dubai Marina; Dubai International Financial Centre (DIFC) District; Silicon Oasis, Dubai (DSO); International City; Downtown Burj Dubai; Dubai Mall; the Gold and Diamond Park; Dubai Waterfront; Ibn Battuta Mall; and UPTOWN Mirdiff.

The following websites represent the major developers in the commercial property market:

- Al Fattan, **www.alfattan.com**: Currency House; Dubai Festival City (**www.dubaifestivalcity.com**).
- Al Mazroui, **www.theoneme.com**: The One Tower.
- DAMAC, **www.damacproperties.com**: XL Tower.
- DEC, **www.dheerajeastcoast.com**: DEC Business Towers; The Sanctuary and Corporate Bay.
- Dubai International Financial Centre (DIFC), **www.difc.ae**.
- Dubai Mall, **www.thedubaimall.com**.
- Dubai Marina, **www.dubai-marina.com**.
- Dubai Properties, **www.dubai-properties.ae**: Business Bay (**www.businessbay.ae**); Vision Tower; Culture Village; The Walk at Jumeirah Beach Residence.
- Dubai Silicon Oasis (DSO), **www.dso.ae**.

- Dubai Sports City, **www.dubaisportscity.ae**.
- Dubai Waterfront, **www.dubaiwaterfront.ae**.
- Emaar Properties, **www.emaar.com**: Downtown Burj Dubai; Saaha Offices; Boulevard Plaza.
- Fortune Group, **www.fortunegroup.ae**: Burj Al Alam (**www.burjalalam. com**): Fortune Bay; Pearl Commercial Tower; Crystal Tower.
- Gold and Diamond Park, **www.goldanddiamondpark.com**.
- IBN Battuta Mall, **www.ibnbattutamall.com**.
- IFA Hotels & Resorts, **www.thepalmgoldenmile.com**; Kingdom of Sheba.
- International City, **www.nakheel.ae**.
- Le Solarium, **www.credouae.com**.
- Tatweer, **www.tatweerdubai.com**: Bawadi Strip.
- Union Properties, **www.up.ae**: UPTOWN Mirdiff.

Volunteering

Dubai's charity and volunteer sector isn't as established as you might imagine, although some interesting opportunities exist for those prepared to ask around. Volunteering in any country offers excellent opportunities to interact with the local community from schools, playgroups, charities, hospitals and all manner of projects connected with young people, the elderly, conservation and animal shelters.

In Dubai, volunteer roles exist with the **Make-a-Wish Foundation, t** 368 0217, **www.makeawish.ae**, a charity that grants special wishes to children who are sick. Several expatriate clubs and societies organise fund-raising events for local animal charities including **Feline Friends Dubai, www.felinefriendsdubai.com**. Another resource to try is the **International Humanitarian City (IHC)**: an innovative humanitarian hub that draws volunteer skills from an array of non-profit organisations, companies, donors and individuals – apply via an online volunteer database, **www.ihc.ae**, or telephone **t** 368 0202.

The **Dubai Cares** educational charity, **www.dubaicares.ae**, launched by His Highness Sheikh Mohammed bin Rashid Al Maktoum, has raised a sum of over US$220,000 via numerous local projects.

References

Dubai at a Glance

Capital city: Dubai (city)

Official name of country: Dubai (emirate)

Region: The United Arab Emirates (comprised of 7 sheikdoms along with Abu Dhabi, Sharjah, Ajman, Umm Al Quwain, Ras Al Khaimah and Fujairah)

Type of government: Federal (With Abu Dhabi, Dubai is one of only two emirates to possess veto power over critical matters of national importance in the UAE)

Head of government: H.H. Sheikh Mohammed bin Rashid Al Maktoum

Area: 3,885 km²

Latitude/Longitude: 25°16' N 55°20' E

Time zone: (UTC) +4

Geographical highlights: Situated on the Persian Gulf in the Arabian Desert roughly at sea level (16m) in the northeast of the UAE. A flat sandy desert gives way to the Western Hajar Mountains, which run alongside Dubai's border with Oman at Hatta.

Official language: Arabic

Bordering countries: Abu Dhabi in the south, Sharjah in the northeast, and the Sultanate of Oman in the southeast.

Surrounding seas: The Persian Gulf borders the western coast

Population: 1.24-million

Religion: Islam

GDP: Dh198 billion

GDP growth rate: 11 %

GDP per capita: US$20,000

Main exports: Oil, gas

Unemployment: 2.4 %

Internet domain: .ae

Internet Resources

Dubai Department of Tourism and Commerce Marketing, **www.dubaitourism.ae**.

Dubai Tourism, **www.dubai-tourism.net**.

Dubai Online, **www.dubai-online.com**.

Go Dubai, **www.godubai.com**.

Dubai City Info, **www.dubaicityinfo.com**.

Tourism Dubai, **www.tourismdubai.org**.

Dubai e-Guide, **www.dubaieguide.com**.

Further Reading

Travel

Carter, Terry and Lara Dunston, Lara, *Dubai*, Lonely Planet Publications (4th rev ed 2006).

Dunston, Lara and Sarah Monaghan, *Top 10 Dubai & Abu Dhabi (DK Eyewitness Top 10 Travel Guides)*, DK Publishing (Dorling Kindersley) (2007).

Where Dubai Popout Cityguide (Where Cityguides), GPP Travel; 1st edition (2008).

Thomas, Gavin, *Rough Guide DIRECTIONS to Dubai*, Rough Guides Ltd; 1st ed (2007).

Dunston, Lara and Terry Carter, *Dubai Lonely Planet ENCOUNTER*, Lonely Planet Publications; Pap/Map edition (2007).

Dubai (AA TwinPack), AA Publishing, Automobile Association (2008).

Carter, Terry and Lara Dunston, *Dubai (Lonely Planet Best of...)*, Lonely Planet Publications (2006).

AA Essential Spiral Dubai (AA Essential Spiral Guides), AA Publishing (2007).

Gilmore, Zee, *Dubai (Footprint Pocket Guides)*, Footprint, 2nd rev ed (2007).

Time Out Shortlist Dubai, Time Out Group Ltd (2009).

Time Out Dubai: Abu Dhabi and the UAE, Time Out Group Ltd; 2nd rev ed (2005).

Dubai Berlitz Pocket Guide, Berlitz Publishing (2006).

Luxe Dubai (LUXE City Guides), LUXE Asia Limited; 4th rev ed (2007).

Vlahides, John & Mathew Lee, *Dubai (Lonely Planet City Guides)*, Lonely Planet Publications; 5Rev Ed edition (2008).

Dubai Insight Pocket Guide, APA Publications Pte Ltd, Singapore; 2nd rev ed (2003).

Dubai Insight Step-by-Step, APA Publications Pte Ltd, Singapore (2008).

Dubai Wallpaper* City Guide, Phaidon Press Ltd (2007).

Dubai Baedeker Guide, Mairs Geographischer Verlag, Kurt Mair (2008).

Quinn, Fiona, *Dubai InsideOut Guides*, Compass Maps (2004).

Bennett, Lindsay, *Dubai (Globetrotter Travel Pack)*, New Holland Publishers Ltd; Pap/Map edition (2008).

Darke, Diane, *Dubai (Travellers)*, Thomas Cook Publishing (2007).

Fodor's in Focus Dubai, Fodor's Travel Publications Inc., U.S. (2009).

Maps

Dubai PopOut Map, Compass Maps (2004).

Dubai Street Map Explorer, Explorer Publishing (2004).

Dubai Mini Map Explorer, Explorer Group (2006).

Dubai Atlas, Explorer Publishing & Distribution, Spi edition (2008).
Dubai Jumbo Atlas, Explorer Publishing & Distribution, Spi edition (2008).
Dubai Tourist Map, Explorer Publishing & Distribution, Map Mil edition (2006).
Dubai map, ITMB Publishing (2007).
Dubai map, Borch (2007).
Dubai City Map, Freytag & Berndt (2007).

Business

Davidson, M. Christopher, *Dubai: The Vulnerability of Success*, C. Hurst & Co Publishers Ltd (2008).

Pagones, Rachel, *Dubai Millennium: A Vision Realised; A Dream Lost*, Highdown (2007).

Rehman, A. Aamir, *Dubai & Co.: Global Strategies for Doing Business in the Gulf States*, McGraw-Hill Professional; 1st ed (2008)

Tamimi, Al Essam, *Setting Up in Dubai: Business Investor's Guide*, Cross Border Legal, 3rd rev ed (2003).

Dubai Business and Investment Opportunities Yearbook (World Strategic and Business Information Library), USA International Business Publications, 6th ed (2007) .

Dubai Investment and Business Guide (World Foreign Policy and Government Library), USA International Business Publications (2007).

Parker, M. Phillip, *Economic and Product Market Databook for Dubai*, United Arab Emirates ICON Group International, Inc. (2006).

Dubai Business Law Handbook (World Strategic and Business Information Library), USA International Business Publications (2007).

Davidson, M. Christopher, *The United Arab Emirates: A Study in Survival*, Lynne Rienner Publishers Inc, US (2005)

Jenson, Broman Boris, *Dubai: Dynamics of Bingo Urbanism* (2006).

Setting Up in the Dubai International Financial Centre, Cross Border Legal (2006).

Havlicek, Svetlana, *Economic Diversification in the United Arab Emirates. Entrepreneurial Opportunities in Dubai*, Verlag Dr. Kovac (2006).

Dubai: Property Investment Guide, Cross Border Legal (2004).

History

Nowell, Simone and Robert Nowell, *Dubai: Now & Then*, Zodiac Publishing, 3rd ed (2000).

Mezrich, Ben, *Rigged: The True Story of an Ivy League Kid Who Changed the World of Oil, from Wall Street to Dubai*, Bloomsbury Publishing plc (2008).

Senzig, A. Theresa, *Gates of Dubai*, AuthorHouse (2007).

Amirsadeghi, Hossein, *Dubai: The Dream Realised*, TransGlobe Publishing Ltd (2009).

Kanna, Ahmed, *The Superlative City: Dubai and the Urban Condition in the Early Twenty-First Century*, Harvard UP (2008).

Burdett, Anita L,P., *Records of Dubai 1820–1965*, Archive Editions (2000).

Architecture and Interiors

Pagones, Rachel, *Dubai Millennium: A Vision Realised; A Dream Lost*, Highdown (2007).

Campbell, Hallie, *Dubai Chic (Chic Guides)*, Kuperard (2008).

Katodrytis, George and Richard Powers, *Dubai: Growing Through Architecture*, Thames & Hudson Ltd; Arabic edition (2008).

Customs and Culture

Gallant, Monica, *Emirati Women in Dubai*, VDM Verlag Dr. Muller Aktiengesellschaft & Co. KG (2008).

Dubai Customs Guide (World Strategic and Business Information Library) International Business Publications USA (2007).

Rizvi, Rajid and Shirley Rizvi: *Arts & Artists in Dubai*, Clearway Logistics Phase (1996)

Fakhro, Bahia, *Customs of the Arabian Gulf: Drawings and Paintings by School Children in Bahrain and Dubai*, Design for Print Ltd (1978).

Murr, al Muhammad, *Dubai Tales*, Forest Books (1996).

Food and Drink

Dubai Posh Nosh, Cheap Eats and Star Bars (Restaurants Cafés Clubs Bars), The Explorer Group (2006).

Marreiros, Sabina, *Dubai Cool Restaurants (Cool Restaurants)*, teNeues Publishing (UK) Ltd (2006).

Jakel, Lutz, *Dubai New Arabian Cuisine*, Parkway Publishing (2007).

Various authors, *Seasoned with Sunshine in Dubai: UAE: Favourite Recipes from Around the World*, Airline of the United Arab Emirates (1995).

Dubai Star Bars, Explorer Group (2008).

Dubai Star Restaurants, Explorer Group (2008).

Fiction

Wilkins, Stephen, *Dubai Creek*, Matador Publishing (2006).

Reeley, Andy, *Dubai Dream*, Exposure Publishing (2005).

Morimoto, Tom, *Breaking Trail: From Canada's Northern Frontier to the Oil Fields of Dubai*, Fifth House Publishers (2007).

Till, Julie, *Dominoes: Drive to Dubai Level 2*, Oxford University Press (2004).

Photographic

Dubai Discovered, Explorer Group; 3rd ed (2005).

Wheeler, Julia, Telling Tales: An Oral History of Dubai, Explorer Group (2006).

Lichfield, Patrick, *Dubai: A City Portrait, Motivate Publishing Ltd* (2005).

Images of Dubai and the UAE, Explorer Group; 2nd rev ed (2006).

Fairservice, Ian and Charles Crowell, *Dubai: A Pictorial Tour* (Arabian Heritage Pictorials), Motivate Publishing (1996).

Dubai: Tomorrow's City Today, Explorer Publishing (2004).

Codrai, Ronald, *Dubai: A Collection of Mid-twentieth Century Photographs* (Arabian Album), Motivate Publishing Ltd (1993).

Films

Modern Times Wonders: Burj Al Arab (DVD), Global Television (2007).

Discover Dubai: Official CD-ROM Guide (CD-ROM) Absolute Entertainment Ltd (2005)

Rishi Rich Project, the, Aj Kal (DVD), Two Point Nine (2004).

Dubai City: Boomtown on the Arabian Gulf (Ear Books); *Sounds and Sights of the Desert* (Ear Books, Compilation, audio CD) (2007).

Climate Charts

Average Maximum Temperature °C

Jan	Feb	Mar	April	May	June	July	Aug	Sept	Oct	Nov	Dec
24.0	25.4	28.2	32.9	37.6	39.5	40.8	41.3	38.9	35.4	30.5	26.2

Average Minimum Temperature °C

Jan	Feb	Mar	April	May	June	July	Aug	Sept	Oct	Nov	Dec
14.3	15.4	17.6	20.8	24.6	27.2	29.9	30.2	27.5	23.9	19.9	16.3

Mean Rainfall (mm)

Jan	Feb	Mar	April	May	June	July	Aug	Sept	Oct	Nov	Dec
15.6	25.0	21.0	7.0	0.4	0.0	0.8	0.0	0.0	1.2	2.7	14.9

Mean No. of Days with Rain

Jan	Feb	Mar	April	May	June	July	Aug	Sept	Oct	Nov	Dec
5.4	4.9	5.9	2.6	0.3	0.0	0.5	0.6	0.1	0.2	1.3	3.6

Sunshine Hours per day

Jan	Feb	Mar	April	May	June	July	Aug	Sept	Oct	Nov	Dec
8.2	8.5	8.6	10.2	11.3	11.5	10.7	10.5	10.4	9.9	9.3	8.2

Mean Sea Temperature °C

Jan	Feb	Mar	April	May	June	July	Aug	Sept	Oct	Nov	Dec
20.9	20.7	22.3	25.0	28.5	31.2	32.2	32.9	31.9	29.9	27.0	23.4

Dubai Meteorological Office

Festivals and Public Holidays

The *Hijra* (Islamic) calendar is lunar, with each month beginning and ending with a new moon. Each of the 12 months in the *Hijra* calendar: Muharram, Safar, Rabi' Al Awwal, Rabi' Al Akhir, Jumada' Al Ula, Jumada' Al Akhirah, Rajab, Sha'baan, Ramadhan, Shawwal, Dhul-Qi'dah, Dhul-Hijjah – is 29–30 days long, making the *Hijra* year shorter than the Gregorian year.

Unlike the Gregorian day, which is from midnight to midnight, the Muslim day starts and ends at sunset.

Islamic dates are not fixed, and depend on the sighting of the new moon each month.

Public Holidays

1 Jan New Year's Day
9 Jan *Al Hijra* (Islamic New Year)
20 Mar *Mouloud* (Birth of the Prophet)
30 July *Leilat al-Meiraj* (Ascension of the Prophet)
Late Aug Ramadan
Sept *Eid al-Fitr* (End of Ramadan)
28 Nov *Eid al-Adha* (Feast of the Sacrifice)
2 and 3 Dec UAE National Day

The Holy Month of Ramadan

Ramadan is the ninth month of the Islamic calendar. Fasting during this month is one of the fundamental acts of worship for all adult Muslims. It requires abstaining from eating, smoking, drinking, sex and unclean thoughts from dawn to sunset for each of the 29–30 days of Ramadan. While earning blessings from Allah, Muslims are also rewarded socially, economically, spiritually, culturally, psychologically and physically for this self-control and discipline. During Ramadan, Muslims are reminded that they should not tell lies, break promises, talk slander or commit any deceitful act. In other words, all parts of the body (eyes, ears, tongue, hands, heart, and mind) should be fasting. The abstention is observed until the new moon is sighted again, signalling the completion of one lunar cycle. Ramadan is a social time for Muslims who experience a strong sense of unity and brotherhood through the pains of hunger and thirst. Fasting also serves to remind Muslims of the people who are starving or experiencing hardship each day across the world. Those that are sick, travelling, pregnant, breast feeding, menstruating, elderly, mentally ill or engaged in military action are exempt from fasting.

During Ramadan, two meals are eaten: *sahoor* is consumed an hour before dawn and finished before first light while *iftar* takes place once the sun has set. Reduced working hours operate throughout Ramadan to a maximum of six hours per day. Muslims ask that food may not be consumed openly during the day by non-Muslims or Muslims who are not fasting.

After the fast is broken, *Eid Al Fitr* follows: a three-day celebration that centres on feasting. On the first day, before dawn, Muslims will eat something (probably dates) before washing and putting on new clothes for the first prayer gathering of the day. After prayer, the day is spent visiting friends and family as homes welcome people in steady droves for many hours and sweets, fruits, and snacks are shared.

Calling Codes and Postal Codes

The dialling code for Dubai from the UK is: 00 971 (4), using the UAE prefix 971 and adding the local code for Dubai but dropping the first zero. Each emirate has its own suffix, as follows:

Abu Dhabi	02
Ajman	06
Al Ain	02
Aweer	04
Dubai	04
Fujairah	09
Jebel Ali	04
Kalba	09
Khor Fakkan	09
Masafi	09
Ras Al Khaimah	07
Sharjah	06
Umm Al Quwain	06

The UAE does not currently have a postal code system.

Dubai Municipal Departmental Numbers

Civil Aviation Department	**t** 206 6333
Courts Department	**t** 334 7777
Department of Economic Development	**t** 222 9922
Department of Emigration	**t** 345 1100
Development Board	**t** 228 8866
Dubai Airport Free Zone Authority	**t** 2995555
Dubai Electricity and Water Authority	**t** 324 4444
Dubai Government Workshop	**t** 334 2999
Dubai Internet City	**t** 399 8888
Dubai Municipality	**t** 221 5555
Dubai Police	**t** 229 2222
Dubai Ports Authority	**t** 345 1545
Dubai Ship Docking Yard	**t** 334 1217
Dubai Tourism and Commerce Marketing	**t** 223 0000
Endowments and Islamic Affairs Dept	**t** 266 3535
Finance Department	**t** 353 1076
Federal National Council	**t** 282 4531
General Information Authority	**t** 282 1565
General Postal Authority	**t** 337 1500
General Secretariat of UAE Municipalities	**t** 223 7785
Health and Medical Services	**t** 337 0031
Heritage and History Committee	**t** 222 7498
HH The Ruler's Affairs and Petroleum Affairs	**t** 353 1060
Institute of Administration	**t** 282 1575
Jebel Ali Free Zone Authority	**t** 881 5000
Jebel Ali Free Zone Administration	**t** 881 3000
Lands Department	**t** 222 2253
Ministry of Agriculture and Fisheries	**t** 295 8161
Ministry of Communications	**t** 295 3330
Ministry of Defence	**t** 353 2330
Ministry of Economy and Commerce	**t** 295 4000
Ministry of Education	**t** 299 4100
Ministry of Electricity and Water	**t** 262 6262
Ministry of Finance and Industry	**t** 353 2323
Ministry of Foreign Affairs	**t** 222 1144
Ministry of Health	**t** 334 8000

Ministry of Information and Culture	**t** 261 5500
Ministry of Islamic Affairs and Endowments	**t** 269 1220
Ministry of Justice	**t** 282 5999
Ministry of Labour and Social Affairs	**t** 269 1666
Ministry of Public Works and Housing	**t** 269 3900
Ministry of Youth and Sports	**t** 269 1680
Ports and Customs Dept	**t** 345 9575
Prime Minister's Office	**t** 345 1900
Protocol Dept	**t** 353 1086
Public Prosecutor	**t** 334 6666
Real Estate Dept	**t** 346 1444
State Audit Institution	**t** 228 6000
UAE Radio and Television Dubai	**t** 336 9999

Index

NOTES